Multimodal Approaches to Chinese-English Translation and Interpreting

Multimodal approaches to translation and interpreting studies is a burgeoning area of research. This volume includes a broad and well-motivated set of papers which apply multimodal approaches to studies on English-Chinese translation and interpreting. The book sets the agenda and makes a significant contribution in this research area. It will serve as a unique resource for researchers in the field of multimodal discourse analysis and translation studies.

Professor Chang Chenguang, Sun Yat-sen University, China

Nowadays, discourse analysis deals with not only texts but also paratexts and images; so do translation and interpreting studies. Therefore, the concept of multimodality has become an increasingly important topic in the subject areas of linguistics, discourse analysis and translation studies. However, up to now not much research has been done systematically on multimodal factors in translation and interpreting, and even less in exploring research models or methodologies for multimodal analysis in translation and interpreting.

This book aims to introduce and apply different theories of the multimodal discourse analysis to the study of translations, with case studies on Chinese classics such as the *Monkey King, Mulan* and *The Art of War*, as well as on interpretations of up-to-date issues including the Chinese Belt and Road Initiatives and Macao tourism.

The chapters reflect the first attempts to apply multimodal approaches to translation and interpreting with a special focus on Chinese-English translations and interpreting. They provide new understandings of transformations in the multimodal translation process and useful reference models for researchers who are interested in doing research of a similar kind, especially for those who are interested in looking into translations related to Chinese language, literature and culture.

Zhang Meifang is Professor of Translation Studies in the Department of English and Master of Cheung Kun Lun College of the University of Macau. She is also the Co-Editor-in-Chief of *Babel: International Journal of Translation*.

Feng Dezheng (William), PhD, is Associate Professor and Associate Director of the Research Centre for Professional Communication in English at the Department of English, Hong Kong Polytechnic University.

Routledge Advances in Translation and Interpreting Studies

49 Translation and Hegel's Philosophy
A Transformative, Socio-Narrative Approach to A.V. Miller's 'Cold-War' Retranslations
David Charlston

50 Indigenous Cultural Translation
A Thick Description of *Seediq Bale*
Darryl Sterk

51 Translating Molière for the English-speaking Stage
The Role of Verse and Rhyme
Cédric Ploix

52 Mapping Spaces of Translation in Twentieth-Century Latin American Print Culture
María Constanza Guzmán Martínez

53 A Century of Chinese Literature in Translation (1919–2019)
English Publication and Reception
Edited by Leah Gerber and Lintao Qi

54 Advances in Discourse Analysis of Translation and Interpreting
Linking Linguistic Approaches with Socio-cultural Interpretation
Edited by Binhua Wang and Jeremy Munday

55 Institutional Translation and Interpreting
Assessing Practices and Managing for Quality
Edited by Fernando Prieto Ramos

56 Multimodal Approaches to Chinese-English Translation and Interpreting
Edited by Zhang Meifang and Feng Dezheng (William)

For more information about this series, please visit www.routledge.com/Routledge-Advances-in-Translation-and-Interpreting-Studies/book-series/RTS

Multimodal Approaches to Chinese-English Translation and Interpreting

Edited by Zhang Meifang and
Feng Dezheng (William)

LONDON AND NEW YORK

First published 2021
by Routledge
2 Park Square, Milton Park, Abingdon, Oxon OX14 4RN

and by Routledge
52 Vanderbilt Avenue, New York, NY 10017

Routledge is an imprint of the Taylor & Francis Group, an informa business

© 2021 selection and editorial matter, Zhang Meifang and Feng Dezheng (William); individual chapters, the contributors

The right of Zhang Meifang and Feng Dezheng (William) to be identified as the authors of the editorial material, and of the authors for their individual chapters, has been asserted in accordance with sections 77 and 78 of the Copyright, Designs and Patents Act 1988.

All rights reserved. No part of this book may be reprinted or reproduced or utilised in any form or by any electronic, mechanical, or other means, now known or hereafter invented, including photocopying and recording, or in any information storage or retrieval system, without permission in writing from the publishers.

Trademark notice: Product or corporate names may be trademarks or registered trademarks, and are used only for identification and explanation without intent to infringe.

British Library Cataloguing-in-Publication Data
A catalogue record for this book is available from the British Library

Library of Congress Cataloging-in-Publication Data
Names: Zhang, Meifang, 1979- editor. | Feng, Dezheng, editor.
Title: Multimodal approaches to Chinese-English translation and
　interpreting/edited by Meifang Zhang and Dezheng Feng.
Description: London; New York: Routledge, 2021. | Series: Routledge
　advances in translation and interpreting studies | Includes
　bibliographical references and index.
Identifiers: LCCN 2020035494 (print) | LCCN 2020035495 (ebook)
Subjects: LCSH: Chinese language – Translating into English. | Translating
　and interpreting – China. | Audio-visual translation. | Semiotics.
Classification: LCC PL1277 .M85 2020 (print) | LCC PL1277 (ebook) | DDC
　428/.02951 – dc23
LC record available at https://lccn.loc.gov/2020035494
LC ebook record available at https://lccn.loc.gov/2020035495

ISBN: 978-0-367-33196-2 (hbk)
ISBN: 978-0-429-31835-1 (ebk)

Typeset in Times New Roman
by Apex CoVantage, LLC

Contents

List of figures vii
List of tables ix
List of contributors xi
Acknowledgements xiii

Introduction: multimodal approaches to Chinese-English translation and interpreting 1
ZHANG MEIFANG AND FENG DEZHENG (WILLIAM)

1 **Intersemiotic shifts in the translation of Chinese costume drama subtitles: a multimodal analysis approach** 16
QIAN HONG (SUNNY) & FENG DEZHENG (WILLIAM)

2 **A multimodal study of paratexts in bilingual picturebooks on Mulan** 43
CHEN XI (JANET)

3 **Intersemiotic translation of rhetorical figures: a case study of the multimodal translation of *The Art of War*** 66
LUO TIAN (KEVIN)

4 **Reshaping the heroic image of Monkey King via multimodality: a hero is back** 91
WANG HUI (WANDA) AND LI XIAOWEI

5 **"Dis"covering *Hamlet* in China: a case analysis of book covers of the Chinese *Hamlet*** 124
XIE GUIXIA (ROSIE)

6 **Belt and Road Initiatives in texts and images: a critical perspective on intersemiotic translation of metaphors** 148
ZHANG XIAOYU (HEATHER)

7 **A corpus-assisted multimodal approach to tourism promotional materials of Macao: a case study of three signature events** 168
LAM SUT I (MICHELLE) AND LEI SAO SAN (SUSANN)

8 **Effects of non-verbal paralanguage capturing on meaning transfer in consecutive interpreting** 192
OUYANG QIANHUA (TASHA) AND FU AI (IVY)

Index 219

Figures

2.1	Classification of paratexts in this study	47
2.2	Front cover and back cover of *China's Bravest Girl: The Legend of Hua Mu Lan* (1993)	52
2.3	Inside page layout of *Song of Mulan* (2010)	57
2.4	Inside page layout of *China's Bravest Girl: The Legend of Hua Mu Lan* (1993)	59
3.1	RFs in the ST and TT	76
3.2	RF translation strategies	77
3.3	Omission of metaphor	78
3.4	Omission of paradox and parallelism	79
3.5	Equivalence of parallelism	80
3.6	Equivalence of parallelism	81
3.7	Equivalence of simile	82
3.8	Addition of antithesis	83
3.9	Addition of metonymy and parallelism	84
3.10	Replacement of antithesis with hyperbole	85
3.11	Replacement of anaphora with reshaption	86
3.12	Replacement of anaphora with reshaption	87
4.1	A multimodal analytical framework (adapted from Chaume 2014, 172)	94
5.1	Cover of Zhu Shenghao's translation by Lianhe Press in 2014	128
5.2	Cover of Cao Weifeng's translation by Cultural Cooperation Company in 1946 (public domain image)	129
5.3	Narrative and conceptual representational meanings of images	135
5.4	Narrative and conceptual representational meanings in images with reference to participants	135
5.5	Types of elements on book covers over the four stages	139
5.6	Information value on book covers over the four stages	140
5.7	Distribution of titles, images, and blurb on vertical covers	141
5.8	Drawing after the covers of Shao Ting's translation by Commercial Press in 1930 (public domain image)	142
6.1	Three-dimensional analytical framework for metaphor translation analysis (based on Fairclough 1995, 98)	152

viii *Figures*

6.2	Conceptual mapping of the metaphor "BRI IS A PLANT"	162
7.1	Processes in verbal resources of selected news releases	177
7.2	Actors of material processes in verbal resources of selected news releases	178
7.3	Carrier/token in verbal resources of selected news releases	179
7.4	Sensor in verbal resources of selected news releases	179
7.5	Shot addressing viewers off-screen	181
7.6	Shot addressing vector formed from actors to visualized goal	181
7.7	Example of analytical process (Senado Square – historic and cultural building)	182
7.8	Example of analytical process (Galaxy Macau on the Cotai Strip – commercial building)	182
7.9	Example shot of creating social affinity (with kiss)	184
7.10	Example shot of low angles to show the solemnity of architecture	184
7.11	Example shot of high modality (with sensory coding orientation)	185
7.12	Example shot of low modality (with sensory coding orientation)	185
8.1	Paralanguage at clause 4–1	204
8.2	Paralanguage at clause 4–2	204
8.3	Paralanguage at clause 12–1	205
8.4	Paralanguage at clause 12–2	205
8.5	Paralanguage at clause 15–1	205
8.6	Paralanguage at clause 15–2	205
8.7	Paralanguage at clause 42–1	210
8.8	Paralanguage at clause 42–2	210
8.9	Paralanguage at clause 49–1	210
8.10	Paralanguage at clause 49–2	210

Tables

1.1	Semiotic shifts across codes (adapted from Delabastita 1990)	19
1.2	A proposed model of intersemiotic shifts in AVT	20
1.3	Summarizing multimodally contextualized intersemiotic shifts	22
1.4	Transcription of case 1	24
1.5	Transcription of case 2	26
1.6	Transcription of case 3	27
1.7	Transcription of case 4	28
1.8	Transcription of case 5	29
1.9	Transcription of case 6	31
1.10	Transcription of case 7	32
1.11	Transcription of case 8	33
1.12	Transcription of case 9	34
1.13	Transcription of case 10	35
1.14	Transcription of case 11	35
4.1	Meaning codes in audiovisual translation (Chaume 2014, 172)	93
4.2	Multimodal analysis of scene 1	97
4.3	Multimodal analysis of scene 2	100
4.4	Multimodal analysis of scene 3	103
4.5	Multimodal analysis of scene 4	106
4.6	Multimodal analysis of scene 5	109
4.7	Multimodal analysis of scene 6	112
4.8	Multimodal analysis of scene 7	115
4.9	Multimodal analysis of scene 8	118
5.1	Coding framework of representational meanings	131
5.2	Coding framework of interactive meanings	131
5.3	Coding framework of compositional meanings	132
5.4	Number of book covers and samples	133
5.5	Interactive meanings of Hamlet and other human participants	138
6.1	Source speeches involved in the narration of DDZX	153
6.2	Metaphorical expressions in the source text and the target text of data	155
6.3	Classifying translation method by metaphor type	156
6.4	Analysis of the metaphor "BRI IS A VENTURE"	157

6.5	Cheng'yu based on the metaphor "DEVELOPMENT IS A VOYAGE"	159
6.6	Examples of HUMAN-related metaphors in the ST	160
6.7	Examples of HUMAN-related metaphors in DDZX	161
6.8	An example of translating metaphor by rearrangement	162
7.1	Types of processes (based on Halliday 1985, 1994, 2000)	171
7.2	Representations in visual grammar (based on Kress and van Leeuwen 1996/2006)	172
7.3	Elements of different modalities	173
7.4	Selected data of present study	174
7.5	Lexical words in top 30 of word lists of C2016, C2017 and C2018	176
7.6	Visual realizations of representations	186
8.1	Interpreters' gaze and the resulted grouping	200
8.2	Short gaze of three selected interpreters of different frequency groups	200
8.3	Recapped instantiations of interpersonal meaning	201
8.4	Transcripts and discourse assessment of the three interpreters' output in case 1	202
8.5	Clause-level realizations of the interpersonal meaning in case 1	203
8.6	Interpreters' recapping of appraisal resources in case 1	206
8.7	Discourse assessment of the three interpreters' output in part 1 of case 2	208
8.8	Clause-level realizations of the interpersonal meaning in part 1 of case 2	208
8.9	Interpreters' recapping of appraisal resources in part 1 of case 2	211

Contributors

Chen Xi (Janet) is Assistant Professor at Macau University of Science and Technology. Her research interests are in multimodal discourse analysis, picturebook translation and cross-cultural studies.

Feng Dezheng (William), PhD, is Associate Professor and Associate Director of the Research Centre for Professional Communication of Hong Kong Polytechnic University. His research focuses on the critical and multimodal discourse analysis of various media and communication practices. His publications appeared in journals such as *Journal of Pragmatics, Discourse and Communication, Visual Communication* and *Critical Arts*.

Fu Ai (Ivy) is Assistant Lecturer at the School of Interpreting and Translation Studies, Guangdong University of Foreign Studies. Her research interests are in interpreting pedagogy and multimodality.

Lam Sut I (Michelle) is a resident fellow who received her PhD in linguistics at the University of Macau. Her research interests include discourse analysis, multimodal analysis and corpus analysis to translation studies.

Li Xiaowei is Academic Liaison and Reference Librarian, Xi'an Jiaotong–Liverpool University. Her research interests are audiovisual translation and media translation.

Lei Sao San (Susann) is a PhD candidate in education in the Faculty of Education at University of Macau. Her research interests include media literacy, educational technology and multimedia in education.

Luo Tian (Kevin) is Professor in the Department of Foreign Languages at Chongqing Jiaotong University, China. He received his PhD degree in English linguistics (specialized in translation studies) from the University of Macau. His main research interests include discourse analysis, military translation history, multimodal translation and corpus-based translation studies.

Ouyang Qianhua (Tasha) is Associate Professor of Translation Studies at School of Interpreting and Translation Studies, Guangdong University of Foreign Studies. Her research interests range from interpreting pedagogy and interpreting quality assessment to discourse analysis in interpreting.

Qian Hong (Sunny), PhD, is Assistant Professor and Programme Director of Applied Translation Studies Programme at the BNU–HKBU United International College, Zhuhai, China. She is interested in critical discourse analysis and translation, multimodality and translation and technology-infused translation pedagogy.

Wang Hui (Wanda) is Associate Professor and Head of the Department of Translation and Interpreting at Xi'an Jiaotong–Liverpool University (XJTLU). Her research interests include media translation, web translation, web localization and discourse analysis. Her papers have appeared in prestigious journals like *Meta, The Interpreter and Translator Trainer* and *Chinese Translators Journal*.

Xie Guixia (Rosie) is a lecturer and the Programme Director of the Master of Translation and Interpreting Programme (MTI) at Sun Yat-sen University, China. Her research interests range from Shakespeare translation in China and abroad to translator training and translation pedagogy. She is also a practicing translator.

Zhang Meifang is Professor of Translation Studies and Master of Cheung Kun Lun College of the University of Macau. Her research interests are in critical discourse analysis of media and political texts and translation. Her publications appeared in journals such as *Target, Perspectives, Babel* and *The Translator*. She is also the co-editor in chief of *Babel: International Journal of Translation*.

Zhang Xiaoyu (Heather) is a PhD candidate in linguistics at the University of Macau. Her main research interest centers on metaphor use and translation in political discourse. Her doctoral research investigates how metaphors have been used as tools to frame Chinese political realities in Xi Jinping's public speeches and translated into English to reach the international audience.

Acknowledgements

Acknowledgement is due to copyright holders for their kind permission to include the following material in this book:

Screenings used in Chapter 1 are from the Chinese costume drama *Zhenhuan Zhuan*, with Netflix's online grant of permission for one-time educational and research purposes. Figures 2.2 and 2.4 are from *China's Bravest Girl: The Legend of Hua Mu Lan*, with the permission of Lee & Low Books Inc., New York. Figure 2.3 is from the book *Song of Mulan* (Chinese-English Illustrated Series of Ancient Chinese Classical Narrative Poems), with the permission of Shanghai People's Fine Arts Publishing House. Figure 5.1 is used with the permission of the China Pioneer Publishing Technology Co., Ltd. Screen shots used in Chapter 4 are from the Chinese movie *Monkey King: Hero is Back* with the permission of October Media. Images used in Chapter 7 with the permission of the Advertising & Production Division, Macao Government Tourism Office. Images used in Chapter 8 are screenshots from a videotaped mock conference, with the permission of the speaker Joshua Benjamin Greenfield.

Introduction
Multimodal approaches to Chinese-English translation and interpreting

Zhang Meifang and Feng Dezheng (William)

Nowadays, discourse analysis deals with not only verbal texts but also images and sound; so do translation and interpreting studies. Therefore, the concept of multimodality has become an increasingly important topic in the subject areas of linguistics, discourse analysis and translation studies. This introductory chapter gives an overview of the development of multimodal approaches to discourse analysis and of previous research on multimodal translation and interpreting. It introduces the main approaches to multimodal discourse analysis, including visual grammar (Kress and van Leeuwen 2006), visual metaphor (e.g. Forceville 1996) and image-text relations (e.g. Martinec and Salway 2005). It also provides a bird's-eye view of each chapter of the whole book, which applies different frameworks to the analysis of intersemiotic shifts in Chinese-English translation and interpreting. The topics of the chapters range from translations of Chinese classics such as the *Monkey King, Mulan* and *The Art of War*, to interpretations of up-to-date issues such as those related to city branding and the Chinese Belt and Road Initiatives. It is argued that the research results will provide insights for readers and researchers to rethink about traditional and newly emerged translational phenomena in both print and digital media.

1 From interlingual to intersemiotic translation

Over the past few decades, definitions of translation were centring around "language" and "text." For example, Catford defined translation "as the replacement of textual material in one language by equivalent textual material in another language" (1965, 20). Nida and Taber considered translation as consisting "in reproducing in the receptor language the closest natural equivalent of the source language message, first in terms of meaning, and secondly in terms of style" (1969, 12), and Newmark viewed translation as "rendering the meaning of a text into another language in the way that the author intended the text" (1988, 5). In the 1990s, translation was redefined as a manipulation, "a rewriting of an original text" (Bassnett and Lefevere 1990, in Gentzler 1993, ix), "an act of communication" (Hatim and Mason 1997, vii) and "a purposeful activity" (Nord 1997).

Parallel with these definitions, translation studies have experienced different approaches in the past few decades, such as the contrastive linguistic approach, discourse analytical approaches, functionalist approaches, philosophical approaches, cultural approaches and cognitive approaches. Although translation and interpreting, as other kinds of human communication, involve not only language and texts but also other modes such as images, gesture, voices and music, very few translation researchers pay attention to para-linguistic modes. Munday (2004, 216), when discussing advertising, realised that almost all translation studies were focusing on the conventional, progressively outdated, written text, and he urged that translation should be seen in a broader perspective to incorporate multimodal features of texts.

The term multimodality only began to appear in translation studies in the last decade or so. Take the two representative works in the field as examples. The first one is the *Routledge Encyclopedia of Translation Studies*; the first edition, published in 1998, was edited by Baker and Malmkjaer, and the second edition, published in 2009, was edited by Baker and Saldanha. The first edition of this book did not touch any topic or concept of multimodal translation. In its second edition (2009, 6–8), the encyclopaedia introduced the terms related to multimodality and discussed audiovisual translation as well as advertising translation. Terms such as "multimodal nature," "multimodal approach" and "translation of advertisement and promotional material" are discussed. Similar things happened in Munday's book. In the first edition of *Introducing Translation Studies: Theories and Applications* (2001), Munday did not mention anything about multimodal translation. In the second edition he contributed a chapter on audiovisual translation (2008, 182–190), and in the third edition (2012) he brought in the concept of multimodality in his discussion of audiovisual translation, in which he proposed a "multimodal transcription model" (ibid., 276) based on research results by Thibault (2000) and Taylor (2003).

What is multimodality, and what is a multimodal approach? According to Kress, multimodality is "representations in many modes, each chosen from rhetorical aspects for its communicational potentials" (2010, 22). "Anyone working with multimodality needs to be clear what theoretical frame they are using; and make that position explicit" (ibid., 54). In other words, researchers from different academic backgrounds might refer to different theories and use different theoretical frameworks.

The term "multimodality" or "multimodal approach" is still quite new in translation and translation studies; however, its underlying meaning is shared with the term "intersemiotic" translation, proposed by Roman Jakobson over half a century ago in his seminal paper "On Linguistic Aspects of Translation." Drawing on semiotics, Jakobson (1959/2004, 139) categorises translation into three types: (1) intralingual translation, (2) interlingual translation and (3) intersemiotic translation. His categorisation and definitions "draw on semiotics, the general science of communication through signs and sign systems, of which language is but one" (Malmkjaer 2011, quoted in Munday 2012, 9). Translation and interpreting indeed involve more than just the linguistic mode; for example, intersemiotic translation "occurs when a written text is translated into a different mode, such as music, film or painting" (Munday 2012, 9). Moreover, we can easily see mixing codes, which are results of intersemiotic translation, in our living surroundings, such as road signs and advertisements.

According to Kress, "social-semiotic theory is interested in meaning, in all its forms. Meaning arises in social environments and in social interactions" (2010, 54). Similarly, many translation scholars are interested in the transfer of meaning from one set of language signs to another set of language signs, and see translation in semiotic terms as "an interpretation of verbal signs by means of some other language" (Jakobson 1959, 233). Kress also notes that "translation is a process in which meaning is moved. It is moved 'across,' 'transported' – from mode to mode; from one modal ensemble to another" (2010, 124).

Over the last two decades, scholars working in various disciplines have developed a growing interest in multimodality, and have come up with some theoretical models to conceptualise communication and social interaction as processes of semiotic negotiation. However, very few translation scholars have extended their attention from the linguistic mode to other modes in their research. Academic interest in non-verbal semiotic resources and their role in the processes of interlingual and intercultural communication has so far been unevenly spread across the different constitutive domains of translation and interpreting studies. Audiovisual translation and sign interpreting are perhaps the only types of non-verbal semiotic resources that have become widely recognised in translation studies to date. Areas such as picturebook translation, visual publicity translation, dialogue interpreting, advertising and drama translation still lack theoretical and methodological concepts and tools to systematically analyse semiotic resources such as gestures, facial expressions, choice of fonts, colours and patterns of textual-visual interaction in real communicative events or in printed materials.

This volume aims to fill in some gaps in this research area. Taking multimodal perspectives, the authors examine the combined use of different meaning-making resources. They pay close attention to communicative encounters involving semiotic resources drawn from more than one mode, for example image, gestures, colour and music. The case studies would be among the first attempts to adopt multimodal approaches to Chinese-English translation and interpreting. This volume covers the introduction and application of different theories of the multimodal discourse analysis to the study of translations of Chinese classics such as *Mulan*, *The Art of War* and *Monkey King*, and of translations and interpretation on up-to-date issues in relation to the Chinese Belt and Road Initiatives.

In sum, this volume will introduce some multimodal research approaches and demonstrate the application of those models with case studies of Chinese-English translation and interpreting. It is hoped that this volume will provide some reference research models for young researchers who are interested in doing research on intersemiotic translation and interpreting.

2 Overview of multimodal discourse analysis

In the last few decades, linguists have come to realise that language is neither the sole nor even the dominant system for meaning-making. "Comments on the multimodal nature of communication, texts and media are increasingly commonplace across a wide range of disciplines, such as anthropology, education, design, linguistics, media and culture studies, sociology and so on" (Jewitt 2009, 1). In linguistics, since the late 1990s, researchers have developed a range of theoretical approaches and methods (e.g. Forceville 1996; Kress and van Leeuwen 1996; O'Toole 1994) to analyse discourses which involve more than one semiotic resource. In this section, we will first address the question "What is mode and what is multimodality?" and then briefly introduce different approaches to multimodal discourse analysis.

There are two different meanings of "mode" that are currently in use: (1) multimodal texts and artefacts combining the use of various semiotic modes such as language, images, gesture, typography, graphics, icons or sound; and (2) semiotic modes that are transmitted via different perceptual modes (i.e. sensory modes), namely visual, auditory, haptic, olfactory and gustatory perception. In favour of the first definition, the leading scholar on multimodality, Kress (2010), defines mode as "a socially shaped and culturally given resource for making meaning." They need to be able to represent (1) states, actions or events (ideational function); (2) social relations of participants in a given communicative act (interpersonal function); and (3) both of the above need to be represented as coherent (both internally and within their environments) texts (textual function).

Multimodality then simply means the representation, communication and interaction using multiple modes. Kress and van Leeuwen (2001, 20) define multimodality as "the use of several semiotic modes in the design of a semiotic product or event." And this "semiotic product or event" is called multimodal discourse. Multimodal studies are concerned with the production, dissemination and reception of multimodal discourse from a wide range of perspectives, for example, psychology, sociology, anthropology, cultural studies and so on. Multimodal discourse analysis (MDA), which is the focus of this book, is just one part of multimodal studies. MDA focuses on the analysis of meaning-making in different individual modes, such as images, gestures and music, and the complex interaction between the modes (O'Halloran and Smith 2011). The former is referred to as intrasemiotic analysis and the latter intersemiotic analysis.

Each of these focuses entails two aspects of research: the mapping of domains of enquiry and the exploring of theoretical and methodological issues (O'Halloran and Smith 2011, 1). On the one hand, scholars are exploring an increasing range of domains, for example, visual image (Kress and van Leeuwen 1996/2006; O'Toole 1994), scientific/mathematical discourse (Lemke 1998; O'Halloran 2005), three-dimensional objects (Martin and Stenglin 2007; O'Toole 1994), websites (Djonov 2005) and film (Bateman and Schmidt 2012; Feng 2012); on the other hand, different issues arising from the exploration of the new domains are addressed, giving rise to new theoretical approaches and methodologies. The two most influential approaches to MDA are the systemic functional or social semiotic approach, represented by O'Toole (1994) and Kress and van Leeuwen (1996/2006), and the conceptual metaphor approach, represented by Charles Forceville (Forceville 1996; Forceville and Urios-Aparisi 2009). In what follows, we will provide a brief introduction of these two approaches which are drawn upon in various chapters in this volume.

The social semiotic approach is based on systemic functional linguistics (SFL) (Halliday 1994). According to SFL, the grammar of a language is not a set of rules for producing correct sentences but linguistic resources for "meaning making" (Halliday 1978, 192). Kress and van Leeuwen (1996/2006) extend this conceptualisation of "grammar" to visual images. According to visual grammar, visual images are analysed in terms of the representation of reality (representational meaning), the interaction between the image participants and the viewers (interactive meaning) and the arrangements of different elements in the visual space (compositional meaning). Representational meaning is analysed in terms of the "processes" that participants are engaged in. Kress and van Leeuwen (2006, 45–113) identified two types of processes, namely, narrative processes and conceptual processes. The distinction between them lies in the ways in which the image participants are related to each other, that is, whether they are based on the "unfolding of actions and events, processes of change" or based on their "generalised, stable and timeless essence." The former mainly includes the depiction of various types of actions and reactions, such as walking, playing, driving, laughing and crying. The latter includes taxonomic relations (i.e. classificational process, such as the books on a library shelf), part-whole relations (i.e. analytical process, as in descriptions of body parts in biology textbooks) and symbolic relations (i.e. symbolic process, such as the cross for Christianity). Interactive meaning includes contact, social distance and attitude. Contact refers to whether the (human) participants in the image interact with viewers, mainly through gaze. Social distance is constructed by shot distance. In a long shot, image-viewer relation is represented as distant, and in a close shot the relation is intimate. Attitude includes involvement and power relations, which are realised through frontal/oblique and high/low camera angles, respectively. If a frontal angle is used, viewers are maximally involved with what is represented; if an oblique angle is used, the visual participants are depicted as "others" or "strangers." For vertical angles, high-angle representation symbolises the power of the viewer, and low-angle representation symbolises the power of image participants. Compositional meaning relates the representational and interactive meanings into a meaningful whole through information value, salience, and framing (Kress and van Leeuwen 2006, 177). Information value is concerned with the placement of visual elements, such as centre or margin, top or bottom. Salience deals with "how some elements can be made more eye-catching, more conspicuous than others, through size, sharpness of focus and color contrast" (Kress and van Leeuwen 2006, 202). Framing is concerned with the disconnection and connection of different visual elements.

The framework is used in several chapters for a systematic description of the images in translated picturebooks (Chapter 2), TV shows (Chapter 4), book covers (Chapter 5) or city promotional materials (Chapter 7). Such application expands the domain of multimodal analysis to the field of translation on the one hand and provides effective analytical tools for dealing with new issues in translation studies on the other hand. As Machin (2009, 182) explains, describing multimodal texts on the basis of a semiotic theory is "to replace commonsensical terms such as evoke and suggest that we often use with systematic and stable terms that allow us to talk in concrete terms about how such a composition communicates." Such systematic descriptions provide new understandings of translation as a multi-semiotic behaviour, rather than merely a linguistic behaviour.

The second approach is multimodal metaphor analysis based on the conceptual metaphor theory (CMT) (Lakoff and Johnson 1980). In the CMT paradigm, metaphor is conceptualised as understanding one thing (which is the target domain) in terms of the other (which is the source domain), and is represented in a formula of A IS B (e.g. LOVE IS A JOURNEY). A metaphor can be realised in both language and other communication modes, such as visual images, gesture and architecture (e.g. Forceville 1996). Multimodal metaphor researchers have developed theoretical models to identify visual metaphor (e.g. El Refaie 2003; Forceville 1996; Feng and O'Halloran 2013) and have analysed metaphor in advertising, political cartoons, comics, picturebooks, films and so on. In Forceville's (1996) seminal work, three types of pictorial metaphor are identified, namely, contextual metaphor, hybrid metaphor and simile. In contextual metaphor, a visually depicted object is compared to something else because of the visual context it appears in. In Forceville's (1996) example in which a shoe is put in the place of a tie in a suit, the metaphor SHOE IS TIE is formed because of the context where it appears. In hybrid metaphor, the source and target are represented as one entity with mixed features. El Refaie (2009) analysed a cartoon in which George Bush is compared to a baby. This is constructed by depicting Bush crawling on the floor like a baby. In animal protection advertisements, animals are sometimes depicted as human beings (e.g. in clothing, facial expression and posture) to raise our awareness. In pictorial simile, the target is compared to a source typically through juxtaposition. For example, a cigarette can be put together with a bullet to highlight its danger. Feng and O'Halloran (2013) analysed an example in which a group of weightlifting athletes are juxtaposed with minivans to suggest that the latter is as strong as the former. Multimodal metaphors pose a challenge for translation and various strategies have been developed. Such issues are dealt with in Chapters 3 and 6.

Aside from the two main theoretical approaches to multimodality, which primarily focus on the analysis of visual images (i.e. intrasemiotic analysis), many studies are concerned with the relations between different semiotic resources (i.e. intersemiotic analysis; e.g. Bateman 2014; Kong 2006; Martinec and Salway 2005; Liu and O'Halloran 2009; Royce 2007; O'Halloran 1999). We will briefly introduce several social semiotic frameworks for such analysis. Royce (2007) proposed the concept of intersemiotic complementarity and developed a system of multimodal sense relations for describing the relations between text and images, such as antonymy, hyponymy, meronymy, and collocation. Liu and O'Halloran (2009) proposed a model of intersemiotic texture "that can account for the integration of information from different modalities rather than simply documenting their 'linkages'" (Bateman 2014, 171). The model includes several new intersemiotic cohesive devices compared with Royce (2007), for example, intersemiotic parallelism and intersemiotic polysemy. Intersemiotic parallelism refers to "a cohesive relation that interconnects both language and images when the two semiotic components share a similar form" (Liu and O'Halloran 2009,

372). Intersemiotic polysemy refers to "the cohesive relation between verbal and visual components which share multiple related meanings in multisemiotic texts" (Liu and O'Halloran 2009, 375). Liu and O'Halloran (2009) also proposed three types of discourse relations, namely, comparative relations, addictive relations, and consequential relations. Comparative relations refers to cases where language and images represent similar meanings. In additive relations, language or image adds new information to one another. In consequential relations, one semiotic message is the cause or effect of the other message. The most widely adopted model is perhaps the logical semantic relations proposed by Martinec and Salway (2005), which provides an explicit framework for analysing the semantic relationships between texts and images based on SFL (Halliday 1994). The relations include elaboration, extension and enhancement. Elaboration refers to the restatement of the information at the same level of generality, or the exemplification of information, in which case either the text is more "general" than the image or vice versa. Extension refers to cases where new information is added in text or image. Enhancement provides "qualifying information about time, place, manner, reason, purpose and other generally 'circumstantial' restrictions" (Bateman 2014, 196). Several chapters in this book are concerned with intersemiotic shifts in translation (e.g. Chapters 1, 3, and 6), which draw upon the aforementioned frameworks (e.g. Martinec and Salway 2005).

3 Previous research on multimodal translation and interpreting

Since the time Jakobson (1959) brought the concept of "intersemiotic translation" to translation studies, developments have happened in intersemiotic translation and research, especially in the last decade. As early as the 1970s, Katharina Reiss (1971/2000) proposed the term "audio-medial" text type in her text typology, but this was very much overlooked, owing to various reasons. One major reason might be that the term did not share the same nature of other three text types (expressive, informative and operative) that refer to language and textual functions. Audio-medial text type seems to fall into fields of study such as advertising translation and film translation. Another reason may be the lack of audio-medial text type in the 1970s. Even in the 1980s, audiovisual translation was "still a virgin area of research" (Delabastita 1989), as most research had a strong focus on the verbal component of texts, whether from a linguistic or a cultural perspective. However, some innovative translators and scholars more than ever found themselves working on texts in which the message is communicated by more than just words.

Delabastita was among the earliest scholars to discuss audiovisual translation, who considered film and TV translation "as evidence of cultural dynamics," and he "sought to identify some of the important characteristics of this type of translation, namely that film establishes a multi-channel and multi-code type of communication" (Munday 2012, 269). The codes described by Delabastita (1989, 199–200) include (a) the verbal (with various stylistic and dialectal features); (b) the literary and theatrical (plot, dialogue, genre); (c) the proxemic and kinetic (relating to a wide range of non-verbal behaviour); and (d) the cinematic (camera techniques, film genres and so on). Based on classical rhetoric (repetition, addition, reduction, transmutation and substitution), Delabastita proposed a number of possible translation procedures to deal with both subtitling and dubbing, but it was "only a first step towards the development of a competence model" (ibid., 201). Munday has commented on Delabastita's model as a "norm-based descriptive framework that encompassed not only linguistic phenomena but also the sociocultural and historical environment" (2012, 270). This framework has been widely read and quoted in later literature on audiovisual translation, such as in Zabalbeascoa (1996), Shuttleworth and Cowie (1997), Chaume (2004) and Munday (2012), to name just a few.

From existing literature, we can see that translation studies have engaged with multimodality in two major ways. One is the conceptualisation and identification of theoretical and methodological frameworks with insights from multimodal discourse analysis for translation studies; the other is the application of multimodal approaches to the study of multimodal translated texts and dialogue interpreting.

Gorlée (1994, 2010, 58) is among the pioneers to suggest that the categorisation of translation should take into consideration the concept of multimodality. Munday (2012) takes the lead in a broad review of relevant literature and conceptualising theoretical frameworks for audiovisual translation studies research. In the chapter "New Directions from the New Media" (2012, 268–280), Munday explores various aspects of audiovisual translation, among others. He first reviews the early days of audiovisual translation as a "virgin area of research" and "the name and nature of the field." Then he points out "the linguistic and prescriptive nature of subtitling research" and "the norms of audiovisual translation." He also discusses how scholars record and analyse the "transcriptions," the "code and narratives," and the "fansubs and video games." After reviewing various scholars' works on audiovisual translation in the past few centuries, Munday comments: "although they do not represent a new theoretical model, the emergence and proliferation of new technologies have transformed translation practice and are now exerting an impact on research and, as a consequence, on the theorisation of translation" (2012, 268).

Kaindl (2013, 261) does propose a detailed model of translation categorisation based on the concepts of mode, media and culture. In this model, he differentiates between "intramodal translation" and "intermodal translation" and between "intramedia translation" and "intermedia translation." For Kaindl, "mode" and "media" are different but overlapping categories. Mode can be realised via the medium: for example, language becomes written words through the medium of writing, and becomes sound through the medium of speech. According to Kaindl, both mode and media should be taken into consideration in translation. Kaindl's categorisation of translation thus expands Jakobson's (1959) tripartite categorisation and contributes to a more accurate positioning of some translation phenomena that used to be difficult to define. However, Kaindl's categorisation of translation is not at all perfect and used for all. As pointed out by Pérez-González (2014a):

> The lack of consensus on where the referential boundaries between seemingly interchangeable terms – such as "medium," "mode" or "sign system" – lie

ultimately exposes the need for a more comprehensive and sophisticated understanding of the semiotic fabric of translated and interpreted texts.

The introduction of concepts of multimodality to translation studies enables a better understanding of intersemiotic translation and widens the scope of translation studies. Nowadays, translation is no longer considered as only a textual activity, but rather it is an act of communication involving mode, media and culture, or in Kress and van Leeuwen's (2001) terms, "transcultural multimodal communication." When we study the multimodal elements involved in intercultural communication, we need to move "from the centrality of 'language' to a focus on 'meaning'; and in terms of disciplines, a move from a linguistic to a semiotic frame" (Kress 2020, 24). Social semiotic theory suggested by Kress "draws on the work of the semiotician-linguist Michael Halliday," and specifically on two assumptions.

> The first assumption asserts that the semiotic resources of a society are the outcome of their shaping in social (inter-)actions. The second asserts that in order for any semiotic resource to be a fully functioning means for human communication, it has to deal with meanings which arise in each of these three distinct yet entirely integrated social domains.
> (ibid., 28)

Hence, multimodality is considered a resource and meanwhile a challenge for translation scholars (O'Sullivan 2013).

Paralleling with the conceptualisation and identification of theoretical and methodological frameworks for translation studies, the application of multimodal approaches to the analysis of intersemiotic translated texts and dialogue interpreting is also expanding in the field. The integration of multimodal analysis in translation studies is specially embraced by researchers in audiovisual translation, advertising translation, game translations, webpage translation and picturebook translation. Among these text types, audiovisual translation has been discussed most extensively since the late 1990s. Stöckl (2004) is perhaps one of the first few scholars to have noticed the vital importance of non-verbal elements and integrated multimodal analysis in translation studies. He thinks that multimodality can be modelled "as a networked system of choices" (in Pérez-González 2014b, 191). He put forward a specific framework to systemise different semiotic resources, in which there are four core modes: sound, music, image and language. The research of audiovisual translation has expanded to include all forms of translation that use any media (or format) to edit programmes, including subtitling, dubbing, revoicing, simultaneous interpreting, living subtitles, surtitling for opera and theatre and so on. Luis Pérez-González's (2014b) *Audiovisual Translation: Theories, Methods and Issues* is a very comprehensive introduction to the study of audiovisual translation in its different forms, providing a detailed examination of the concept of multimodality as well as an exploration of fansubbing and other emerging practices. He brings together modes of audiovisual translation and offers a systematic framework for analysis of examples from subtitling, dubbing, audio description and even multilingual versions (215–217).

The influence of audiovisual translation is so profound that it is easy to form the impression that multimodality only refers to audiovisual phenomena, whereas in fact audiovisual translation constitutes merely a single manifestation of multimodality in translation (Boria and Tomalin 2020, 5). Apart from audiovisual translation, advertising translation and picturebook translation also require visual analysis and have become important points of engagement with multimodal theories. Some scholars apply visual grammar in analysing TV advertisement; other scholars have shifted their attention to the translation of picturebooks for children (e.g. Oittinen 2008; Lathey 2006, 2010; Joosen 2010; Sonzogni 2011; Oittinen, Ketola, and Garavini 2018; Chen 2017). In addition, some studies have specifically explored the paratextual elements in picturebook translation (e.g. Gerber 2012; Kung 2013; Tsai 2013). New text types such as game translation and experimental literary translation (e.g. Lee 2012) which emerged alongside the development of multimodality have also received theoretical support from insights derived from studies of multimodality. Interpreting, a traditional field in translation studies, also resorts to multimodal theories to deal with non-verbal elements such as facial expression and gestures that might affect the communication process.

Although various efforts have been made in the study of words and images in translation from multimodal perspectives, up to now not much research has been done systematically on multimodal factors in translation and interpreting, even less in relation to the Chinese cultural context. In line with the continuous effort in translation studies to develop more relevant frameworks in order to support developments in the discipline with adequate theoretical tools, this monograph intends to introduce several models for multimodal analysis of translation and interpreting in the Chinese cultural context.

4 Content of the book

This collection addresses a wide range of issues arising in multimodal translation. The first four chapters are concerned with the translation of classic Chinese literary works into English, while Chapter 5 takes the opposite direction and examines the translation of the English classic *Hamlet* in China. Chapters 6 and 7 shift their focus to the translation of modern Chinese themes, working with text and images from the Belt and Road Initiatives and tourism promotional materials of Macao, respectively. Chapter 8 is concerned with multimodal meaning-making in consecutive interpreting. In what follows, we will provide an overview of each chapter.

Chapter 1 by Qian Hong (Sunny) and Feng Dezheng (William) analyses the intersemiotic shifts in the English subtitle of the popular Chinese costume drama, *Zhenhuan Zhuan*. A framework is developed to model the types of shifts in multimodal translation and to examine the role of non-verbal modes in the translation process. Five kinds of intersemiotic shifts are identified, namely, addition, omission, omission + addition, compensation, and typographic transformation. These shifts are all cross-modal, resulting from the role of non-verbal modes in meaning-making. This study furthers our understanding of the new forms of transformations in the translation process when non-verbal resources are involved. Chapter 2 by Chen Xi (Janet) investigates the paratexts in picturebook translation. It analyses how the Chinese classic "Mulan Ci" is repackaged in contemporary bilingual picturebooks through the verbal and non-verbal paratexts in translation. It proposes a framework to classify different types of verbal and non-verbal paratexts in picturebooks and elucidates the functions the paratexts in picturebook translation. The study contributes to multimodal translation studies by providing an effective method for categorising and analysing paratextual materials in picturebooks. Chapter 3 by Luo Tian (Kevin) is concerned with the intersemiotic translation of rhetoric figures. It conducts a corpus-based case study of the Chinese classic *The Art of War* with a focus on verbal-to-visual translation of rhetorical figures. The study shows both the infeasibility and feasibility in intersemiotic translation of rhetorical figures. It identifies four strategies employed in the intersemiotic translation of rhetorical figures, namely, equivalence, replacement, addition and omission. Along the same line as Chapter 1, the study sheds some light on intersemiotic shifts in the translation of rhetoric figures. Chapter 4 by Wang Hui (Wanda) and Li Xiaowei focuses on the reshaping of the image of Monkey King in translating the animated movie *Monkey King: Hero Is Back* for Western audiences. It conducts a comparative visual, verbal and vocal analysis of the 4-minute Chinese-English episodes and explores the way the translator sets the lines to the same visual image in the dubbing process and the impact of the interplay between the same image and different dubbing on meaning-making. The analysis shows that the "humanised" heroic image of Monkey King, as presented in the Chinese movie, is reshaped as a flawed hero in the English movie, which is more in line with the taste of American viewers. Chapter 5 by Xie Guixia (Rosie) analyses the diachronic changes of paratextual elements in the book covers of the Chinese translations of *Hamlet*. Drawing upon Kress and van Leeuwen (2006) and Martinec and Salway (2005), this study analyses the representational, interactive and compositional meanings of 70 book covers of *Hamlet* across the last hundred years. The study shows that the Chinese *Hamlet* is received differently in different periods, that is, as serious literary book, as fiction and as commercialised reading material. These three types of reception reflect attitudes towards *Hamlet* influenced by socio-cultural factors as well as the change of readership. This study contributes to multimodal translation research by connecting textual features to the broad socio-historical context through diachronic analysis.

Shifting to modern themes, Chapter 6 by Zhang Xiaoyu (Heather) takes a critical approach to investigating the intersemiotic translation of metaphors in the publicity discourse of the Chinese government's Belt and Road Initiatives (BRI). The study focuses on how metaphors are transformed from verbal to visual mode and how they reshape the reality and persuade the audience in political communication. The analysis shows that not all metaphorical instances related to BRI have been faithfully translated into visuals; they could also be selected, rearranged and foregrounded to fulfil the communicative needs. The chapter further argues that the change of medium, audience and socio-political background may be reasons for the different representations of BRI metaphors in the speeches and video. Chapter 7 by Lam Sut I (Michelle) and Lei Sao San (Susann) investigates the promotional materials of Macao with a case study of three signature events of the city. The study employs a corpus-assisted multimodal approach to examine the intersemiotic translation of news release and videos, with a focus on the interplay between verbal and visual resources in contributing to the tourism image of Macao. Their analysis shows that with the verbal and visual realisation, Macao is transformed from a gaming city to a historical and cultural city with love, joy and festivals, and the shifts are realised in the intersemiotic translation process due to different nature of the sorts of materials. The study broadens the scope of multimodal translation research to include multilingual communicative practices. The final chapter by Ouyang Qianhua (Tasha) and Fu Ai (Ivy) explores whether the capturing of non-verbal paratextual elements, specifically facial expressions and gestures, has a positive impact on meaning transfer in consecutive interpreting. A mock conference that involved one speaker and nine interpreters was videotaped, transcribed and tagged. Findings suggest that non-verbal paratextual elements facilitate interpreters' rendition of meaning, in that interpreters having more frequent eye contact with speakers during the input stage present meaning more accurately and consistently in their output than those who do not. The findings are valuable for interpreting pedagogy and professional interpreting practices.

We hope that this volume will showcase how multimodal discourse analysis in its various forms is a powerful tool for uncovering intersemiotic translations and the process of interpreting, and at the same time for explaining the motivation behind the author's and the translator's choices. Intersemiotic translation is a complex, motivated component of multimodal, multilingual communication in which the translator's various linguistic and social interventions can be systematically uncovered and explained only with the help of comprehensive multimodal discourse analysis built on solid interdisciplinary foundations.

References

Baker, M., and K. Malmkjaer, eds. 1998. *The Routledge Encyclopedia of Translation Studies*, 1st ed. London & New York: Routledge.
Baker, M., and G. Saldanha, eds. 2009. *The Routledge Encyclopedia of Translation Studies*, 2nd ed. London & New York: Routledge.
Bassnett, S., and A. Lefevere, eds. 1990. *Translation, History and Culture*. London & New York: Pinter Publishers.
Bateman, J.A. 2014. *Text and Image: A Critical Introduction to the Visual/Verbal Divide*. London: Taylor and Francis.
Bateman, J.A., and K.H. Schmidt. 2012. *Multimodal Film Analysis: How Films Mean*. London & New York: Routledge.
Catford, J. 1965. *A Linguistic Theory of Translation*. London: Oxford University Press.
Chaume, F. 2004. "Film Studies and Translation Studies: Two Disciplines at Stake in Audiovisual Translation." *Meta* 49(1): 12–24.
Chen, X. 2017. "Representing Cultures through Language and Image: A Multimodal Approach to Translation of Chinese Classic Mulan." *Perspectives* 26(2): 1–18.

Delabastita, D. 1989. "Translation and Mass Communication: Film and TV Translation as Evidence of Cultural Dynamics." *Babel* 35(4): 193–218.
Delabastita, D. 1990. "Translation and the Mass Media." In *Translation, History and Culture*, edited by S. Bassnett and A. Lefevere, 97–109. London & New York: Pinter Publishers.
Djonov, E. N. 2005. *Analyzing the Organisation of Information in Websites: From Hypermedia Design to Systemic Functional Hypermedia Discourse Analysis*. Unpublished doctoral dissertation, University of New South Wales, Sydney.
El Refaie, E. 2003. Understanding Visual Metaphor. *Visual Communication* 2(1): 75–95.
El Refaie, E. 2009. "Metaphor in Political Cartoons: Exploring Audience Responses." In *Multimodal Metaphor*, edited by C. Forceville and E. Urios-Aparisi, 173–196. Berlin: Mouton de Gruyter.
Feng, D. 2012. *Modelling Appraisal in Film: A Social Semiotic Approach*. Unpublished PhD thesis, National University of Singapore.
Feng, D., and K. O'Halloran. 2013. The Visual Representation of Metaphor: A Social Semiotic Perspective. *Review of Cognitive Linguistics* 11(2): 320–335.
Forceville, C.J. 1996. *Pictorial Metaphor in Advertising*. London & New York: Routledge.
Forceville, C., and E. Urios-Aparisi, eds. 2009. *Multimodal Metaphor*. Berlin: Mouton de Gruyter.
Gentzler, E. 1993. *Contemporary Translation Studies*. London & New York: Routledge.
Gerber, L. 2012. "Marking the Text: Paratextual Features in German Translations of Australian Children's Fiction." In *Translation Peripheries: Paratextual Elements in Translation*, edited by A. Gil-Bardají, P. Orero, and S. Rovira-Esteva, 43–61. Berlin: Peter Lang.
Gorlée, D. 2010. "Metacreations." *Applied Semiotics* 24(9): 54–67.
Gorlée, D. 1994. *Semiotics and the Problem of Translation: With Special Reference to the Semiotics of Charles S. Peirce*. Amsterdam & Atlanta: Rodopi.
Halliday, M.A.K. 1978. *Language as Social Semiotic: The Social Interpretation of Language and Meaning*. London: Arnold.
Halliday, M.A.K. 1994. *An Introduction to Functional Grammar*, 2nd ed. London: Arnold.
Hatim, B., and I. Mason. 1997. *The Translator as Communicator*. London & New York: Routledge.
Jakobson, R. 1959. "On Linguistic Aspects of Translation." In *On Translation*, edited by R. Brower, 232–239. Cambridge, MA: Harvard University Press.
Jewitt, C. 2009 "Different Approaches to Multimodality." In *The Routledge Handbook of Multimodal Analysis*, edited by C. Jewitt, 28–39. London & New York: Routledge.
Joosen, V. 2010. "True Love or Just Friends? Flemish Picture Books in English Translation." *Children's Literature in Education* 41(2): 105–117.
Kaindl, K. 2013. "Multimodality and Translation." In *The Routledge Handbook of Translation Studies*, edited by C. Millán, and F. Bartrina, 257–269. London & New York: Routledge.
Kong, K.C. 2006. "A Taxonomy of the Discourse Relations between Words and Visuals." *Information Design Journal* 14(3): 207–230.
Kress, G. 2010. *Multimodality: A Social Semiotic Approach to Contemporary Communication*. London & New York: Routledge.
Kress, G. 2020. "Transposing Meaning: Translation in a Multimodal Semiotic Landscape." In *Translation and Multimodality: Beyond Words*, edited by M. Boria, Á. Carreres, M. Noriega-Sánchez, and M. Tomalin, 24–40. London & New York: Routledge.
Kress, G., and T. van Leeuwen. 1996/2006. *Reading Images: The Grammar of Visual Design*, 2nd ed. London & New York: Routledge.

Kress, G., and T. van Leeuwen. 2001. *Multimodal Discourse: The Modes and Media of Contemporary Communication*. London: Edward Arnold.

Kung, S. 2013. "Paratext, an Alternative in Boundary Crossing: A Complementary Approach to Translation Analysis." In *Text, Extratext, Metatext and Paratext in Translation*, edited by Valerie Pellatt, 49–68. Newcastle: Cambridge Scholars Publishing.

Lakoff, G., and M. Johnson. 1980. *Metaphors We Live By*. Chicago: University of Chicago Press.

Lathey, G. 2006. *The Translation of Children's Literature: A Reader*. Bristol: Multilingual Matters Ltd.

Lathey, G. 2010. *The Role of Translators in Children's Literature: Invisible Storytellers*. London & New York: Routledge.

Lee, T. 2012. "Performing Multimodality: Literary Translation, Intersemioticity and Technology." *Perspectives: Studies in Translatology* 21(1): 245–256.

Lemke, J.L. 1998. "Multiplying Meaning: Visual and Verbal Semiotics in Scientific Text." In *Reading Science: Critical and Functional Perspectives on Discourses of Science*, edited by J.R. Martin and R. Veel, 87–113. London & New York: Routledge.

Liu, Y. and K. L. O'Halloran 2009. "Intersemiotic Texture: Analyzing Cohesive Devices between Language and Images." *Social Semiotics* 19(4): 367–388.

Machin, D. 2009. "Multimodality and Theories of the Visual." In *The Routledge Handbook of Multimodal Analysis*, edited by C. Jewitt, 181–190. London: Routledge.

Martin, J.R., and M. Stenglin. 2007. "Materialising Reconciliation: Negotiating Difference in a Post-colonial Exhibition." In *New Directions in the Analysis of Multimodal Discourse*, edited by T. Royce and W. Bowcher, 215–238. Mahwah, NJ: Lawrence Erlbaum Associates.

Martinec, R. and A. Salway. 2005. "A System for Image-Text Relations in New (and Old) Media." *Visual Communication* (4): 337–371.

Munday, J. 2001/2008. *Introducing Translation Studies: Theories and Applications*, 1st and 2nd ed. London & New York: Routledge.

Munday, J. 2004. "Advertising: Some Challenges to Translation Theory." *The Translator* 10(2): 199–219.

Munday, J. 2012. *Introducing Translation Studies: Theories and Applications*, 3rd ed. London & New York: Routledge.

Newmark, P. 1988. *A Textbook of Translation*. London & New York: Prentice Hall.

Nida, E., and C. Taber. 1969. *The Theory and Practice of Translation*. Leiden: Brill.

Nord, C. 1997. *Translating as a Purposeful Activity: Functionalist Approaches Explained*. Manchester: St. Jerome.

O'Halloran, K.L. 1999. "Interdependence, Interaction and Metaphor in Multisemiotic Texts." *Social Semiotics* 9(3): 317–354.

O'Halloran, K.L. 2005. *Mathematical Discourse: Language, Symbolism and Visual Image*. London: Continuum.

O'Halloran, K.L., and B. Smith. 2011. *Multimodal Studies: Exploring Issues and Domains*. London & New York: Routledge.

O'Sullivan, C. 2013. "Introduction: Multimodality as Challenges and Resource for Translation." *JoSTrans: The Journal of Specialised Translation* (20): 2–14.

O'Toole, M. 1994. *The Language of Displayed Art*. London: Leicester University Press.

Oittinen, R. 2008. "From Thumbelina to Winnie-the-Pooh: Pictures, Words, and Sounds in Translation." *Meta* 53(1): 76–89.

Oittinen, R., A. Ketola, and M. Garavini. 2018. *Translating Picturebooks: Revoicing the Verbal, the Visual, and the Aural for a Child Audience*. London & New York: Routledge.

Pérez-González, L. 2014a. "Multimodality in Translation and Interpreting Studies." In *A Companion to Translation Studies*, edited by Sandra Bermann and Catherine Porter, 119–131. Chichester: Wiley-Blackwell.

Pérez-González, L. 2014b. *Audiovisual Translation Theories, Methods and Issues*. London & New York: Routledge.

Reiss, K. 1971/2000. *Translation Criticism – The Potentials and Limitations, Categories and Criteria for Translation Quality Assessment*. Manchester, UK: St. Jerome Publishing.

Royce, T.D. 2007. "Intersemiotic Complementarity: A Framework for Multimodal Discourse Analysis." In *New Directions in the Analysis of Multimodal Discourse*, edited by T. Royce and W. Bowcher, 63–110. New Jersey: Lawrence Erlbaum Associates.

Shuttleworth, M., and M. Cowie. 1997. *Dictionary of Translation Studies*. Manchester: St Jerome Publishing.

Sonzogni, M. 2011. *Re-Covered Rose: A Case Study in Book Cover Design as Intersemiotic Translation*. John Benjamins Publishing.

Stöckl, H. 2004. "In Between Modes: Language and Image in Printed Media." In *Perspectives on Multimodality*, edited by Eija Ventola, Cassily Charles, and Martin Kaltenbacher, 9–30. Amsterdam & Philadelphia: John Benjamins.

Taylor, C. 2003. "Multimodal Transcription in the Analysis, Translation and Subtitling of Italian Films." *The Translator* 9(2): 191–205.

Thibault, P. 2000. "The Multimodal Transcription of a Television Advertisement: Theory and Practice." In *Multimodality and Multimediality in the Distance Learning Age*, edited by A. Baldry, 311–385. Campobasso: Palladino Editore.

Tsai, Y. 2013. "The Significance of Texts in Children's Picture Books." In *Text, Extratext, Metatext and Paratext in Translation*, edited by Valerie Pellatt, 91–102. Newcastle: Cambridge Scholars Publishing.

Zabalbeascoa, P. 1996. "Translating Jokes for Dubbed Television Situation Comedies." *The Translator* 2(2): 235–267.

1 Intersemiotic shifts in the translation of Chinese costume drama subtitles

A multimodal analysis approach

Qian Hong (Sunny) & Feng Dezheng (William)

1 Introduction

Audiovisual text (hereinafter AVT) is defined by Chaume (2004, 16) as "a semiotic construct comprising several signifying codes that operate simultaneously in the production of meaning" and is regarded as one of the most prominent polysemiotic text types. Subtitling, an indispensable part of AVT study, is defined by Díaz Cintas and Remael (2007, 8) as consisting of the presentation of

> a written text, generally on the lower part of the screen, that endeavors to recount the original dialogue of the speakers, as well as the discursive elements that appear in the image (letters, inserts, graffiti, inscriptions, placards and the like), and the information that is contained on the soundtrack.

Over the past two decades, scholars (Zabalbeascoa 1996; Chuang 2006) have studied film translation from a polysemiotic perspective and claimed that "no text can be made entirely of verbal signs because such signs always need some sort of physical support" (Zabalbeascoa 1996, 338). Other scholars have started to explore the interaction between verbal and non-verbal elements in subtitle translation (Baldry and Thibault 2006; Gottlieb 2008; Kourdis 2015). However, up to now, scholarly attention in translation studies has mainly concentrated on verbal texts while the function of non-verbal elements such as intonation, layout, body language, and facial expression has been largely unnoticed (Zabalbeascoa 2008, 24). As Perez-Gonzalez (2014, 185) observes, "a large proportion of research efforts in audiovisual translation still revolve around elaborating taxonomies of different types of equivalence between short, decontextualized stretches of dialogue in the source and target language."

Although research from the polysemiotic approach started decades ago, it is noticed that the aims of previous studies were rather general and the approaches were lack of theoretical support (Yu and Song 2017, 604; Lee 2018, 58; EI-Farahaty 2018, 37). When it comes to the study of AVT translation between Chinese and English, very few scholarly works could be found. A notable study is Chuang, who noted that "different semiotic modes contribute different kinds of meanings to the film text" (2006, 381). But the author did not give a thorough theoretical account of how those semiotic modes affect the Chinese-English translation. In order to provide further understanding about how the visual track impacts translation choices, this study proposes a theoretical framework to investigate Chinese-English AVT translation and applies it to the analysis of a Chinese costume drama.

Costume dramas, normally setting against historical background and unique conventions in ancient China, have always played an important role in the Chinese TV industry and social media. Recent years have witnessed the export of several popular costume dramas abroad such as *Zhenhuan Zhuan* (*Empresses in the Palace*), *Yanxi Gong Lue* (*Story of Yanxi Palace*), and *Lang Ya Bang* (*Nirvana in Fire*). They have attracted the attention of overseas audiences.

This chapter investigates the English translation of the Chinese costume drama *Zhenhuan Zhuan* by adopting a multimodal discourse analysis approach. Being the first costume drama of its kind officially exported overseas, it has aroused great interest from an international audience (Liu and Zhang 2017, 64). This drama is about the growth of the girl Zhenhuan in the harem of the Qing Dynasty, transforming from an innocent girl to a sophisticated empress dowager. Netflix, the largest media service provider in the United States, released its English-language version in 2014. Due to its high recognition, and the intersemiotic nature and translation quality assured by Netflix, this costume drama serves as good material for translation studies. In recent years, scholars have carried out research on the English translation of this drama. Shi and Fu (2016) took a practical approach and focused on the losses and gains in translating addressing terms and suggested several translation techniques like direct translation and addition to produce more effective translation products. Taking a sociological approach, Xiong (2016) discussed possible reasons for shortening the originally rather long drama into six episodes and commented positively on the translation provided by Netflix. However, very little research has been done on the abundant non-verbal modes of this drama, and even less in relation to translation. It is hoped that by investigating the interaction between verbal and non-verbal modes, this study will be able to systematically map out the intersemiotic shifts in this TV drama and examine the role of non-verbal modes in the translation process. Specific research questions of this study are as follows: (1) What intersemiotic shifts could be observed in the subtitle translation of *Zhenhuan Zhuan*? (2) Why do the shifts happen, and what are the roles of the non-verbal modes?

2 Multimodality: a networked system of choices

Multimodality is defined as "the use of several semiotic modes in the design of a semiotic product or event" (Kress and van Leeuwen 2001, 20). Regarded as an approach to investigate the integration between different modal elements, it can be applied to study various kinds of discourse such as discourses of advertisements, websites, museum exhibitions, textbooks, and comics. The term "mode" is an essential notion, which is defined as "a socially shaped and culturally given resource for making meaning" (Kress 2009, 54).

In the field of AVT, Stöckl is one of the first few scholars to have noticed the vital importance of non-verbal resources and integrated multimodal analysis in translation studies. He thinks that multimodality can be modelled "as a networked system of choices" (quoted in Gonzalez 2014, 191). In order to instantiate the meaning potential of an AVT, various specific modes could be chosen for better communication. He puts forward a specific framework to systemize different semiotic resources, in which there are four core modes – SOUND, MUSIC, IMAGE, and LANGUAGE – and the core modes "need to be instantiated in a specific medial variant" (Stöckl 2004, 14).

To begin with, according to Stöckl (ibid.), each core mode consists of medial variants and is further realized through sub-modes. LANGUAGE, for example, has verbal signifiers such as lexico-grammar and syntax and three medial variants, which are speech para-verbal means, static writing, and animated writing. The medial variants, on the other hand, can be instantiated via volume, intonation, layout, font, and so forth. Speech para-verbal means help to realize LANGUAGE via manners related to sound or hearing. Bosseaux (2008) has realized that the voice, as the combination of prosodic features and phonetic markers of linguistic variation, has been acknowledged as central to perceptions of filmic performance and dramatic characterization. Static and animated writing help to realize LANGUAGE visually.

The core mode IMAGE is related to visual elements. Stöckl refers to the bound-togetherness of visual and verbal elements in AVT as the "language-image-link" (2004, 21). Perez-Gonzalez (2014, 191) argues that normally verbal and visual elements can add to a common mental image, which facilitates the audience's understanding of the multimodal artifact. However, it does not always hold across languages due to linguistic and cultural differences. This actually has challenged professional translators, and solutions have to be found for a better cross-cultural communication. IMAGE includes static (still) images, whose sub-modes are color, lighting, and so forth; and dynamic (moving) images. For the latter, the sub-modes refer to camera panning, body language, and so on. In our study, non-verbal modes mainly refer to visual modes (IMAGE) and para-verbal means (Perez-Gonzalez 2014, 198) such as volume, intonation, and speed. The medial variants proposed in LANGUAGE and IMAGE will be applied to identifying translation cases involving the synergy of these semiotic resources.

3 Analytical framework

To understand how the verbal and non-verbal modes work together to contribute to the translation, theories from multimodal discourse analysis and translation studies will be drawn upon. An intersemiotic shifts model facilitating multimodal costume drama analysis will be adopted (Delabastita 1990; Lambert and Delabastita 1996).

Delabastita (1990) believes that audiovisual texts can transfer meaning via the combination of signs related with acoustic and visual modes: verbal (consisting of linguistic and para-linguistic signs), narrative, vestimentary, moral and cinematic

Intersemiotic shifts in subtitles 19

Table 1.1 Semiotic shifts across codes (adapted from Delabastita 1990)

Semiotic shift	Description
Adiectio (Addition)	The translation of the source text involves the incorporation of additional signs, whether they are "new images, sounds, dialogue or spoken comments."
Detractio (Omission)	The translation results in a reduction of the verbal and non-verbal semiotics deployed in the source text.
Substitutio (Substitution)	Replacing one sign with a (more or less) equivalent one from a different code. It may involve a partial substitution of visual and non-verbal signs by verbal signs conveyed through the visual channel.

(quoted in Perez-Gonzalez 2014, 114). Based on classical rhetoric, he proposed that semiotic shifts across codes cover three categories; Table 1.1 is a summary of the model.

We argue that the model proposed by Delabastita, which consists of three kinds of intersemiotic shifts, is not sufficient to describe the translation process involving different kinds of modes. More specific subcategories of shifts and more methods are needed. Based on our preliminary categorization of the data and careful assessment of the diversified intersemiotic shifts in these cases, the following intersemiotic shifts model is proposed in order to better capture the intersemiotic shifts in the translation process.

In this proposed model (Table 1.2), we identify five types of intersemiotic shifts. Compared with the model proposed by Delabastita (Table 1.1), there are three differences. First of all, *Substitutio* is left out because no typical cases complying with the description provided by Delabastita could be identified. Secondly, the original terms *Adiectio* and *Detractio* are replaced by Addition and Omission respectively, as the latter are commonly used in translation studies. Thirdly, another three intersemiotic shifts are added, which are Omission + Addition, Compensation, and Typographic Transformation. Within each shift, more specific translation shifts and the description of the shift between different modes are specified. It can be seen from the model that each intersemiotic shift involves the participation of non-verbal elements, such as speech para-verbal factors, punctuation marks and images.

In this model, Addition means adding either verbal or non-verbal means in the Target Text (hereinafter TT). We proposed two kinds of Addition. The first one is to add punctuation marks in the TT to transmit the meaning contained in the speech para-verbal modes. For example, if a person is too outrageous, his/her pitch may become very high. When translating into the target language, the high pitch may need due attention since it plays a role in expressing the emotion of the speaker. In this case, non-verbal means such as exclamation marks can be added to reflect the strong emotion. The second kind of addition is to add verbal modes, that is addressing terms to show interpersonal relations in the TT. In the Source Text (hereinafter ST), the interpersonal relations can be reflected via the non-verbal modes such as speakers' gestures or physical movements. When translating, the

Table 1.2 A proposed model of intersemiotic shifts in AVT

Intersemiotic shift	Sub-category of intersemiotic shift
Addition	Adding punctuation marks to transmit the meaning contained in the speech para-verbal modes in source text
	Adding addressing terms to show interpersonal relations reflected via the non-verbal modes in source text
Omission	Omitting expressions with cultural connotations/addressing terms as non-verbal means in the accompanying settings are able to transmit the omitted meanings
Omission + Addition	Omitting modal particles and adding punctuation marks to transmit the meanings contained in the modal particles and in the speech para-verbal modes in source text
	Omitting modal particles and adding verbal modes to transmit the meaning contained in the modal particles and reflected via the non-verbal modes in source text
	Omitting repetition and adding punctuation marks to transmit the meanings contained in the repetition in source text
Compensation	Explaining the meanings verbally in the target text because there are cultural connotations in the verbal or visual modes
	The translational cultural loss compensated by IMAGE
Typographic Transformation	Italicizing the font to differentiate inner monologue/written texts in the drama from the regular spoken form in the subtitle

translator might deem it necessary to add a verbal expression so that the meaning (especially the interpersonal meaning) can be better conveyed. For instance, when receiving a command from a general, the soldier may say "是" (yes) in Chinese while standing upright and saluting. When translated into English, "是" can be translated as "Yes, sir." The verbal mode "sir" is an addition, contextualized by the gestures of the soldier.

Omission means to omit the verbal modes of the ST and resort to non-verbal means which are usually the accompanying settings for transmitting the omitted meanings. The omitted parts are mostly expressions with cultural connotations and addressing terms. For example, in traditional Chinese culture, when greeting a superordinate, people would say "在下拜见大人" (literally "below you pay respects to the superordinate"). While saying so, the speaker usually bows. The bowing is an indication of the different social status between the speaker and the listener. In AVT, when translated into English, the verbal expression "在下" (whose meaning is "your subordinate") will usually be omitted and the gesture like bowing, as an accompanying setting, can in a sense help to reveal the different social identities and the respects from the speaker. One thing that needs to be explained is that though most Chinese addressing terms in a broad sense are culturally loaded, we'd like to separate them from conventional cultural expressions considering the important role of addressing terms in Chinese costume dramas (Shi and Fu 2016, 90).

The third type of intersemiotic shift is Omission + Addition, which involves three different kinds of shifts. The first kind is to omit verbal modes such as modal particles in the translation and add non-verbal modes like punctuation marks to transmit the original meaning of the ST. The second kind is similar to the first, as modal particles are omitted in the translation, but the difference lies in the added part: content words such as "please" are added in the translation. Modal particles in Chinese are expressions such as "啊" (Pinyin: *a*) and "吧" (Pinyin: *ba*), which usually have no concrete meanings but can reflect the emotions of the speaker, especially when used together with the speech para-verbal means. They are usually omitted in translation, and punctuation marks like exclamation marks or verbal modes are added to convey the emotion. In the third kind of shift, the omitted part is the verbal modes; non-verbal modes like punctuation marks are added. A very typical example is the omission of repetition and the addition of non-verbal modes such as punctuation marks, as will be discussed in next section. On the whole, in the category, the addition in translation is not only contextualized by the verbal modes of the ST but also by the speech para-verbal modes. The translation effect may be weakened if the para-verbal mode cannot be well received by the TT audience since prosodic features and phonetic markers are distinct and hard to be transferred.

For the fourth intersemiotic shift, Compensation, the meaning is twofold in our study; both usually happen when the ST contains culture-specific expressions. On the one hand, the translation in the TT is usually an explanation of the ST due to the untranslatability of the source text so as to compensate for the translational loss. On the other hand, the other medial variants in the accompanying setting can help to compensate for the loss of the cultural connotation when they could not be explained explicitly in the TT. For instance, in traditional Chinese culture, people of lower social position would like to call themselves "小人" (little person). It is a self-abasing term to show their respect for the speakers of higher social positions. When saying so, they either make a bow with hands folded in front or lower their heads. The pronoun "I" is usually used to translate the Chinese term "小人," but the rich cultural connotation is lost. Then in AVT, the physical movements like bowing or lowering heads can in a sense supplement the cultural loss. The difference between Compensation and Omission is that in Compensation, the literal meaning of the expression in ST is verbally transmitted and the cultural connotations are supplemented by the accompanying scenes; in Omission, the whole expressions in ST are completely omitted and the IMAGE can function to reveal or supplement the meanings of the original text.

The last kind of shift is Typographic Transformation, which refers to the change of typographic forms of the language when translating from ST into TT. The forms here mainly refer to the font, size, and color of the words, which may be shifted in the translation process resulting from the need to transmit the meaning of non-verbal modes. For example, in the ST, a voice-over may be adopted to show the inner world of the speaker. If no change is made to the form of the words, they seem the same as the form of regular dialogues. Then target text readers have no way to realize that it is an inner monologue, and the typographic transformation can help to differentiate them.

22 *Qian Hong (Sunny) & Feng Dezheng (William)*

In applying the model for analyzing our data, we will adapt the transcription model (Taylor 2003, 191) to describe the full picture of a related scene. In the adapted model, there are four columns. In the first column, the number of images will be indicated. The second column, the screenshot column, will then be presented to give the audience an immediate impression of the scene. In the third column, the visual image will be described in detail. The medial variants such as the speech para-verbal means and static writing will be described in the last column.

We will firstly examine the ST and the TT with a focus on the LANGUAGE and IMAGE core modes and their interactions. There are six episodes of *Zhenhuan Zhuan*, each lasting around 90 minutes. Every episode is carefully examined and relevant examples are selected to build a small corpus for the study. The specific procedures go as follows. Firstly, we go through all the bilingual subtitles in the six episodes to gain a general idea of the translation. Secondly, we adopt the key medial variants put forward by Stöckl to identify the nature of subtitle translation. If one of the medial variants other than verbal mode is involved in the translation process, the example would be marked and the screenshot with the translation would be collected. Through these procedures, we have identified 408 samples altogether involving intersemiotic translation for analysis.

4 Analysis

In this section we will analyze the salient features of intersemiotic shifts in AVT and illustrate them with representative samples. The interpersonal meanings construed in ST and TT will be analyzed and compared to explore the function of non-verbal elements and para-verbal means in Chinese-English subtitle translation.

4.1 Overview

By applying the above proposed intersemiotic shifts model (Table 1.2), the 408 translation examples collected in this research are identified and categorized based on the shifts in translating the ST into the TT. Table 1.3 presents the summary of the intersemiotic shifts.

As is shown in Table 1.3, Addition is the most frequently used, taking up 49% of all the cases collected. There are two subcategories of Addition, which are adding punctuation marks and adding addressing terms. Adding addressing terms (183 times) is the most prominent strategy compared with all the other intersemiotic shifts. The addressing terms are usually added when translating the replies by the eunuchs or maids, whose heads are always lowered to show their submission. As

Table 1.3 Summarizing multimodally contextualized intersemiotic shifts

Addition	Omission	Omission + Addition	Compensation	Typographic Transformation
199	126	53	26	4

this scene frequently happens through the whole drama, we assume it probably explains such a high ratio.

Omission ranks second, taking up 31% of all intersemiotic shifts. When this happens, usually the meaning could be supplemented by IMAGE. In this category, it is noteworthy that the omitted parts are expressions with cultural connotation, especially self-addressing terms. In terms of the intersemiotic shift, it is from verbal mode to non-verbal mode, and IMAGE helps to supplement the meaning lost in the translation.

The total number of Omission + Addition is 53, including three subcategories. The first two are related with modal particles, which are omitted in the TT and punctuations and verbal modes are added. The third subcategory is omitting repetition. Punctuation marks are added in the TT. For the three subcategories, it is noticed usually in the accompanying scenes that the speaker is very excited or angry. Those modal particles and repetitions are employed to express their strong feelings. However, they are omitted in the TT and punctuation marks or verbal modes are added.

The fourth kind of intersemiotic shift is Compensation, with 26 examples in total. In this category, the implied meanings of the expressions are usually translated verbally in the TT, but the cultural connotation is not explained. Instead, the accompanying IMAGE can bring out the connotation.

The last category is Typographic Transformation. Four examples were identified. In this transformation process, the font of the subtitle in the TT is usually changed to indicate the special nature of the expressions such as the inner monologues/written texts. Though there are not as many cases as the previously discussed two shifts, their important role could not be simply ignored. Their functions will be analyzed in detail in the case analysis section.

4.2 Addition

As explained previously, Addition means adding signs such as images, sounds, dialogues, or spoken comments in the TT. In our study, two subcategories of addition are observed. One is to add punctuation marks to convey different kinds of meanings or emotions, and the other is to add extra addressing terms to represent the para-verbal means. Detailed analysis will be carried out in the following section.

4.2.1 Adding punctuation marks to convey meanings or emotions

In our data, there are 16 examples in which punctuation marks are added. Generally, the addition of punctuation marks is related to transferring the strong emotions of the speakers. There are no punctuation marks in the ST-Chinese subtitles. When the speakers are in an excited mood, out of joy or anger, the voice volume will increase and facial expressions can be recognized. Exclamation marks and question marks are often used in the translation to capture the non-verbal meanings. The following are cases in point to illustrate the importance of adding appropriate punctuation marks.

24 *Qian Hong (Sunny) & Feng Dezheng (William)*

Case 1

ST1: 我是这样一个无情无义的女子
TT1: You would not have known I am such a heartless soul!
ST2: 无情无义
TT2: Heartless?
ST3: 无情无义
TT3: Heartless!

In Case 1, the three scenes (Table 1.4, Images 1, 2, and 3) are put together for the convenience of discussing the function of adding punctuation marks in AVT-multimodal translation. In Table 1.4, Image 1, Zhenhuan yells at Marquess Guo,

Table 1.4 Transcription of case 1

Image no.	Screenshot	Visual description	Speech paraverbal means
1		Zhenhuan is extremely upset. She is saying something to Marquess Guo.	When saying these words, she is shouting, and her voice is high-pitched.
2		Upon hearing what Zhenhuan says, Marquess Guo is bewildered.	The volume of Marquess Guo is low, and sounds confused.
3		Marquess Guo opens his mouth loud and his face is a little bit twisted.	He roars.

saying that she is a heartless soul. In this episode, Marquess Guo does not return from an errand on time and is reported dead. Zhenhuan is devastated and finds herself pregnant with Marquess Guo's child. Being determined to keep the baby alive, she finds a way to regain the favor of the Emperor. Just when she is ready to return to the palace, Marquess Guo shows up. Things have been done cannot be undone. Zhenhuan cannot bear to hurt Marquess Guo, and wants him to forget her. She shouts, "You would not have known I am such a heartless soul!" Her emotion is extremely sorrowful and anguished, which can also be seen from her facial expression, and her cry can be well received by the Chinese audience. However, as she speaks Chinese, whose pronunciation and intonation are totally different from that of English, it is hard for the acoustic effect to function the same way for the English-speaking audience. In this case, the addition of an exclamation mark can be regarded as the most suitable way to compensate for the acoustic loss.

It is a similar case for the translation of Marquess Guo's replies (TT2 and TT3). Zhenhuan's returning to the palace is completely out of his expectation. Besides, the word "heartless" is never a word that he would use to describe Zhenhuan. Thus he is bewildered as he cannot understand what is happening in front of his eyes. His voice is also low and connotes a mixture of confusion, grief, and sorrow, as if he is murmuring to himself. Similarly, his voice, which is full of confusion, depression, and grievance, can be well understood by the Chinese audience, but it might not be fully understood by the English-speaking audience. Here a question mark is added to compensate this loss, as it shows the doubt and bewilderment of Marquess Guo. After he has realized what happened, he is furious, which can be observed from his facial expression. His eyes open wide and his face is a little bit contorted when he is crying out the expression in Chinese, "无情无义" (heartless). His grief and desperation are all conveyed in this cry. However, as the cry is in Chinese, which cannot function the same for the target audience, addition is adopted – to add an exclamation mark, which is usually used after an interjection or exclamation to indicate strong feelings or high volume (shouting), or to show emphasis. Thus the strong feelings of Marquess Guo can be revealed to the target audience to a greater extent.

4.2.2 *Adding addressing terms to represent the para-verbal means*

Earlier in this chapter we mentioned that speech para-verbal means helps to realize the language function via manners related to sound or hearing. Throughout this drama, whenever the eunuch or the servant replies to his superordinate, the verbal term "嗻" (Pinyin: *zhe*) is added to realize his humble manners. Altogether, this verbal term appears 183 times in the whole drama, reflecting the strict hierarchy in the palace, as illustrated in Case 2.

Case 2

ST4: 嗻
TT4: Yes, <u>my lady</u>.

Table 1.5 Transcription of case 2

Image no.	Screenshot	Visual description	Speech para-verbal means
1		Consort Hua looks arrogant and bossy. The eunuch lowers his head, replying to Consort Hua.	When saying the word "嗻", the voice is low and the speed is quick.

In Case 2, Consort Hua asks the eunuch to punish the newly taken mistress, First Attendant Xia. Her arrogance and contempt for First Attendant Xia can be seen in her facial expression. When given such an instruction, her servant says "嗻" (Pinyin: *Zhe*) in Chinese. It is a verbal signifier which is used in classical Chinese by servants when replying to the superordinate. The voice of the servant is quick and low, showing his submission and respect. Both the speech para-verbal means and the connotation need to be transferred to the TT. Addition is adopted here, so the TT becomes "Yes, my lady." When the TT audience may not be able to well decode the para-verbal means, the addition of "my lady" is a suitable way to show the different social status of the persons in the scene and the accompanying facial expressions of Consort Hua and the body language of the eunuch and to bring out the cultural connotation of "嗻."

4.3 Omission

Our study finds 126 examples of Omission. As omission occurs mainly under two conditions, the cases in discussion are therefore further divided into two kinds: (1) omitting expressions with cultural connotations which are self-evident in the scene; and (2) omitting self-addressing terms whose meaning may be supplemented by IMAGE.

4.3.1 Omitting expressions with cultural connotations self-evident in the scene

Altogether we have found 71 examples of this type. In these cases, the expressions are usually rich in cultural connotations. If fully translated into English by paraphrasing or adding footnotes, the TT will become rather long and awkward, not complying with the time and space requirements of AVT. Fortunately, the accompanying scene can well show the TT audience what is happening. It is thus what we mean by using the expression "self-evident." Case 3 can well illustrate our point.

Intersemiotic shifts in subtitles 27

Case 3

ST5: 皇后娘娘驾到
TT5: Her Highness the Empress!

In Case 3, "驾到" (arrive) is omitted in the TT. As the camera shots go too fast, we have to use two screenshots to display the subtitle and the scene. "驾到" is used in ancient Chinese to announce the arrival of the royal members like the Emperor or the Empress. When a eunuch is announcing so, all the subordinates and servants are expected to either bow or kneel down to show their respect and greet them. And usually, the announcer will drawl. The drawling here is to draw people's attention and to remind people to pay due respect. Though "驾到" is Chinese, the body language such as bowing or kneeling down can be generally understood by English-speaking audiences since the social meaning carried by these gestures in both language communities is more or less the same, indicating people's reverence or submission. In Table 1.6, Image 1, the audience will find that every maid and eunuch kneels down to welcome the Empress. When the core mode IMAGE can function in such a constructive way, omission seems to be a suitable decision. The meaning conveyed by "驾到" is an obligation to show utmost respect for the Empress, although the expression itself seems only a statement of her arrival. When translated into English, with the omission of "驾到," the degree of the obligation may have been weakened if only the linguistic resource "Her Highness the Empress" is examined. The accompanying scenes (Table 1.6, Images 1, 2) in a sense help to make up for the loss of the obligation.

Table 1.6 Transcription of case 3

Image no.	Screenshot	Visual description	Speech para-verbal means
1		All the people in the scene kneel down, lowering their heads. The Empress is sitting in a sedan, carried by eunuchs, looking straight ahead.	When declaring the arrival of the Empress, the eunuch's voice volume is high, sounding formal. It sounds a little drawled.
2			

28 *Qian Hong (Sunny) & Feng Dezheng (William)*

4.3.2 Omitting addressing terms

In this subcategory there are 55 examples. Omission of addressing terms normally happens in the conversations between the superordinate and the subordinate. The self-addressing terms used by the subordinate are usually omitted. Due to the strict hierarchy in the Chinese imperial palace, whenever addressing the Emperor or other superordinates, the subordinate always has to physically show their respect in the designated manner. Therefore, the power and distance between the two speakers can be well demonstrated through the physical movements, which then further supplement the meaning lost in the omitted self-addressing terms. Case 4 is used as an example to illustrate this type of shift.

Case 4

ST6: 臣妾前来恭喜皇上
TT6: Congratulations. Your Majesty.

In Case 4, when the Empress knows that the Emperor has taken some new concubines, in order to show her virtue, she goes to the Emperor's place to congratulate him on it. She says "臣妾前来恭喜皇上" (subordinate Concubine comes here to congratulate the Emperor). In the scene, she is standing there and keeping a decent distance from the Emperor. While saying those words, she bends her body a little bit as a traditional courtesy used in the palace to show her respect for the Emperor. The Emperor, however, sitting in the armchair that is exclusive to him, leans against one of the arms in a very relaxing way. One eunuch is standing next to him, lowering his head, getting ready to take the Emperor's order at any time. The distance between the Emperor and the Empress and the body language of the Empress, the Emperor, and the eunuch work together to clearly indicate the hierarchical relationship between them.

Table 1.7 Transcription of case 4

Image no.	Screenshot	*Visual description*	*Speech paraverbal means*
1		The Empress bends her body to greet the emperor, who is sitting relaxed in an armchair.	The Empress sounds humble and joyful.

Intersemiotic shifts in subtitles 29

4.4 Omission + addition

In our model, the third kind of shift is Omission + Addition. We find 53 examples. The proportion is smaller when compared with the previous two kinds of shift, but it still represents very typical phenomena of intersemiotic shifts in AVT. For this kind of shift, three subcategories are further proposed, which are omitting modal particles and adding punctuation marks, omitting repetition and adding punctuation marks, and omitting modal particles and adding verbal modes.

4.4.1 Omitting modal particles and adding punctuation marks

Our analysis has found 32 examples of this subcategory (see Table 1.3). In these examples, modal particles are used in the ST. Modal particles are usually employed to express different emotions like joy, contempt, or doubt in Chinese. They are unique in the Chinese language and barely have English equivalents, so omission is a common strategy in translating them. In the accompanying scenes of the examples of this subcategory, the facial expressions and the speech para-verbal means can function in synergy with the modal particles. When omitting modal particles becomes a necessity, the addition of punctuation marks is often adopted to maintain similar effects. The following case can well illustrate the point.

Case 5

ST7: 耳根子未免太软了吧
TT7: How gullible you are!

In the scene of Case 5, Zhenhuan's maid, Huanbi, is fighting for her survival. She and other maids are framed in the palace, and the Emperor has them sent to the Ganlu Temple as punishment. They are bullied in the temple. On a heavily

Table 1.8 Transcription of case 5

Image no.	Screenshot	Visual description	Speech para-verbal means
1		Zhenhuan's maid Huanbi looks scornful and indignant. Her head is raised up a little bit.	Her voice is loud.

snowing day, the nuns in the temple decide to kick them out of the temple and ask them to move to a remote hut. They beg and hope the nuns sympathize with them. However, the nuns show no mercy. Huanbi asks the head nun to help them, but the head nun's personality is too weak to help them. Huanbi is desperate and shouts to her "耳根子未免太软了吧" (your ears are too soft). Perhaps she tries to provoke her so that she can give her a hand. The modal particle "吧" (Pinyin: *ba*) used in the ST is to strengthen her tone of taunting. However, there is no such modal particle in English. In the TT, an exclamation mark is added to reflect the strong emotion of Huanbi. Besides, the sentence type is changed from a statement into an exclamatory sentence, which further helps to intensify the taunt on her face, in her tone, and in her language.

4.4.2 Omitting modal particles and adding verbal modes

This subcategory of Omission + Addition consists of eight examples. The STs of these cases are similar to the ones discussed above, making use of modal particles to express the speaker's emotions. The difference lies in that the meanings of the modal particles can hardly be conveyed by adding punctuation marks. Instead, more concrete verbal expressions have to be added to bring out the meaning potential of the ST and make the irony or other emotions implied in the tones of the speakers more salient.

Case 6

ST8: 臣妾做不到啊
TT8: I <u>truly</u> cannot bear it
ST9: 你何曾明白呀
TT9: How could you <u>truly</u> understand

Case 6 shows two scenes (Table 1.9, Images 1, 2) about the confession of the Empress. It can be regarded as one of the climaxes of the drama, revealing her dark heart. But the Empress feels that she is totally wronged and neglected. She thinks she is well justified for what she does. In the whole process, she cries and shouts. Her voice sounds harsh. She uses many "啊" (Pinyin: *a*) to express her extremely strong emotions. For instance, in the above two examples, she says (ST8) "臣妾做不到啊" (subordinate concubine cannot do it) and "你何曾明白啊" (ST9) (you don't understand). The modal particle "啊" is omitted in the two TTs, and the verbal mode, an adverb "truly," is added to convey the strong emotion.

4.4.3 Omitting repetition and adding punctuation marks

Our analysis has found that the repeated expressions, which are common in Chinese, are often omitted in the translation. In all the 13 collected cases, repetition is mainly used to express the speakers' strong emotion when they feel scared, terrified, excited, furious, and so on. For most of these cases in English, the repetition is omitted and a punctuation mark is added. Case 7 will illustrate our point.

Intersemiotic shifts in subtitles 31

Table 1.9 Transcription of case 6

Image no.	Screenshot	Visual description	Speech para-verbal means
1		The Empress is talking about her loss of the son.	Her face seems a little bit twisted, which indicates her anguish. The volume of her voice is high.
2		The Empress kneels in front of the Emperor, who is sitting uprightly on the chair. A eunuch is standing beside the Emperor, lowering his head.	The Empress increases her voice volume, shouting about the misery she has suffered.

Case 7

ST10: 贵人饶命 贵人饶命
TT10: Please spare me!

In Case 7, the maid is caught poisoning Zhenhuan. Zhenhuan feels outrageous and asks her the reason for doing so. She also realizes that the maid herself does not dare to do so and someone must be behind her. The maid, who is asked to confess, is very terrified. She tells Zhenhuan the whole plot and begs for her life because she has done something that is unforgivable. She says repeatedly (ST10) "贵人饶命, 贵人饶命" (Noble Lady spare my life, Noble Lady spare my life) in this scene. But the ST is translated as "Please spare me!," omitting the repeated part and the addressing term and adding an exclamation mark. The repetition is not kept in the TT, perhaps because the translator considers it too wordy in English, especially regarding the nature of the text as an AVT that is constrained by space and time. In addition, the background scene can provide sufficient information (the IMAGE and the speech para-verbal means) to show the panic of the maid and what she is begging for. Besides, the addition of an exclamation mark can be regarded as an informed choice to supplement the omitted information since the repetition in the ST is out of fear. The exclamation mark, which is used to express the speaker's

32 *Qian Hong (Sunny) & Feng Dezheng (William)*

Table 1.10 Transcription of case 7

Image no.	Screenshot	Visual description	Speech para-verbal means
1		A maid is kneeling down on the floor, kowtowing to Zhenhuan. Zhenhuan is sitting in front of her. Three maids are standing besides Zhenhuan and one eunuch is standing behind the maid, who is begging.	The maid's voice sounds high-pitched and trembling, and her speaking speed is rather fast.

strong emotion, can be adopted to compensate for the loss. For the interpersonal metafunction, in the ST, the utterance by the maid can be regarded as a request. She repeats her request to show her strong desire for life. In the TT, though the repeated request is omitted, it is believed that adding an exclamation mark could also help to instantiate the function in a similar way.

4.5 Compensation

We find 26 examples of Compensation in our study. As discussed in section 3, we find that when taking into consideration the non-verbal elements, the meaning of compensation is twofold: verbal explanation of the ST functions as a compensation on the one hand, and the accompanying setting helps to supplement the translational cultural loss on the other hand. We have two cases to illustrate this point. Case 8 is about conventional expressions with Chinese cultural connotations. It deals with translating addressing terms.

Case 8

ST11: 如今她<u>有喜</u>，更要事事小心照料
TT11: She is <u>with child</u> and should be looked after with extra care.

In the scene of Case 8, the Empress is talking with the Emperor about Zhenhuan's pregnancy. In Chinese language, there is a special term to refer to

Intersemiotic shifts in subtitles 33

Table 1.11 Transcription of case 8

Image no.	Screenshot	Visual description	Speech para-verbal means
1		The Empress wears a smile on her face, and seems peaceful and happy.	The voice sounds gentle and caring.

pregnancy "有喜" (have happiness). The expression itself suggests the importance of conceiving a baby. In traditional Chinese culture, it is believed the offspring is related with the future prosperity of the family. The more children a family has, the more blessing it gets. When it comes to the royal family, this belief becomes almost a kind of religion. The pregnancy of concubines is one of the most important things in the harem. Therefore, when Zhenhuan is found pregnant, in order to show her virtue the Empress says these words to the Emperor (ST11). In TT11, "有喜" is translated into "be with child," which is an explanation of the metaphorical meaning in Chinese. But the connotation of "喜" is lost in the translation. The lost meaning of "喜" is compensated by the facial expression of the Empress, namely she is smiling and her face is radiant with joy, seeming very high-spirited.

Case 9

ST12: 娘娘, <u>微臣</u>恭喜娘娘
TT12: My lady, <u>I</u> congratulate you.

In the scene of Case 9, Zhenhuan does not feel well, so she summons the imperial physician to give her a checkup. After his diagnosis, he reports to Zhenhuan that she is pregnant, saying "娘娘, 微臣恭喜娘娘" (ST12). The self-addressing term "微臣" (humble subordinate) is translated as "I" in the TT. It is regarded as a high courtesy in Chinese culture to use self-abasing terms when people address themselves. However, it is not commonly seen in other cultures. In TT12, "I," an ordinary pronoun is used. But the accompanying setting can work well to compensate. In our case, the physician kneels beside the bed with his head lowered, reporting the pregnancy. The physical distance and his physical gestures together with his low and submissive voice help to maintain the courtesy to an extent, which may function as a compensation.

34 *Qian Hong (Sunny) & Feng Dezheng (William)*

Table 1.12 Transcription of case 9

Image no.	Screenshot	Visual description	Speech para-verbal means
1		Zhenhuan is lying in bed. Two maids are standing by the bed, one of them holding a bowl of Chinese herb medicine. An imperial physician is kneeling besides the bed, lowering his head.	The voice volume of the imperial physician is low, sounding submissive.

4.6 Typographic transformation

This subsection mainly deals with the medial variant: static writing. As it is a special phenomenon in AVT translation, no traditional translation method or term is suitable to refer to the change. Considering the fact that during the translation process, typographic changes happen, we name it as Typographic Transformation. There are four cases in our data. In this scenario, usually a voice-over will be used to describe what is happening in the person's mind or what is written on a piece of paper. The voice-over can differentiate the above discussed situation from the normal dialogues in the drama. But when translated into a written form, the change of the font is adopted to function to make such a difference. The following two cases are expected to illustrate this point.

Case 10

ST13: 我希望你平安喜乐地在这月光下

TT13: *I hope you are enjoying peace and happiness beneath the moonlight*

In this scene of Case 10, Marquess Guo is missing Zhenhuan when looking up at the full moon in the sky. The subtitle in this screenshot is his internal monologue. It can be seen that the TT13 is italicized. For the Chinese version (ST13), Marquess Guo's internal monologue is read out as a kind of voice-over, so the ST audience can immediately understand what is in his mind. However, if this internal monologue is directly translated into English as ordinary dialogues, the TT audience might misunderstand that he is talking with Zhenhuan. Moreover, it will be confusing if the TT audience think he is talking, as in the scene his mouth is closed. Therefore, changing the style of the font can be a possible way to solve this problem, reminding the TT audience this part is different from ordinary dialogues.

Intersemiotic shifts in subtitles 35

Table 1.13 Transcription of case 10

Image no.	Screenshot	Visual description	Speech para-verbal means
1		Marquess Guo is looking up into the sky, musing. His mouth is closed. Subtitles appear on the bottom of this screenshot.	The voice-over is given by Marquess Guo, which sounds sad but loving.

Table 1.14 Transcription of case 11

Image no.	Screenshot	Visual description	Speech para-verbal means
1		Two persons kneel in front of a shut gate in a courtyard. Several eunuchs stand on both sides of them at a distance from each other.	The voice-over is given by the Emperor, which sounds formal and authoritative.

Case 11

ST14: 朕念青海之功
TT14: *Considering his service in calming Qinghai Province*

All through the drama, the form of static writing is changed in several places. For example, in Case 11, in the imperial edict for Nian Gengyao, who used to be a general contributing greatly to the stability and union of the Qing Dynasty, it says "朕念青海之功." These Chinese characters are usually written on a piece of yellow silk cloth which is exclusive to the Emperor. In our case, these are read by the Emperor as a voice-over to the ST audience. Knowing the culture and listening to the voice-over, the ST audience can immediately understand that it is from the imperial edict. The translator italicizes the words to differentiate the content of the edict from ordinary dialogues, so the TT becomes "*Considering his service in calming Qinghai Province.*"

5 Discussion of intersemiotic shifts: scenarios and reasons

By adopting the intersemiotic shifts model, we have examined the intersemiotic shifts occurring in the English translation of *Zhenhuan Zhuan*. In this section, we are going to firstly discuss the functions and applications of those shifts, such as the scenarios in which the intersemiotic shifts happened. Then we will explore the roles of non-verbal modes and find out possible reasons behind the intersemiotic shifts and their impacts.

5.1 Intersemiotic shifts: functions and applications

In this study, we find that the proposed intersemiotic shifts mainly appear in four kinds of scenarios, which are related with addressing terms, modal particles, repeated expressions, and inner monologue and written texts. We will discuss them one by one.

Translating addressing terms in costume dramas is considered a hard nut to crack due to the great cultural difference between Chinese and English (Shi and Fu 2016). Our finding shows that the intersemiotic shift methods Omission, Addition and Compensation could in a sense solve the problem. For Addition, addressing terms which are not used in the ST are added in the TT. For example, when the servants reply to the superordinate, as discussed in Case 2, the title is added. The purpose is to show their respect and submission. It is also usually an echo of the accompanying scene, in which the servant always looks submissive.

Omission is also applied to deal with addressing terms, especially with self-addressing terms. When the accompanying scene can clearly show the relationship between the speakers, as discussed in Case 4, the self-addressing term like "臣妾" can be omitted.

When adopting Compensation, the self-abasing terms in the ST of the drama such as "微臣" (humble subordinate) is generally translated into the first person pronoun. The loss of the hierarchy can usually be compensated by physical movements, such as kneeling or bending their bodies to show respect, and the paraverbal speeches such as voice and volume.

The second scenario is related with translating modal particles. Modal particles can be more often found in Chinese than in English. The various emotions can always be expressed via different modal particles such as "吧," "啊," and "呢," which barely have equivalents in English. One prominent feature of the English translation is to omit the modal particles and add the non-verbal mode: punctuation marks. The most often used one is the exclamation mark, which is a common way to convey the strong emotion of the speaker. Apart from adding punctuation marks, some adverbs are also found being added to reflect the strong feeling of the speaker. The most possible reason for either of the options is that the translator needs to consider the accompanying plot, speech para-verbal means, and non-verbal elements. For example, when the pitch is high or the emotion is very strong, the non-verbal mode such as an exclamation mark is adopted, as is shown in Case 5, in which the nuns are scorned by Huanbi. Our research shows that the

Intersemiotic shifts in subtitles 37

voice volume, the facial expressions, and body language of the speakers and the listeners all work together to realize the intended meaning and effect.

During the research process, we also noticed that in some scenes, the modal particles were omitted completely without adding any verbal or non-verbal modes. For instance, in a scene in which the Empress is asked by the Emperor to confess all the conspiracies, the Empress is desperate, and starts to justify for herself. She recalls her miserable experience, especially the loss of her child. She complains about the ruthlessness of the Emperor, shouting at the top of her voice. Her whole face is twisted because of fury, desperation, and agony. The strong emotion is apparently written on her face. The ST "不治而死啊" (incurable and die) is a four character-expression ended with a modal particle "啊" (Pinyin: *a*). "啊" is a modal particle to indicate very strong emotion like great joy and hatred in Chinese. The dramatic effect of this scene is thus co-created via three channels: the speaker's facial expression, a verbal signifier (the modal particle "啊"), and the para-verbal means. When translated into English, it becomes the statement "He died from an incurable illness," which is far from being sufficient to transfer the strong emotion of the Empress. In other words, the TT is produced without too much consideration of the function of "啊" and the impact of the facial expression and the high-pitched cry of the Empress. In this case, if an exclamatory mark can be added, it would be of some help to express the Empress's strong emotion.

The third scenario is about translating repeated expressions (Case 7). As there are numerous conflicts and climaxes all throughout the story, repeated expressions can always be found in many scenes. The expressions on the whole are very colloquial in Chinese and reflect the strong emotions of the speaker. However, if translated fully and faithfully, the TT might be wordy and even clumsy. Therefore, Omission is often used in rendering the repeated expression. But the strong emotion expressed by the repetition still needs to be kept as much as possible in the TT. As a result, Addition is also needed. As illustrated in Case 7, the addition of a non-verbal mode, the exclamation mark, can in a sense transmit the strong emotion of the speaker. Overall, Omission can help reduce the length of the subtitle, and Addition can help reserve the emotions.

However, we also noticed in *Zhenhuan Zhuan*, some of the repetition is not dealt with via adopting Omission + Addition. The repeated part is omitted, and no verbal or non-verbal modes are added. For example, there is a scene in which three young mistresses are walking in a hurry, looking terrified, because they encounter Consort Hua and witness how she gives a severe lesson to another young mistress First Attendant Xia. One of Consort Hua's purposes is to show them who is the real boss in the harem. The three young and innocent mistresses hastily run away when they are finally dismissed by Consort Hua. After running for a while, they come to a secluded place. They stop and can barely breathe. One of them keeps saying "吓死我了, 吓死我了" (I was scared to death, I was scared to death) very fast while covering her chest with her hand. In this case, Omission is used so in the TT only one sentence "I was scared to death" could be found. Though the omitted part can in a degree be supplemented by the IMAGE, i.e. the above-described setting, if an exclamation mark is added after the English sentence, it could better express the fear they had been through.

The fourth finding is the written form of the translation of the internal monologue (Case 10) and written text (Case 11) in AVT of this costume drama. In order to properly present them to the TT audience, the solution is to change the style of the font of the subtitle and make it different from the way of presenting normal dialogues.

5.2 Intersemiotic shifts: roles of non-verbal modes

When exploring the reasons behind the intersemiotic shifts, we firstly need to emphasize the polysemiotic nature of AVT. This nature makes the consideration of non-verbal modes including IMAGE and para-verbal means indispensable in the translation process. The five types of shifts we analyzed are all cross-modal. In what follows, we will discuss them to examine how they affect the translation process.

Our study has found that IMAGE, which is related with visual elements such as physical movements of the body, facial expressions, and the distance between speakers, can affect the translation decision and lead to intersemiotic shifts. For example, when eunuchs speak to the superordinate, they often have to bow and always lower their heads. They look quite submissive or obsequious, either standing beside the superordinate or keeping a decent distance. As a matter of fact, this also apply to the spatial relation between the Emperor and the Empress and the concubines. In such a harem, where power and hierarchy prevail, these visual images play an important role to show the interpersonal relationship.

Therefore, we find the strategies of Addition, Omission, Addition + Omission, and Compensation appropriate, as addressing terms are added to show the power relations reflected via the IMAGE. In other cases when the meaning is self-evident in the visual modes, Omission is accordingly adopted.

Para-verbal means involve volume, intonation, and speed. The various emotions and feelings like angry, upset, excited, sacred, joyful, and scornful are usually transmitted via para-verbal means. It cannot be denied that the volume or speed can also be received by the TT audience, which seems to debase the importance of para-verbal means. But considering that it is impossible for para-verbal means to function alone, like the scene about Zhenhuan and Marquess Guo (Case 1), their desperation demonstrated via facial expressions and yells could never be conveyed via verbal modes alone. The addition of the punctuation marks seems to be an effective method to be used with such cases.

5.3 Intersemiotic shifts: reasons and effects

Behind the intersemiotic shifts involved in this costume drama, we argue that cultural differences play a role. It can help to explain the adoption of the intersemiotic shifts, especially when dealing with verbal expressions in the ST. We notice the abundant use of expressions with rich cultural connotations such as "有喜" and addressing terms like "臣妾" and "微臣" when dealing with expressions with rich cultural connotations such as "有喜" and addressing terms like "臣妾" and "微臣." As discussed in the case analysis, Omission and Compensation are usually adopted. In Omission, the addressing term like "臣妾" is omitted, and in Compensation, the fundamental meaning of the expressions is provided to the target audience. That the two intersemiotic shifts become involved is probably because the profound cultural information is difficult to transmit to the target audience, especially in the context of AVT, which has a strict requirement on the number of words appearing on the screen. For conventional written text, scholars proposed various ways to deal with culture-loaded expressions such as paraphrasing (Baker 2000, 80), borrowing and calque (Vinay and Darbelnet 1958/2000, 85), semantic translation with Pinyin, semantic translation with annotation, addition and substitution and so forth (Zhang and Chen 2013, 99). It can be seen that due to the cultural differences between Chinese and English, most of the methods recommended tend to either explain the meaning, keep the ST unchanged, or add information to explain the ST. In the AVT context, due to the constraint of the space of time, explaining the complicated cultural connotations such as the addressing system is impossible. How to transmit the meaning without losing too much of the cultural connotation? IMAGE thus plays a role. The physical movements such as kneeling down to greet the Emperor, lowering the head when greeting the people who are superordinate to the speaker, and keeping distance from the superordinate may be considered when dealing with expressions with cultural connotation as they can supplement the cultural loss in the verbal translation process, like what happens in the intersemiotic shifts Compensation and Omission.

We have examined 408 examples in which Addition, Omission, Omission + Addition, Compensation, and Typographic Transformation are adopted. The general feature is that on the whole, the translation is simpler or shorter in the multimodal context. It is easy to understand that omission often leads to the shortening of the ST. Then why do Addition, Omission + Addition, and Compensation also result in shorter translations? There might be various reasons, but one of them is very possible. For Addition, in most of the cases, punctuation marks are added to supplement the omitted parts. Punctuation marks can not only preserve the omitted textual meaning but also compensate and convey the meaning implied in the accompanying scene. For Compensation, as only the fundamental meaning is provided to the target audience, the verbal expressions are usually concise too. The cultural connotation gets supplemented via the accompanying setting.

Taking from this finding, we can argue that, for AVT translation in the multimodal context, one important measure is to reduce the linguistic expressions to fit in with the needs of the limited time and space, and to add other codes such as punctuations and to make use of the IMAGE to realize the intended meaning in the multimodal contexts for the target audience.

Last, we argue that the proposed intersemiotic shifts is an attempt to expand the boundary of translation shift theories proposed by previous scholars (Vinay and Darbelnet 1958/2000; Catford 1965; Loh 1958a, 1958b, quoted in Zhang and Pan 2009). The previous translation shift theories, regardless from which perspective they are discussed, are based on the understanding of the translation process between verbal modes, without considering the function of the non-verbal modes such as IMAGE and para-verbal means as illustrated in our study. The integration of the non-verbal modes in translation studies is a small step forward in the further exploration of the interaction of various modes in translation process.

6 Conclusion

In this chapter, we have examined the translation of costume drama subtitles in the context of polysemiotics, using the ST and TT of *Zhenhuan Zhuan* as the study object. We argue that various medial variants such as IMAGE and speech para-verbal means must be taken into consideration during the translation process so as to convey the textual meaning and non-verbal meaning on the one hand, and to maintain as much as possible the meaning potential of the ST on the other hand.

Based on the model of semiotic shifts across codes proposed by Delabastita, we proposed the intersemiotic shifts model as the analytical framework, which includes Addition, Omission, Omission + Addition, Compensation, and Typographic Transformation. A total of 408 cases were analyzed in our study. When the method of Addition is used, punctuation marks or addressing terms are often added to clarify the hidden meaning or cultural connotation in the LANGUAGE or IMAGE. The method of Omission + Addition is applied to deal modal particles. Some Chinese modal particles are often omitted while exclamation marks are added to transfer the strong emotions of the speaker, which is always reflected through the accompanying scenes. The method of Omission is often used to render repeated expressions or to omit some modal particles. The method of Compensation is used to handle cultural differences, para-verbal means, and other non-verbal aspects, and the addressing terms, especially self-addressing terms, are replaced with general pronouns "I" and "you." The hierarchical relations between addressers and addressees are often compensated by the IMAGE in the accompanying scenes. In addition, Compensation is used to explain an expression which is absent in the target language. When the non-verbal variants are considered, the loss of meaning can in a sense be made up. The last method, Typographic Transformation, is mainly used to differentiate normal dialogues from internal monologues or written texts.

The roles of non-verbal modes including IMAGE and para-verbal elements are discussed in detail, demonstrating the vital importance of them in helping to transmit the meaning of the ST to the TT reader. It is argued that cultural differences between Chinese and English is one of the possible reasons leading to the intersemiotic shifts such as Omission and Compensation in AVT translation. By proposing the intersemiotic shifts model, we believe that it is a meaningful attempt to expand the boundary of current translation shift theories as they focus on the verbal modes.

In terms of the limitations of the research, during our research we found there are still some other aspects that need further exploration. For example, will the synergy of verbal and non-verbal modes (such as the makeup, the costumes, and the facial expressions) of Zhenhuan in the TT exert an influence on her identity reconstruction? More studies of the translation of a wide range of audiovisual texts can be conducted to further develop the model and investigate various issues arising from the translation process.

Acknowledgement

This work is supported by the UIC Research Grant Project (R201925) of BNU–HKBU United International College; Zhuhai Philosophy and Social Sciences Foundation and UIC Research Grant Project (R202042) of BNU–HKBU United International College.

References

Baker, M. 2000. *In Other Words: A Coursebook on Translation*. Beijing: Foreign Language Teaching and Research Press.
Baldry, A., and Thibault, P.J. 2006. *Multimodal Transcription and Text Analysis: A Multimedia Toolkit and Coursebook*. London: Equinox.
Bosseaux, C. 2008. "Buffy the Vampire Slayer Characterization in the Musical Episode of the TV Series." *The Translator* 14(2): 343–372.
Catford, J. C. 1965. *A Linguistic Theory of Translation: An Essay in Applied Linguistics*. Oxford: Oxford University Press.
Chaume, F. 2004. "Film Studies and Translation Studies: Two Disciplines at Stake in Audiovisual Translation." *Meta* 49(1): 12–24.
Chuang, Y-T. 2006. "Studying Subtitle Translation from a Multi-Modal Approach." *Babel* 52(4): 372–383.
Delabastita, D. 1990. "Translation and the Mass Media." In *Translation, History and Culture*, edited by Susan Bassnett and Andrew Lefevere, 97–109. London & New York: Pinter Publishers.
Diaz Cintas, J. and A. Remael. 2007. *Audiovisual Translation: Subtitling*. Manchester: St Jerome.
El-Farahaty, H. 2018. "A Multimodal Analysis of Political Satire: Webcomics and GIFs in Post-Arab Spring Egypt." *Linguistica Antverpiensia, New Series: Themes in Translation Studies* 17: 37–57.
Gottlieb, H. 2008. "Multidimensional Translation." In *Understanding Translation*, edited by A. Schjoldager, H. Gottlieb and I. Klitgard, 39–65. Copenhagen: Academica.
Kourdis, E. 2015. "Semiotics of Translation: An Interdisciplinary Approach to Translation." In *International Handbook of Semiotics*, edited by P.P. Trifonas, 303–320. Dordrecht: Springer.
Kress, G. 2009. "What is a Mode?" In *The Routledge Handbook of Multimodal Analysis*, edited by C. Jewitt, 54–67. London & New York: Routledge.
Kress, G., and T. van Leeuwen. 2001. *Multimodal Discourse: The Modes and Media of Contemporary Communication*. London: Edward Arnold.
Lambert, J. and D. Delabastita. 1996. "La traduction de textes audiovisuels: Modes et enjeux culturels." In *Les transferts linguistiques dans les médias audiovisuels*, edited by Yves Gambier, 33–58. Villeneuve d'Ascq: Septentrion.
Lee, T.Y.E. 2018. "Communicative Functions and Characterization in the Chinese Graphic Novel Adaptation of *Little Women*." *Linguistica Antverpiensia, New Series: Themes in Translation Studies* 17: 58–70.

Liu, X. H. 刘晓辉, and L. Zhang. 张亮. 2017. "影视剧字幕翻译及跨文化传播 – 以美版《甄嬛传》为例." (YING SHI JU ZI MU FAN YI JI KUA WEN HUA CHUAN BO: YI MEI BAN *ZHEN HUAN ZHUAN* WEI LI). *View on Publishing* (6): 64–66.

Loh, D. 陆殿扬. 1958a. *Translation: Its Principles and Technique*. Book One. Beijing: Times Publishing.

Loh, D. 陆殿扬. 1958b. *Translation: Its Principles and Techniques*. Book Two. Beaijing: Times Publishing.

Perez-Gonzalez, Luis. 2014. *Audiovisual Translation Theories, Methods and Issues*. London & New York: Routledge.

Shi, C. R. 石春让, and X. Fu.付秀丽. 2016. "《甄嬛传》美版字幕中称谓词翻译的失与得." (*ZHEN HUAN ZHUAN* MEI BAN ZI MU ZHONG CHENG WEI CI FAN YI DE SHI YU DE). *Journal of Changji University* (4): 90–93.

Stöckl, H. 2004. "In Between Modes: Language and Image in Printed Media." In *Perspectives on Multimodality*, edited by Eija Ventola, Cassily Charles, and Martin Kaltenbacher, 9–30. Amsterdam & Philadelphia: John Benjamins.

Taylor, C. 2003. "Multimodal Transcription in the Analysis, Translation and Subtitling of Italian Films." *The Translator* 9(2): 191–205.

Vinay, J.P. and J. Darbelnet. 1958/2000. "A Methodology for Translation, translated by J.C. Sager and M.J. Hamel, in *The Translation Studies Reader*, edited by Lawrence Venuti, 84–93. London & New York: Routledge.

Xiong, J. 2016. "Translation of Films and TV Series from the Perspective of Bourdieu's Field-habitus Theory – A Case Study of *Empresses in the Palace*." *Foreign Language and Literature Research* (2): 73–78.

Yu, H. and Z. Song. 2017. "Picture – Text Congruence in Translation: Images of the Zen Master on Book Covers and in Verbal Texts." *Social Semiotics* 27(5): 604–623.

Zabalbeascoa, P. 1996. "Translating Jokes for Dubbed Television Situation Comedies." *The Translator* 2(2): 235–267.

Zabalbeascoa, P. 2008. "The Nature of the Audiovisual Text and its Parameters." In *The Didactics of Audiovisual Translation*, edited by Jorge Diaz Cintas, 21–37. Amsterdam & Philadelphia: John Benjamins.

Zhang, M. F. 张美芳, Chen X. 陈曦. 2013. "巧传信息 适应读者 – 以故宫博物院网站材料翻译为例" (QIAO CHUAN XIN XI, SHI YING DU ZHE: YI GU GONG BO WU YUAN WANG ZHAN CAI LIAO WEI LI). *Chinese Translators Journal* 6(4): 99–103.

Zhang, M. and L. Pan. 2009. "Introducing a Chinese Perspective on Translation Shifts." *The Translator* 15(2): 351–374.

2 A multimodal study of paratexts in bilingual picturebooks on Mulan

Chen Xi (Janet)

1 Introduction

The picturebook is an art form "based on the combination of two levels of communication, the visual and the verbal" (Nikolajeva and Scott 2001, 29). They are also regarded as "multimodal texts, where image and writing come together to convey a message and constructing meaning" (Coifman 2013, 21). In picturebooks, not only the verbal texts can convey information, but the visual materials, such as book covers and illustrations, also influence readers' overall reading experiences. The abundant paratextual elements in picturebooks provide the potential of paratextual and multimodal perspectives for picturebook studies.

Up to now, various studies on picturebooks have explored their characteristics, structures and functions (Arizpe and Styles 2003; Kiefer 2011; Nikolajeva and Scott 2001), or have focused on the text-image interaction in picturebooks (Doonan 1993; Evans 2009; Nodelman 1988). However, few studies were conducted on the paratexts of picturebooks before 2001. (Nikolajeva and Scott 2001) Since 2001, after the publication of *How Picturebooks Work* (2001), several scholars have particularly investigated the meaning potentials of different paratextual elements in picturebooks (Beckett 2012; Duran and Bosch 2011; Kümmerling-Meibauer and Meibauer 2013; Sipe and McGuire 2006).

Moreover, the interplay between images and texts in picturebooks has attracted the interest of scholars in the field of multimodality, and many multimodal studies have been conducted on picturebooks, especially with the use of systemic functional linguistics (SFL) and the visual social semiotics (Moya Guijarro and Sanz 2008; Moya Guijarro 2011, 2014; Painter, Martin, and Unsworth 2013), which expands the multimodal approaches to picturebook studies.

During the past decades, more studies have shifted their attention to the translation of picturebooks (Lathey 2006, 2010; Oittinen 2003, 2008, 2010; Oittinen et al. 2018; O'Sullivan 1999, 2005). Some studies have specifically explored the paratextual elements in picturebook translation (Gerber 2012; Kung 2013; Tsai 2013). However, compared with the variety of studies in this field in other countries, picturebook translation is still sidelined in China. To date, there are only a few Chinese monographs on the study of picturebooks (Fang 2012; Hao 2009; Peng 2006). Few Chinese journal articles focus on the translation of picturebooks

(Fu 2016; Xu and He 2015) and even fewer on paratextual studies in picturebook translation. These results reflect the research limitations on picturebook translation in China on the one hand, and indicate a great demand for more specialized paratextual studies on picturebook translation in the Chinese cultural context on the other.

This study aims to investigate the role of paratexts in the translation of picturebooks on Mulan, in the hope of providing a specialized paratextual study on picturebook translation of the Chinese cultural classic. Based on the concept of paratext (Genette 1997; Pellatt 2013) and the theory of visual grammar (Kress and van Leeuwen1996, 2006), this study explores how the Chinese classic "Mulan Ci" is repackaged in contemporary bilingual picturebooks through the paratextual elements in translation.

2 Paratexts in picturebook translation

The term "paratext" was originally coined by Gérard Genette (1997, 2) as

> a zone between text and off-text, . . . a zone not only of transition but also of transaction: a privileged place of a pragmatics and a strategy, of an influence on the public, an influence that – whether well or poorly understood and achieved – is at the service of a better reception for the text and a more pertinent reading of it.

Paratexts have "spatial, temporal, substantial, pragmatic and functional characteristics" (ibid., 4), and the function of paratexts is "to make present, to ensure the text's presence in the world, its 'reception' and consumption in the form of a book" (ibid., 1). According to Genette's classification, paratexts can be further divided into peritexts and epitexts. Peritexts refer to the elements within the same volume, such as front covers, titles, authorial names, prefaces and notes, while epitexts refer to more distant elements located outside the book, such as interviews, conversations, letters and diaries (ibid., 5). Genette's analysis of paratext provides a solid theoretical basis for further studies; however, he mainly focuses on literature and does not involve the issues of paratext in translation or translation as paratext. Expanding Genette's ideas into translation studies, Pellatt (2013) examines different types of paratexts in translation in his anthology. According to Pellatt (2013, 1), paratext is "the text that surrounds and supports the core text, like layers of packaging that initially protect and gradually reveal the essence of the packaged item." Nowadays, as the forms of paratexts become increasingly varied, this interpretation of paratexts includes more non-verbal materials in the research scope. In this highly digitalized era, paratexts and their cultural, political or commercial implications have caused growing concerns in translation studies (Armstrong 2007; Gil-Bardají, Oreo, and Rovira-Esteva 2012; Pellatt 2013; Tahir-Gürçağlar 2002). Meanwhile, paratextual studies in China have also experienced a rapid surge during the past decade, with translation studies becoming a new research focus (He and Shen 2013; Huang 2018; Zhang 2014).

On the basis of paratext concepts (Genette 1997; Pellatt 2013), in this study paratext is broadly referred to as, in Pellatt's (2013, 1) words, "any material additional to, appended to or external to the core text which has functions of explaining, defining, instructing, or supporting, adding background information, or the relevant opinions and attitudes of scholars, translators and reviewers". In terms of the basic structure, a picturebook usually contains the front cover, endpaper, title page, inside page and back cover. In line with the essential elements of a picturebook, the paratexts in picturebooks mainly include the following types: footnote or endnote, preface/foreword, introduction and afterword, index, title and subtitle, front or back cover, illustration, blurb on dust jacket and flap, frontispiece, dust jacket design, endpaper design, title page design, font, page layout and so forth.

The aforementioned paratexts play different functions in picturebooks and their translations. On the one hand, paratexts such as notes, prefaces/forewords, introductions and afterwords may reveal translators' preferences and strategies in the translation process. For example, translators may introduce the translated works and give their translation views in the preface, introduction or afterword. They may also provide explanations of some social, historical or cultural background information in footnotes or endnotes to help target readers better understand the translated works. Sometimes, prefacing and footnoting can even be an effective tool for translators to oppose cultural hegemony and highlight gender identity (von Flotow 1991, 69–84). On the other hand, paratexts such as front covers, illustrations, blurbs on dust jacket and flap and dust jacket design are usually influenced by patrons or publishing agencies; therefore, these paratexts help to understand the production and reception of the translated works in the historical and cultural environment of the target language.

3 Visual grammar

Kress and van Leeuwen (1996) propose a "grammar of visual design" based on Halliday's (1978, 1994) systemic functional grammar (SFG). In their framework, in accordance with the three metafunctions by SFG, four major elements are used to describe the semiotic resources of images: (1) representational resources that visually represent the material world; (2) interactive resources that visually interpret the interaction between the viewer and what is represented in a visual design; (3) modality judgments that concern the reliability or credibility of visual messages; and (4) compositional arrangements that relate to the value of the information and visual emphasis of visual resources. As a useful tool for visual analysis, the visual grammar has been adopted to analyse various types of visual materials, such as magazine covers (Bell 2001), posters (Jewitt and Oyama 2001), print advertisements (Friedman and Ron 2017) and textbooks (Vu and Febrianti 2018).

According to visual grammar, ideational metafunction is "the ability of semiotic systems to represent objects and their relations in a world outside the representational system or in the semiotic system of a culture" (Kress and van Leeuwen 1996, 47). The semiotic resources to realize the ideational function include represented participants, processes and circumstances. Represented participants (RPs) refer to the depicted participants "about whom or which we are speaking or writing or producing images" (ibid., 48), such as the people, places and things in the image. Processes refer to the depicted actions and relations in the image. Circumstances refer to the depicted settings in the image.

The interpersonal metafunction in visual images is to establish relations between the represented participants (in the visual image), the viewer and the represented participant, as well as the producers (artists/designers) of the image and the viewer. (Kress and van Leeuwen 1996, 114) The semiotic resources to realize the interpersonal metafunction include image act and gaze, social distance and intimacy, horizontal angle and involvement, vertical angle and power, and modality. Kress and van Leeuwen (2006, 124–129) further elaborate that social distance relates to the degree of intimacy established between the viewer and the RPs depicted in a composition, and the scale of intimacy or distance varies between close-up shots, long shots and medium shots. The visual attitude in the image is established by the way the viewer and the RPs are located in terms of the vertical and horizontal planes (ibid., 129–143). Modality in the image refers to the truth value or credibility of the visual mode about the real world. The resemblance of an image to the objects or the RPs in the real world is defined by eight different modality markers: colour saturation, colour modulation, colour differentiation, contextualization, representation, depth, illumination and brightness (ibid., 160–162). Take colour saturation as an example. If colour conveys emotion, then saturation is the fullness of that emotion, and the saturation scale is a scale that runs from maximum emotive intensity to maximally subdued, maximally toned-down emotion (van Leeuwen 2013, 65). High saturation may be positive, adventurous or vigorous, while low saturation may express a feeling of blandness, repression and gloom.

The textual metafunction in visual images integrates the representational and interactive meaning of the image. The semiotic resources to realize the textual metafunction include information value, salience and framing. According to Kress and van Leeuwen (2006, 177), the placement of elements endows them with the specific informational values attached to the various zones of the image: Give-New (left and right), Ideal-Real (top and bottom), and Centre-Margin. Salience contains elements that "are made to attract the viewer's attention to different degrees, as realized by such factors as placement in the foreground, or background, relative size, contrasts in tonal value (or colour), differences in sharpness, etc." (ibid.). Framing is achieved through "the presence or absence of framing devices (realized by elements which create dividing lines, or by actual frame lines) disconnects or connects elements of the image" (ibid.).

4 Methodology

The picturebooks under investigation are based on the legend of Mulan, a woman who disguises herself as a man to take her father's place in the army and thus becomes a legendary heroine in Chinese history. The earliest written account of the legend of Mulan is an anonymous folk ballad titled "The Ballad of Mulan (Mulan Ci)" dated to the fourth to sixth centuries ce. This ballad consists of 392 words and 31 couplets, in which Mulan is vividly portrayed as a courageous girl displaying the Chinese traditional values of *xiao* (filial piety) and *zhong* (loyalty) in the patriarchal society. In the past decades, Mulan's legend has been adapted into different art forms such as books, films, TV series and dramas. Among the different adaptations, several bilingual picturebooks represent the legendary Mulan in different ways. This study attempts to explore how the Chinese classic "Mulan Ci" is repackaged in contemporary bilingual picturebooks through the paratextual elements in translation. The data for analysis are selected from four bilingual picturebooks listed in the following section.

The Legend of Mu Lan: A Heroine of Ancient China (1992) is the first English picturebook of Mulan published in the United States. *China's Bravest Girl: The Legend of Hua Mu Lan* (1993) is published by Children's Book Press, the first independent press in the United States to focus on publishing children's literature by and about people of colour. *The Ballad of Mulan* (1998) is published by Pan Asian Publications, a publisher aiming to "promote Chinese culture and to encourage children to learn a second language" (Pan Asian Publications homepage). *Song of Mulan* (2010) is published by Shanghai People's Fine Arts Publishing House in China. In its bilingual foreword, it states that this bilingual picturebook is one of the "Chinese-English Illustrated Series of Ancient Chinese Classical Narrative Poems" and aims to "assist overseas readers to better appreciate the charm and beauty of Chinese poetry and Chinese paintings."

As shown in Figure 2.1, the paratexts in these four bilingual picturebooks are mainly divided into two types: verbal paratexts and non-verbal paratexts. Verbal paratexts include footnotes or endnotes, prefaces and forewords, and introductions and afterwords. Non-verbal paratexts consist of front or back covers, pictures in endpapers or title pages, and the page layout. This study covers all the verbal paratexts and non-verbal paratexts in the four bilingual picturebooks on Mulan.

The analysis involves three steps. The first step is to identify and examine the different functions of verbal paratexts in picturebooks on Mulan through textual

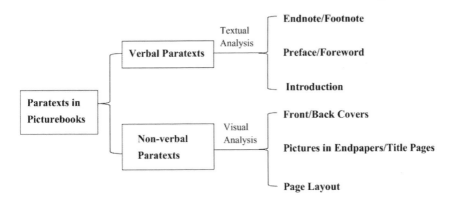

Figure 2.1 Classification of paratexts in this study

48   *Chen Xi (Janet)*

analysis, which includes a detailed comparative analysis of the Chinese texts and the English translations. The second step will employ visual grammar (Kress and van Leeuwen 1996, 2006) to assist in the visual analysis of non-verbal paratexts in picturebook translation, with a special focus on the representation of Mulan's image in the front or back covers of picturebooks. The third step is to explore how these verbal and non-verbal paratexts collaborate and interact with each other to repackage the Chinese classic *Mulan* in contemporary picturebooks and at the same time disseminate Chinese culture to Western readers.

5   Paratexts in the translation of picturebooks on Mulan

This section investigates the verbal paratexts in picturebooks through a textual analysis and then conducts a visual analysis of non-verbal paratexts in picturebook translation.

5.1   Verbal paratexts

Through the investigation, there are different verbal paratexts inserted in the translations of the four bilingual picturebooks on Mulan, namely endnotes, footnotes, preface and foreword. In this section, examples of these four types of paratexts will be presented so as to see what kind of information they carry.

5.1.1   Footnote/endnote

Among these four picturebooks, footnotes and endnotes are more extensively used as verbal paratexts in the translation of *Song of Mulan* (2010) and *The Ballad of Mulan* (1998). In *Song of Mulan*, footnotes are most widely used compared with other types of paratexts. In the target text, in addition to the English translation of the ballad, there are eight footnotes added, most of which aim to supplement the cultural or historical background information of words in the target text specific to Chinese culture.

Example 1

Source text

当窗理云鬓，
对镜帖花黄。

Target text

She combs by window her cloud hair,
And mirror finds her brow decked hair*.

* Fashion had it that, during the Later Wei Dynasties (493–556), females other than those in an imperial palace were only allowed to paint the face and brow with yellow and black colours, though they had been free to use red and dark green colours before, according to Yu Shenxing's *Gushan's Sketches* (*Gushan Bizhu*).

Back translation

By the window she combs her cloud hair,
And in the mirror, she pastes Hua Huang.

Example 1 illustrates the scene when Mulan changes back into female clothes and dresses up after returning from the battlefield. In the source text, "云鬓 (Yun Bin)" and "花黄 (Hua Huang)" are two culture-specific words that are loaded with specific cultural background information. "云鬓 (Yun Bin)" describes the ancient Chinese maiden's beautiful hairstyle; "花黄 (Hua Huang)," which refers to a kind of facial ornament of ancient Chinese women, is perhaps an unfamiliar word to foreign readers. Therefore, in the target text, a detailed footnote about the translation of "花黄" (Hua Huang) as "brow decked hair" is added, which introduces the historical background of the custom of using brow decked hair in ancient China and helps English readers understand this culturally loaded word in Chinese.

Example 2

Source text

朔气传金柝，
寒光照铁衣。

Target text

The watchman gongs* in northland air,
And coats of mail in chill light flare.

* Gong: here refers to the act of clapping a cauldron. In ancient wartime, the cauldron served to cook during the day and announce the time at night.

Back translation

The cold air in the north is transmitting the sound of night watch;
The chill moonlight shines on the soldiers' iron armour.

Example 2 describes the harsh environment that Mulan has experienced on the battlefield. In the source text, "金柝 (Jin Tuo)" is a culture-specific item that refers to a kind of iron cauldron used in ancient Chinese armies for cooking during the day and for the reporting of night watch at night. In the target text, "朔气传金柝" is translated into "The watchman gongs in northern air," with a footnote of "gong" added. This footnote assists readers to understand the cultural and historical backgrounds of the period when Mulan's legend happened, which also produces a faithful translation of the ballad.

Apart from footnotes, endnotes have also been employed as a translation method to supplement necessary background information for target readers. For instance, in *The Ballad of Mulan* (1998), Zhang Songnan, the illustrator, writer and translator of this picturebook, has added a one-page endnote titled "Historical Notes on Mulan." In this long endnote, he explains in detail the history from the end of the Han Dynasty to the Northern Wei Dynasty, the cultural fusion of Xianbei culture into Han culture and the development of Mulan's legend in different historical periods in China. It is worth noting that in this endnote, Zhang (1998) particularly emphasizes:

> It was during the Northern Wei period that the ballad of Mulan was composed as a popular song before being officially sanctioned by the court. Whether Mulan's story was based on an actual case of a victorious female general is unknown, but her independent spirit and martial skills clearly suggest her origin in the nomadic-warrior Xianbei culture, rather than Han culture, where women's roles were rigidly defined.

The Ballad of Mulan is a well-designed picturebook with particular images of Mulan and special layout arrangement. Therefore, this supplementary endnote is significant as it sets the historical and cultural backgrounds in this picturebook as the Northern Wei Dynasty and Xianbei culture, which might help target readers better understand the image of Mulan in this picturebook and corresponds to the special layout arrangement with added pictures in the endpapers of this picturebook.

5.1.2 Preface/foreword

Compared with footnotes or endnotes, prefaces or forewords usually contain more supplementary information as verbal paratexts. For example, *Song of Mulan* (2010) is the only one that includes a foreword among these four picturebooks. In this picturebook, there is a seven-page bilingual foreword offering a comprehensive introduction of the whole picturebook. The foreword first introduces the features and development of Chinese narrative poetry, especially the *yuefu* folksong, which is the literary genre of "Mulan Ci". It then provides in detail the personal information of the illustrator and the translator and their illustrating and translating strategies in this picturebook, through which readers might get a clue that the illustrator and the translator both make efforts to produce a faithful representation of Mulan in the Chinese classics. In addition, it talks about the intricate relationship between Chinese traditional poetry and Chinese traditional painting, which seems to be irrelevant information but in fact is closely related to the aim of this book, to "assist overseas readers to better appreciate the charm and beauty of Chinese poetry and Chinese paintings". Therefore, the detailed and comprehensive bilingual foreword in *Song of Mulan* functions as a useful verbal paratext to provide essential information of this culture-loaded picturebook both for Chinese and Western readers. Moreover, in this picturebook, several small pictures are added

A multimodal study of paratexts on Mulan 51

in the inside pages as non-verbal paratexts (see Figure 2.4), with the function to help foreign readers better appreciate and comprehend the essence of Chinese painting. This special layout echoes the discussion on Chinese traditional poetry and Chinese traditional painting in the introduction. In this way, readers can not only acquire knowledge about Chinese traditional poetry and painting, but also have an intuitive sense of Chinese painting's charm through the images of Mulan and non-verbal paratexts in the picturebook.

5.2 Non-verbal paratexts

In addition to the verbal paratexts, different non-verbal paratexts are also utilized to realize the representation of Mulan in the four bilingual picturebooks under investigation. These non-verbal paratexts are mainly divided into three categories: front or back covers, pictures in endpapers or title pages and the page layout. The front or back covers aim to establish the relationship between readers and the picturebooks, realizing the interpersonal function of non-verbal paratexts. The pictures in endpapers or title pages represent special objects related to the content of inside pages, realizing the ideational function of non-verbal paratexts. Furthermore, the page layout arrangements play the textual function in the picturebook via the integration of the images and texts, and composite the visual narrative of the whole picturebook. For these three categories, specific examples will be presented in this section, illustrating the ideational, interpersonal and textual functions of these non-verbal paratexts.

5.2.1 Front/back covers establishing relations between participants

The ideational, interpersonal and textual functions simultaneously contribute to the meaning potentials in book covers. Book covers usually provide the reader with a first impression of the books, and they have significant functions as the "first and foremost marketing devices, and secondarily freestanding art objects" (Mossop 2018, 2). Furthermore, as quoted from Genette (1997, 2–4) earlier in this chapter, the paratext serves as a strategy to have influence on the public and achieve a better reception of the text among target readers. Therefore, the analysis mainly focuses on the interpersonal function of book covers, and regards front and back covers as non-verbal paratexts that prominently function to establish relations between readers and books.

However, within the field of translation studies, there are only a few studies focusing on the translation of book covers (Furukawa 2012; Roditakis 2012; Sonzogni 2011), and even fewer go deeper to explore the paratextual function of cover in translation (Alvstad 2012; Gerber 2012; Tahir-Gürçağlar 2002). To provide a more systematic visual analysis of book covers, this study adopts Kress and van Leeuwen's (1996, 2006) visual grammar, especially the interpersonal and textual functions, to analyse the book covers of the bilingual picturebooks on Mulan. The

52 *Chen Xi (Janet)*

visual analysis of covers not only includes the images of Mulan in front covers but also contains the layout arrangements of back covers.

It is found that these four picturebooks all take efforts to reinforce the core image of Mulan through the realization of the interpersonal function in the front covers, which enhances the interactive relations between readers and picturebooks and meanwhile attracts the reader's interest in the book. For example, the long shot is usually adopted to illustrate the whole figure of Mulan, her action and the settings, which enhances the visual narrative of Mulan's story in the front cover. Sometimes, the layout in the back cover also plays a significant role in realizing the textual function. Salience and special layout arrangements are especially used in the back covers to publicize the picturebook and further stimulate readers' desire to buy the book.

Take the front and back covers of *China's Bravest Girl* (1993) as an example (see Figure 2.2). On the front cover, the realization of interpersonal function reinforces Mulan's image as a military figure in profile riding in the battlefield. In terms of the ideational function, the setting is in the azure night sky, with little shining stars and a bright full moon. Under the white moonlight, military camps with soldiers and horses appear in the distance. Mulan rides on a white horse, pulls the rein with one hand, and points a spear to the sky with the other hand. Mulan is dressed in a full set of armour and a helmet, with the helmet rendered in gold and her armour rendered in different colours such as purple, blue, golden, red and green. Her bright red cloak is fluttering in the sky, and there is a golden sword

Figure 2.2 Front cover and back cover of *China's Bravest Girl: The Legend of Hua Mu Lan* (1993)

Source: Text copyright © 1993 by Charlie Chin. Illustration copyright © 1993 by Tomie Arai. Chinese translation copyright © 1993 by Wang Zing Chu. Permission arranged with Children's Book Press, an imprint of Lee & Low Books Inc., New York, NY 10016.

in her waist. Regarding the interpersonal function, the whole figure of Mulan is represented through a "long shot," producing a kind of far social distance between Mulan and readers. Besides, as Mulan's hair is mainly concealed under the helmet and only her side face can be seen in the image, it is difficult to identify her facial expressions and the female quality of the character is thus weakened. Furthermore, warm colours, such as gold and red, are used in large areas of the image of Mulan, whereas the background setting is mainly depicted in cool colours, such as white and azure, which conveys a sense of coldness and loneliness on the battlefield. The use of different colours in the depiction of Mulan enhances the degree of colour differentiation, and the high degree of colour saturation creates a sense of vigour in the visual expression.

Textually, with no framing in the cover image, the salience of Mulan's image is established by the colour contrast between Mulan's figure and the background setting. The layouts of the bilingual book titles are different. The Chinese title "巾帼英雄花木兰" is printed in traditional Chinese in vertical on the right side of the front cover, while the English title *China's Bravest Girl* is arranged in horizontal on the top left corner, which shows the publisher's consideration about the reading traditions of both Chinese and Western readers. As to the translation of book titles, there is a culture-specific item "巾帼英雄 (Jin Guo Ying Xiong)" in the Chinese book title. In ancient China, noble women often wore a headdress made of silk or hair in sacrifice ceremonies. This kind of headdress is called "巾帼 (Jin Guo)," and it is usually decorated with precious jewels such as gold and jade. As "巾帼" is the noble ornament of ancient Chinese women, people begin to call the great heroine as "巾帼英雄," and "巾帼" is then used to address respectable women. In the English book title, the culture-specific item "巾帼英雄" is translated into *China's Bravest Girl*, which removes the cultural connotation of this Chinese idiom but highlights the bravery of Chinese heroine Mulan in the concise expression. Meanwhile, the subtitle *The Legend of Hua Mu Lan* is added on the back cover to clearly indicate to readers that this book is based on Mulan's legendary story. Through the interaction between texts and images, the translation of book titles echoes the image of Mulan on the book covers: a brave military warrior in the battlefield.

While the front cover demonstrates the core image of Mulan in the picturebook, the back cover provides essential related information, which works as a blurb to help the reader directly and efficiently get the main storyline and the representative image of Mulan in this picturebook. Therefore, the role of the textual function seems more prominent on the back cover. On the one hand, on the back cover, the unframed English book title is reprinted in red horizontally against the yellow background. The colour contrast achieves the salience, making the title more eye-catching for readers. On the other hand, the Chinese book title is printed in traditional Chinese characters in vertical on the left side of the back cover, and it is specially framed by lines and colour contrast with a small picture as its background setting. In the small picture, there is a golden pheasant and several peonies in full bloom, which are both auspicious images in traditional Chinese culture. This special layout not only produces a strong sense of Chinoiserie but is also consistent with the inside page design in this picturebook. Below the English book title, there is a short English poem: "For love of her elderly father / she will dress in warrior's clothes, / walking and talking like a man, / so no one ever knows." This short poem tactfully summarizes the main storyline of Mulan's ballad. Meanwhile, as the legend of Mulan is adapted into Pipa lyric (a poetic form like Chinese traditional poetry) in this picturebook, this poetic form just echoes the poetic bilingual texts in inside pages. Furthermore, beneath the short English poem, a concise introduction tells us that the author tries to show us "a heroine who is courageous and wise, respectful and loving, and able to meet men on equal terms", which laconically sums up the representative image of Mulan in this picturebook for readers.

Amidst the four picturebooks, the covers of *The Legend of Mu Lan: A Heroine of Ancient China* (1992) have some similarities with *China's Bravest Girl*, in which the interpersonal function of the front cover and the textual function of the back cover work together to establish relations between readers and the core image of Mulan. However, in *The Legend of Mu Lan* (1992), a different image of Mulan is represented with different layout arrangements. In the front cover, it depicts a dynamic image of Mulan fighting on the battlefield. Ideationally, the main setting is in bright yellow with the high degree of colour saturation. In the sub-setting, a soldier holds a large blue flag printed with the Chinese character "Hua" (Mulan's family name), and several soldiers gallop on horseback. Mulan rides on a grey horse, pulls the rein with her left hand and holds a spear in her right hand. Dressed in red clothes, blue pants, black boots and a cerulean hat, Mulan wears brown armour, with her purple cloak fluttering in the wind. With regard to the interpersonal function, the use of different colours constitutes a high degree of colour differentiation in the image. In addition, the figure of Mulan is presented through a long shot: through her fluttering cloak, her fighting gesture and the galloping movement of the horse, the courageous and heroic behaviour of Mulan is expressed in the image. The long shot shows the whole figure of Mulan in the distance, creating a far social distance between Mulan and readers. Meanwhile, through the long shot, more background settings are included in the front cover, such as a soldier holding an army flag and several soldiers galloping on horseback. These detailed depictions in the setting help to convey a scene of a fierce battle, strengthening Mulan's military image. Additionally, Mulan's image is seen from a slightly low angle, with the four hooves of the horse raising off the ground as it gallops forward. As pointed out by Kress and van Leeuwen (2006, 140), "if the represented participant is seen from a low angle, then the relation between the interactive and represented participants is depicted as one in which the represented participant has power over the interactive participant". The representation of Mulan's image in this picture indeed produces a sense of power, and thus reinforces the powerful and valiant image of Mulan. In terms of the textual function, the image of Mulan is framed by thick blue lines in the centre, and the colour contrast establishes the salience of the image of Mulan in the picture. The bilingual book titles are printed horizontally in the upper part of the front cover, reflecting modern reading habits.

On the back cover of this picturebook, a short bilingual introduction is framed in the centre through lines and colour contrast, briefly describing the legend of Mulan

A multimodal study of paratexts on Mulan   55

and telling readers that this ballad is based on an ancient Chinese poem "Mulan Ci" in the Song Dynasty (ad 960–1279). In addition, a striking circular symbol labelled "Seal of Approval" is printed on the top left corner of the back cover. As the first English picturebook of Mulan published in the United States, *The Legend of Mu Lan* (1992) was awarded this seal of approval for a multicultural classic by the Multicultural Publishers and Education Council, and has been regarded as a required reading for the University of California Berkeley and San Francisco State Asian American Studies departments. This layout arrangement shows one of the publisher's common strategies: to arrange the rewards and recognition of picturebooks in salience so as to achieve effective publicity and arouse readers' interest in purchasing.

5.2.2 Pictures in endpapers/title pages representing objects and their relations

Endpapers are the

> pages glued inside the front and back covers of a book, and are thus the first parts of the interior of the book to be seen when the book is opened, as well as the last to be seen after the story has been read and the book is about to be closed.
>
> (Sipe and McGuire 2006, 292)

Although endpapers are a relatively trivial part of a book that might be ignored occasionally, they are, in fact, a significant paratext in picturebooks with different functions to "mediate the reader's transition to the interior of the book" (ibid.). The title page is the page at or near the front, which contains the title and subtitles of the book, the author, the name and address of the publisher and the publication date. On some occasions, special patterns or pictures are printed in endpapers or title pages with particular functions for the meaning construction in picturebooks. Endpapers and title pages may have ideational or interpersonal meanings in different cases. In this study, the pictures in endpapers or title pages are examined as non-verbal paratexts in picturebooks. From our investigation, the pictures in endpapers or title pages in these four picturebooks mainly play the ideational function to represent some specific objects related to the visual narratives in the inside pages, which may supplement essential information for readers.

For instance, in *The Ballad of Mulan* (1998), pictures as non-verbal paratexts are added on the endpapers to visually supplement the historical and cultural background information about Mulan's legend. In this picturebook, the endpapers cover two pages, including little pictures of different artefacts from the Northern Wei Dynasty. On the left of the verso page, from top to bottom, there are five little pictures: (a) baked clay figurines from a tomb: dancing girl, scholar-official and general; (b) detail from a painted lacquer screen: illustrated stories of virtuous men and women; (c) calligraphy in the Tablet style: rubbing from Wei stone stele announcing the dedication of a sculpted Buddha to a gentleman's son; (d) porcelain: celadon (gray-green) jar with lotus pattern, with the background of stone carving of mythical creatures; and (e) sculpture: Xianbei boy, from Maijishan Grottos in Gansu province. On the right of the recto page, from top to bottom, there are five additional little pictures: (a) sculpture: large Buddha from Yungang Grottos in Shanxi province; (b) wall painting: hunting scene from Mogao Grotto in Dunhuang of Gansu province; (c) a 40-volume geography text *The Water Chronicles* (*Shui Jing Zhu*) by Li Daoyuan; (d) a coin worth 5 ju minted in the reign of Emperor Xiaowen with the background of woven silk brocade fabric with stylized tree pattern; and (e) sculpture: Xianbei girl, from Maijishan Grottos in Gansu province. In the middle of the endpapers, there is a map showing the Xianbei nation's rise and migration, Mulan's journey to the front line, the Great Wall and the Chinese borders today.

Why are such detailed non-verbal paratexts about different historical and cultural background information of the Northern Wei Dynasty provided in this picturebook? The historical endnote which has just been analysed in the previous sections can answer this question. The historical endnote indicates that Mulan's legend in this picturebook is based on the historical and cultural backgrounds of the Northern Wei Dynasty. Therefore, the little pictures representing the political, economic and cultural lives of the Northern Wei Dynasty are added as non-verbal paratexts on the endpapers of this picturebook. Through the pictures of different artefacts from the Northern Wei Dynasty and the map on the Xianbei nation's migration and Mulan's military journey, foreign readers are provided with historical and cultural background information about the period when Mulan's legend happened, which corresponds to what the illustrator Zhang Songnan has mentioned in the preface "for everyone with an interest in ancient Chinese culture and literature".

5.2.3 Page layout integrating the images to each other

Page layout is related to "the simultaneous display of two facing pages" and "the drama of the turning of page" (Bader 1976, 1). With an important role in the visual narrative of picturebooks, page layout includes many issues that attend to the materiality of picturebooks, such as facing pages, frames, borders and typology. In this study, page layouts are the non-verbal paratexts that integrate images and texts to each other through the realization of textual function. These four picturebooks on Mulan all have their ingenious designs in inside page layout arrangements, but the page layouts in *China's Bravest Girl* (1993) and *Song of Mulan* (2010) seem to be more special compared with other ones.

Song of Mulan (2010) has the most unique inside page layout arrangement as it is the only one to include added pictures in inside pages. In *Song of Mulan*, six small pictures are added as non-verbal paratexts in different inside pages, which play the textual function to unify different images to each other. Figure 2.3 shows that in this picturebook the verbal texts are printed on the verso page and the picture corresponding to the verbal texts appears on the recto page, with a simple and helpful bilingual introduction of the ballad below each picture. Throughout this picturebook, different small pictures are supplemented as non-verbal paratexts

A multimodal study of paratexts on Mulan 57

Figure 2.3 Inside page layout of *Song of Mulan* (2010)

Source: Reproduced with the permission of Shanghai People's Fine Arts Publishing House. Copyright © 2010 by Yongli Tang.

alongside the verbal materials on the verso page. These small pictures are closely related to the images of Mulan on the recto page or correspond to the historical background of Mulan's legend, such as the picture of a plan of marketplace copied from a brick relief of the Eastern Han Dynasty, the picture of a pottery figure of a military officer in the Northern Dynasties, the picture of a cavalryman of the Northern Dynasties copied from the Dunhuang murals and so on. For instance, Figure 2.3 shows the texts and the image in which Mulan's father is drafted to the army. On the verso page, the verbal texts are listed as follows:

Example 3

Source Text	**Target Text**
"女亦无所思，	She says, "I'd not be deep in thought,
女亦无所忆，	Nor would I be by reveries caught,
昨夜见军帖，	But for the warfare bills last night,
可汗大点兵。	That Khan will draft all men of might.
军书十二卷，	On twelve enrolments to recruit,
卷卷有爷名。	My daddy's name is absolute."

58   *Chen Xi (Janet)*

Example 3 describes Mulan's worry and anxiety that her father's name has been included in the conscription list. Knowing that her father will be drafted into the army, Muian is seriously worried that her elderly father cannot endure the hardship in the battlefield. The image on the recto page also corresponds to the verbal texts on the verso page: the horses and military officials herald the emergency of the warfare, while the hunchbacked father holding a stick is hardly able to join the army. In addition, a picture of the painted pottery figurine of a fully armed cavalryman in the Northern Dynasty is added alongside the verbal texts on the verso page. A brief bilingual introduction of conscription system in ancient China is printed in smaller font below this added picture. The bilingual introduction tells readers:

> In the early stage of the Northern Wei Dynasty, soldiers of different areas were enlisted on a rotating basis, so they were also called "rotating soldiers." In the Northern Qi Dynasty, wars broke out more frequently than ever, and the term of service and scope of enlistment often exceeded what was set out by law. All civilian families were required to serve the army in the Western Wei and Northern Zhou Dynasties.

This bilingual introduction explains what the conscription system is and the situation in the period when Mulan's legend happened, supplementing the verbal texts in the inside pages. The supplementary information may help readers know more about the historical background of the conscription system in ancient China, and thus understand why Mulan has no other choice but to join in the army instead of her father. Moreover, the added picture of a painted pottery figurine of a fully armed cavalryman corresponds to the image of military soldiers on the recto page, which textually integrates the two images with each other and meanwhile provides the historical information through non-verbal paratexts.

Apart from *Song of Mulan*, the inside page layout of *China's Bravest Girl* (1993) also achieves the successful textual function. In this picturebook, bilingual texts are arranged on each verso page, while the image of Mulan occupies the whole recto page. Textually, the framing and salience in this picturebook produce a different sense of perception for readers. On each verso page, the English text is printed in the white background on the right side, while the Chinese text is framed by lines and highlighted in the background setting of a small picture on the left side. In the small picture, the patterns with auspicious meanings in traditional Chinese culture are presented, such as dragons, phoenix, red-crowned cranes, butterflies and peonies, producing a strong sense of Chinoiserie.

For example, Figure 2.4 shows the texts and the image of Mulan in the male clothes in *China's Bravest Girl*. On the verso page, the verbal texts depict Mulan's dressing before she joins in the army.

A multimodal study of paratexts on Mulan 59

Figure 2.4 Inside page layout of *China's Bravest Girl: The Legend of Hua Mu Lan* (1993)
Source: Text copyright © 1993 by Charlie Chin. Illustration copyright © 1993 by Tomie Arai. Chinese translation copyright © 1993 by Wang Zing Chu. Permission arranged with Children's Book Press, an imprint of Lee & Low Books Inc., New York, NY 10016.

Example 4

Source Text	**Target Text**
月牙长枪手中握，	The crescent moon spear in her hand,
柳叶大刀挂腰旁。	the willow leaf sword by her side,
紧身盔甲好威武，	her armor is laced and tightened,
战马长啸斗志昂！	her war horse is saddled to ride.

Through the verbal texts in Example 4, a valiant and heroic image of a military soldier is presented to readers. Fully equipped with all the military necessities, Mulan is ready to go to the battlefield. She wears a set of tightened armour, with a willow leaf sword in the waist and a crescent moon spear in the hand. Meanwhile, on the recto page, the image of Mulan echoes the depiction of Mulan in the verbal texts: a neutral image of Mulan is represented through the interpersonal function realized by the social distance, horizontal angle and modality. Mulan's full figure is presented with a long shot, and her figure almost occupies the height of the entire page. Holding a golden sword in her left hand and a spear in her right hand, Mulan seems especially taller, stronger and more heroic compared with her little sister. Moreover, different warm colours are used in the depiction of Mulan's image, such as golden armour and red cloak, which constitutes the high degrees of colour saturation and colour differentiation. On the verso page, a small picture is arranged on the left side as the background setting of Chinese texts, on which is printed a golden dragon treading on auspicious clouds and a colourful phoenix with a pink flower in its mouth. As the symbols of the male and the female in traditional Chinese culture, the dragon and the phoenix correspond to Mulan's neutral image in this picture: she dresses like a valiant and heroic army soldier, but her real identity is female.

6 Discussion

The detailed analysis of verbal and non-verbal paratexts in the four picturebooks shows that both the verbal and non-verbal paratexts interplay with each other and repackage different images of Mulan with the collaboration of ideational, interpersonal and textual functions in picturebooks. In addition, these different paratexts are influenced by the choices of publishing agencies in the picturebooks.

6.1 Interplay between verbal and non-verbal paratexts

First, different verbal paratexts, such as endnotes, footnotes, forewords or prefaces, supplement the necessary historical and cultural background information of Mulan's legend, assisting foreign readers to better understand the English translation of this classic ballad. Second, various forms of non-verbal paratexts contribute to the visual representation of Mulan's image in the picturebook and meanwhile complement the verbal paratexts. For instance, the front covers illustrate the core image of Mulan, strengthening the readers' first impression of her, and inviting the reader to go into the book. The interpersonal function of the visual materials plays an important role here. The back covers, which contain the information of the design and publicity strategies of publishing agencies, showcase the realization of the textual function of the picturebooks. Moreover, the use of non-verbal paratexts, such as pictures in endpapers or added pictures in inside pages, also visually supplements the related cultural and historical information, which works with the similar functions like footnote and endnote in the verbal paratexts. In addition, layout arrangement plays an important role not only in the cover design but also in the inside pages. The framing and salience of essential verbal and visual information contribute to integrating images and texts into a whole combination, which functions to attract readers' attention to where the illustrator and the publisher want our focus.

Although these picturebooks adopt different forms of verbal and non-verbal paratexts with different functions, they actually work in concert with each other and demonstrate the consistent preferences and strategies of the author, the illustrator, the translator and the publisher within a picturebook. For example, in *The Ballad of Mulan*, the long endnote about the historical and cultural backgrounds of Northern Wei Dynasty and Xianbei culture echoes with the non-verbal paratexts of added pictures in the endpapers, which reveals the ambition of this picturebook for a faithful representation of Mulan's legend, her image and Chinese culture. In *China's Bravest Girl*, the front and back covers are also in line with the layout in inside pages, which indicates the efforts to repackage a courageous, wise, respectful and loving image of Mulan and meanwhile transmits the beauty of Chinoiserie for foreign readers.

6.2 Paratexts and publishing agencies' choices

Furthermore, the employ of these different paratexts reveals different choices of publishing agencies on the repackage of Mulan in the picturebooks. Therefore, the particular historical, social or cultural contexts of these publishing agencies are also discussed, so as to help us understand the reasons of choices behind these different paratexts in the picturebooks.

The three picturebooks under investigation, *The Legend of Mu Lan* (1992), *China's Bravest Girl* (1993) and *The Ballad of Mulan* (1998), were all published by American publishing companies in the 1990s, during the development of multilingualism and multiculturalism in the United States. As a nation of immigrants, the United States is one of the first countries to be concerned about the issues of multilingualism and multiculturalism. Multicultural education has been popular in the United States since the 1960s and is "an approach to school reform designed to actualize educational equality for students from diverse racial, ethnic, cultural, social-class, and linguistic groups" (Banks 2011, 184). With the mission of multicultural education, a number of multilingual and multicultural children's books were published in the 1990s, among which include the bilingual picturebooks on Mulan in this study.

The Legend of Mu Lan is published by Victory Press and has been awarded a seal of approval for a multicultural classic by Multicultural Publishers and Education Council. It is noteworthy that Victory Press has not only paid special attention to the publishing of multicultural books with a Chinese background but is also dedicated to publishing books, especially on women, such as female scientists, heroines of modern-day and ancient China, and female writers and artists. This meets the purpose of multicultural education, to provide equal education for people of different genders or with different racial, religious and cultural backgrounds. In the cover layout of this picturebook, such emphasis on multiculturalism has also been reinforced through non-verbal paratexts.

China's Bravest Girl is published by Children's Book Press, a non-profit publisher dedicated to producing quality multicultural literature for children. In 2012, it became a branch of Lee & Low Books, which is the largest multicultural children's book publisher in the United States, with the mission to promote multilingualism and multiculturalism. In this picturebook, through the front and back covers as well as the special layout in inside pages, we can find the publisher's strategies and preferences to introduce Mulan's legend as well as Chinese culture and fulfil the mission of multicultural transmission.

The Ballad of Mulan is published by Pan Asian Publications, whose aim is to bridge East and West through publishing bilingual picturebooks. With the specific mission to "promote Chinese culture and to encourage children to learn a second language", it has published several picturebooks that adapt classic stories, legends and folk tales for English and bilingual editions, such as the legend of lady Snake and Monkey King. *The Ballad of Mulan* is an important one of these bilingual picturebooks adapted from Chinese legend. Through the historical endnote and the added pictures in the endpapers in this picturebook, it shows the publisher's multicultural prospect to

> proffer a possibility for the child readers as well as their parents to enjoy the cross references of the legend of the warrior woman in classical Chinese and English, in storytelling and retelling, in premodern text and contemporary Chinese American re-creation.
>
> (Dong 2006, 226)

7 Conclusion

This study has investigated how the Chinese classic "Mulan Ci" is repackaged in contemporary bilingual picturebooks with the examination of paratextual elements in translation. The research results demonstrate that the verbal and non-verbal paratexts work in accordance with each other to repackage Mulan's image as a whole. On the one hand, the use of verbal and non-verbal paratexts in the picturebooks contributes to the different repackages of the Chinese classic Mulan; on the other hand, these paratexts also reflect the different preferences and strategies of the authors, illustrators, translators and publishers in transmitting Chinese culture for different target readers. Multicultural picturebooks offer young children a multitude of opportunities to understand diverse ethnic, racial and cultural communities. Through the verbal and non-verbal paratexts, the legend and images of Mulan in these bilingual picturebooks may better provide "a positive representation for Chinese American youngsters, a female heroic image for all children, and an imaginative cultural adventure for all readers" (Dong 2011, 129). This research shows a new perspective to examine the paratextual materials in picturebooks through their multi-semiotic meanings, expanding the paratextual and multimodal approaches to picturebook translation. It is hoped that it can also shed light on future paratextual studies in the Chinese cultural context.

Acknowledgement

This work is supported by the FRG Project (FRG-17–049-UIC) of Macau University of Science and Technology.

References

Alvstad, C. 2012. "The Strategic Moves of Paratexts: World Literature through Swedish Eyes." *Translation Studies* 5(1): 78–94.
Arizpe, E. and M. Styles. 2003. *Children Reading Pictures: Interpreting Visual Texts*. London & New York: Routledge.
Armstrong, G. 2007. "Paratexts and Their Functions in Seventeenth-Century English 'Decamerons.'" *The Modern Language Review* 1: 40–57.

Bader, B. 1976. *American Picturebooks From Noah's Ark to the Beast Within*. New York: Macmillan Publishing Co.
Banks, J. A. 2011. *The Routledge International Companion to Multicultural Education*. London & New York: Routledge.
Beckett, S. L. 2012. *Crossover Picturebooks: A Genre for All Ages*. London & New York: Routledge.
Bell, P.. 2001. "Content Analysis of Visual Images." In *Handbook of Visual Analysis*, edited by Theo van Leeuwen and Carey Jewitt, 11–34. Thousand Oaks & New Delhi: Sage Publications.
Chin, C.. 1993. *China's Bravest Girl: The Legend of Hua Mu Lan*. Emeryville, CA: Children's Book Press.
Coifman, R. C. 2013. "Giving Texts Meaning through Paratexts: Reading and Interpreting Endpapers." *School Library Monthly* 30(3): 21–23.
Dong, L. 2006. "Writing Chinese America into Words and Images: Storytelling and Retelling of The Song of Mu Lan." *The Lion and the Unicorn* 30(2): 218–233.
Dong, L. 2011. *Mulan's Legend and Legacy in China and the United States*. Philadelphia: Temple University Press.
Doonan, J. 1993. *Looking at Pictures in Picture Books*. Stroud: Thimble Press.
Duran, Teresa, and Emma Bosch. 2011. "Before and After the Picturebook Frame: A Typology of Endpapers." *New Review of Children's Literature and Librarianship* 17(2): 122–143.
Evans, J. 2009. *Talking beyond the Page: Reading and Responding to Picturebooks*. London & New York: Routledge.
Fang, W. P. 方卫平. 2012. 享受图画书：图画书的艺术与鉴赏. (*Xiang Shou Tu Hua Shu: Tu Hua Shu de Yi Shu Yu Jiang Shang*). Jinan: Tomorrow Publishing House.
Friedman, A., and S. Ron. 2017. "Unlocking the Power of Visual Grammar Theory: Analyzing Social Media Political Advertising Messages in the 2016 US Election." *Journal of Visual Literacy* 36(2): 90–103.
Fu, L. L. 傅莉莉. 2016. "符际翻译视角下的儿童绘本翻译" (Translation of Children's Picture Book from the Perspective of Intersemiotic Translation). 北京第二外国语学院学报 (*Journal of Beijing International Studies University*) 3: 61–73.
Furukawa, H. 2012. "Representations are Misrepresentations: The Case of Cover Designs of Banana Yoshimoto's Kitchen." *TTR* 25(2): 215–233.
Genette, G. 1997. *Paratexts: Thresholds of Interpretation*. Translated by Jane E. Lewin. London: Cambridge University Press.
Gerber, L. 2012. "Marking the Text: Paratextual Features in German Translations of Australian Children's Fiction." In *Translation Peripheries: Paratextual Elements in Translation*, edited by A. Gil-Bardají, P. Orero, and S. Rovira-Esteva, 43–61. Berlin: Peter Lang.
Gil-Bardají, A., P. Orero, and S. Rovira-Esteva. 2012. *Translation Peripheries: Paratextual Elements in Translation*. Berlin: Peter Lang.
Halliday, M. A. K. 1978. *Language as Social Semiotic: The Social Interpretation of Language and Meaning*. London: Edward Arnold.
Halliday, M. A. K. 1994. *An Introduction to Functional Grammar*, 2nd ed. London: Edward Arnold.
Hao, G.C. 郝广才. 2009. 好绘本如何好. (*Hao Hui Ben Ru He Hao*). Nanchang: 21st Century Publishing House.
He, S. B. 贺赛波, and D. Shen 申丹. 2013. "翻译副文本、译文与社会语境 – 女性成长小说视角下《大地的女儿》中译考察" (Translation Paratext, Translated Text and

Social Context: A Translation Study of Daughter of Earth from the Angle of Female Bildungsroman). 外国语文 (*Foreign Language and Literature*) 1: 109–113.

Huang, P.X. 黄培希. 2018. "副文本与翻译文化建构 – 以艾尔萨·威斯《黄帝内经·素问》英译为例" (Paratexts and Cultural Construction in Translation – A Case Study of English Translation of *Huangdi Neijing Suwen by Ilza Veith*). 上海翻译 (Shanghai Journal of Translators) 3: 73–79.

Jewitt, C. and R. Oyama. 2001."Visual Meaning: A Social Semiotic Approach." In *Handbook of Visual Analysis*, edited by Theo van Leeuwen and Carey Jewitt, 134–156. London, Thousand Oaks & New Delhi: Sage Publications.

Kiefer, B. 2011. "What Is a Picturebook? Across the Borders of History." *New Review of Children's Literature and Librarianship* 17: 86–102.

Kress, G. and T. van Leeuwen. 1996. *Reading Images: The Grammar of Visual Design*. London & New York: Routledge.

Kress, G. and T. van Leeuwen. 2006. *Reading Images: The Grammar of Visual Design*, 2nd ed. London & New York: Routledge.

Kümmerling-Meibauer, B. and J. Meibauer. 2013. "On the Strangeness of Pop Art Picturebooks: Pictures, Texts, Paratexts." In *Picturebooks: Beyond the Borders of Art, Narrative and Culture*, edited by Evelyn Arizpe, Maureen Farrell, and Julie MacAdam, 23–41. London & New York: Routledge.

Kung, S. 2013. "Paratext, an Alternative in Boundary Crossing: A Complementary Approach to Translation Analysis." In *Text, Extratext, Metatext and Paratext in Translation*, edited by Valerie Pellatt, 49–68. Newcastle: Cambridge Scholars Publishing.

Lathey, G. 2006. *The Translation of Children's Literature: A Reader*. Bristol: Multilingual Matters Ltd.

Lathey, G. 2010. *The Role of Translators in Children's Literature: Invisible Storytellers*. London & New York: Routledge.

Li, X. 李新. 2010. 木兰辞. (*Song of Mulan*). Shanghai: Shanghai People's Fine Arts Publishing House.

Mossop, B. 2018. "Judging a Translation by Its Cover." *The Translator* 24(1): 1–16.

Moya Guijarro, A. J. 2011. "Engaging Readers through Language and Pictures: A Case Study." *Journal of Pragmatics* 43(12): 2982–2991.

Moya Guijarro, A. J. 2014. *A Multimodal Analysis of Picture Books for Children: A Systemic Functional Approach*. Sheffield: Equinox.

Moya Guijarro, A. J. and M. J. P. Sanz. 2008. "Compositional, Interpersonal and Representational Meanings in a Children's Narrative: A Multimodal Discourse Analysis." *Journal of Pragmatics* 40(9): 1601–1619.

Nikolajeva, M. and C. Scott. 2001. *How Picturebooks Work*. London & New York: Routledge.

Nodelman, P. 1988. *Words about Pictures: The Narrative Art of Children's Picture Books*. Athens & London: The University of Georgia Press.

O'Sullivan, E. 1999. "Translating Pictures." *Signal* 90: 167–175.

O'Sullivan, E. 2005. *Comparative Children's Literature*. London & New York: Routledge.

Oittinen, R. 2003. "Where the Wild Things Are: Translating Picture Books." *Meta* 48(1–2): 128–141.

Oittinen, R. 2008. "From Thumbelina to Winnie-the-Pooh: Pictures, Words, and Sounds in Translation." *Meta* 53(1): 76–89.

Oittinen, R. 2010. "On Translating Picture Books." *Perspectives: Studies in Translatology* 9(2): 109–125.

Oittinen, R., A. Ketola, and M. Garavini. 2018. *Translating Picturebooks: Revoicing the Verbal, the Visual, and the Aural for a Child Audience*. London & New York: Routledge.

Painter, C., J. R. Martin, and L. Unsworth. 2013. *Reading Visual Narratives: Image Analysis of Children's Picture Books*. Sheffield: Equinox.

Pellatt, V. 2013. *Text, Extratext, Metatext and Paratext in Translation*. Newcastle: Cambridge Scholars Publishing.

Peng, Y. 彭懿. 2006. 图画书：阅读与经典. (*Tu Hua Shu: Yue Du Yu Jing Dian*). Nanchang: 21st Century Publishing.

Roditakis, A.E. 2012. "A Paratextual Look at the Greek Translations of Turkish Novels." *IU Journal of Translation Studies* 5(1): 39–68.

Sipe, L. R., and C. E. McGuire. 2006. "Picturebook Endpapers: Resources for Literary and Aesthetic Interpretation." *Children's Literature in Education* 37(4): 291–304.

Sonzogni, M. 2011. *Re-Covered Rose: A Case Study in Book Cover Design as Intersemiotic Translation*. Amsterdam: John Benjamins.

Tahir-Gürçağlar, Ş. 2002. "What Texts Don't Tell: The Uses of Paratext in Translation Research." In *Crosscultural Transgressions: Research Models in Translation Studies, II: Historical and Ideological Issues*, edited by Theo Hermans. Manchester: St. Jerome Publishing.

Tsai, Y. 2013. "The Significance of Texts in Children's Picture Books." In *Text, Extratext, Metatext and Paratext in Translation*, edited by Valerie Pellatt, 91–102. Newcastle: Cambridge Scholars Publishing.

van Leeuwen, T. 2013. "Color Schemes." In *Multimodality and Social Semiosis: Communication, Meaning-Making, and Learning in the Work of Gunther Kress*, edited by Margit Bock and Norbert Pachler, 62–70. London & New York: Routledge.

von Flotow, L. 1991. "Feminist Translation: Context, Practices, Theories." *TTR* 2: 69–84.

Vu, T. and Y. Febrianti. 2018. "Teachers' Reflections on the Visual Resources in English Textbooks for Vietnamese Lower Secondary Schools." *TEFLIN Journal* 29(2): 266–292.

Xu, D. R. 徐德容, and F. F. He 何芳芳. 2015. "论图画书文字突出语相的翻译" (On the Translation of Words with Distinct Graphological Features in Picturebooks). 外语研究(*Foreign Language Research*) 6: 78–82.

Zhang, L. 张玲. 2014. "汤显祖戏剧英译的副文本研究 – 以汪译《牡丹亭》为例" (The Paratextual Study of the English Translation of Tang Xianzu's Dramas – A Case study of the English Translation of *The Peony Pavilion* by Wang Rongpei). 中国外语(*Foreign Languages in China*) 3: 106–111.

Zhang, S. N. 1998. *The Ballad of Mulan*. Union City, CA: Pan Asian Publications.

3 Intersemiotic translation of rhetorical figures

A case study of the multimodal translation of *The Art of War*

Luo Tian (Kevin)

1 Introduction

Rhetorical figures (RFs), or figures of speech, are artful deviations from readers' expectations with the goal of communicating more than is literally expressed (e.g. McQuarrie and Mick 1996; Theodorakis, Koritos, and Stathakopoulos 2015). RFs are rich in almost all literary texts, such as poems, novels and literary essays, and in non-literary texts such as print advertisements (Leigh 1994; McQuarrie and Mick 1996), because they help beautify, enrich and upgrade the form of expression. Compared with non-figurative language, figures of speech are advantageous to some extent in capturing the reader's attention, demanding a higher degree of information processing, arousing aesthetic and pleasurable reading experience, adding persuasive power, ensuring longer time of memory and encouraging a positive attitude toward the text (McQuarrie and Mick 1996, 427).

RFs constitute a significant topic that needs to be examined in depth, especially when multimodal texts become prevalent. As we are living in a world featured with multiple modes of communication, scholars in linguistics, discourse studies and communications inevitably engage with multimodal texts which involve, besides written language, many other modes of communication such as sound, image and gestures. Kress (2010, 11) maintained that we should be "looking at the field of meaning as a whole and see how meaning is handled modally across the range of modes in different societies." In this scenario, the discussion of RFs has reached beyond the scope of verbal language and engaged new aspects such as visual, musical or multimodal RFs. Visual RF becomes the subject of investigation by a large number of researchers, especially those in ads (e.g. Cook 2001; Peterson 2019). They find that visual RFs, commonly used in ads (van Mulken 2003), contribute positively to effective communication (e.g. Maes and Schilperoord 2009; McQuarrie and Mick 2003). Some scholars focus on the multimodal metaphor or metonymy in discourses (Feng 2017, 2019; Feng and O'Halloran 2013), while still others look into rhetoric of sound (Kjeldsen 2018). Rather than treating RFs only as a linguistic phenomenon, these researchers are attending to RFs in multimodal texts, bringing up fresh insights about multimodal RFs and pushing forward the frontier of RF studies.

The issue of RFs translation across modes, however, remains under-researched or almost neglected by translation scholars despite the fact that multimodality has already gained much visibility in translation studies. Munday (2004, 216) points out that, instead of focusing on the conventional, progressively outdated written text, translation should be seen in a broader perspective to incorporate multimodal features of texts. The recent increasing academic interest in the translation of multimodal texts, including intersemiotic translation, has brought out a wealth of insightful studies (e.g. Boria, Carreres, Noriega-Sánchez, and Tomalin 2020; O'Halloran, Tan, and Wignell 2016; Pârlog 2019). These studies cover a wide range of themes and fields such as film (e.g. Mubenga 2009), theatre and drama (Bigliazzi 2013), music and song (e.g. Susam-Saraeva 2019), museum (Liao 2018), picturebooks (e.g. Chen 2018), comics (e.g. Borodo 2015), translation pedagogy (e.g. Zhang 2015) and accessibility for people (Hurtado and Gallego 2013). Although multimodal RFs are rich and sometimes constitute key elements in the aforementioned genres or fields, scanty attention has been devoted to the translation of RFs.

Against such backdrop, the present study aims to investigate the issue of RFs in multimodal translation. We are particularly interested in finding out the translatability of RFs across different semiotic modes, and the strategies in intersemiotic translation of RFs if any. The study addresses the following three key questions: (1) Can RFs be translated across different modes (e.g. from verbal mode to visual)? (2) If yes, what are the strategies in translating verbal RFs into visual ones? If not, why? (3) What are the dimensions involved in intersemiotic translation of RFs?

2 Rhetorical figures in multimodal context

Among copious discussions about rhetorical figures, some examine them as artful deviations only in verbal discourse, some approach them only in visual settings, still others consider them as both verbal and non-verbal at the same time. These discussions deal with issues such as definition, taxonomy, function and audience response to RFs in a wide range of discourses and genres including scientific discourse, advertising, poems, media texts and online documents. In this section, we will identify elementary issues concerning investigating and practising RFs intersemiotic translation with a literature review.

2.1 Verbal rhetorical figures

The earliest traditional discussion of RFs focused on verbal ones. Rhetoric, in its traditional sense, operates on the basis of logical and aesthetic dimensions to affect interaction in verbal discourses. The object of rhetoric is to produce effective text or speech so as to persuade readers to believe, or to influence their actions. According to Ehses (1984), the key term of rhetoric is choice, or "making appropriate selections of means to achieve a desired end," while being communication-oriented and governed by pragmatic motivations and functional considerations.

A rhetorical figure is "a form of speech artfully varied from common usage" (Corbett 1971, 460), and "an expression deviates from expectation, the expression is not rejected as nonsensical or faulty" (McQuarrie and Mick 1996, 425). In other words, verbal RFs are considered deviations that violate the norms of the common use of language in its different linguistic forms (phonic, grammatical and semantic). The key issue of RFs has always been "how to discover the most effective way to express a thought in a given situation, and how to alter its expression to suit different situations" (McQuarrie and Mick 1996, 424).

McQuarrie and Mick (1996) approached verbal RFs by focusing on its operation dimension. He categorized RFs into four types of rhetoric operations: repetition, reversal, substitution and destabilization. Repetition "combines multiple instances of some element of the expression without changing the meaning of that element" (McQuarrie and Mick 1996, 429). Rhyme, chime and alliteration are examples of repetition. Reversal is an operation used in an expression that contains concepts or elements in inversed syntactic arrangements with one another. A typical example of reversal would be a device such as antimetabole. Substitution means replacing one item with another, which relies on readers to reason out the correction. Synecdoche is a figure of substitution which replaces a part with a whole, or a whole with a part. Destabilization requires multiple interpretations since a single and specific interpretation of meaning may not be resolved. Metaphor, pun and irony are typical examples of destabilization.

Among the four rhetorical operations, repetition and substitution are easier, more regular and less complex, and are categorized as tropes; the other two, reversal and destabilization, are subsumed as schemes. Rhyme and alliteration, for instance, are schematic figures that are rather regular in sound patterns, while metaphors and puns are tropes with more irregularity. McQuarrie and Mick's (1996) taxonomy of verbal RFs differentiates schemes from tropes and distinguishes simple from complex rhetorical operations. His categorization "makes it possible for the advertiser to vary the degree of processing demand over a substantial range" (McQuarrie and Mick 1996, 434). It also gives a clue to the cognitive and affective consumer response processes and outcomes that may be elicited by each type.

Recently, Miller and Toman (2016) proposed a relatively complex taxonomy of verbal RFs by incorporating dimension of operation and the linguistic resources involved. More than 20 RFs are classified into five types: phonetic, orthographic, morphological, syntactic and semantic. Phonetic RFs engage the sounds of language (e.g. alliteration); orthographic ones involve spelling and the arrangement of symbols within texts (e.g. abbreviation); morphological ones deal with the formation of words with word bases and affixes (e.g. blending), syntactic ones use the patterns of words within sentences and their modification (e.g. chiasmus) and semantic ones involve the interpretation of word meanings (e.g. simile, metaphor and personification). Each of the RFs under the five categories are further classified as scheme, trope or, under rare conditions, both scheme and trope, with detailed descriptions and examples. For instance, assonance is classified as a phonetic device and a scheme, with a definition "repetition of vowel sounds given the limited number of vowel sounds" (Miller and Toman 2016, 481).

Miller and Toman's (2016) taxonomy is relatively comprehensive and provides a clear map of both linguistic resources and operations involved in the construction of RFs. However, it also has its weaknesses, for example, some lexical formations which belong to linguistic devices rather than artful deviations, have been included in the taxonomy of RFs.

2.2 Visual rhetorical figures

From 1980s, scholars began their earnest studies on visual RFs, of which there are two types. One type views visual RFs as devices independent of verbal ones, and develops taxonomies specific to visual communication (e.g. Durand 1987; Gkiouzepas and Hogg 2011). The other type holds that verbal and visual RFs are both semiotic signifying process, and applies verbal principles to visual RFs in the analysis (e.g. Ehses 1984; McQuarrie and Mick 1999, 2003).

Durand (1970, 1987) is among those scholars who investigated visual RFs independent of verbal ones. He proposed two criteria against which visual RFs can be classified and defined: rhetorical operations (addition, suppression, substitution and exchange) and relation between the variable elements (identity, similarity, difference and opposition). According to Durand, the first rhetorical operation, addition, suggests presenting multiple visual elements; suppression, the second operation, involves missing or suppressed elements whose intended message is to be identified and understood by readers; the third operation, substitution, means replacing one visual for another, and the fourth operation exchange is to modify element relationships. Durand based his taxonomy on thousands of ads that he had gathered and his experience working in the French advertising industry. Durand's taxonomy was later applied by Dyer (1982) in an analysis of visual RFs in British advertisements and recently proved to be the most exhaustive one, with the best overall domain coverage compared against many other taxonomies (Huhmann and Albinsson 2019).

Similarly, Phillips and McQuarrie (2004) proposed another typology of visual RFs, which differentiates the ways they are designed. The typology is based on two crossing dimensions: (1) visual structure, or the way elements constituting the visual RF are physically presented (juxtaposition, fusion and replacement); and (2) meaning operation, which is the target or focus of the cognitive processing required to comprehend the picture, and according to which three possibilities are distinguished (connection, comparison for similarity and comparison for opposition). According to the typology, there are nine fundamentally distinct kinds of visual rhetorical figures (Phillips and McQuarrie 2004, 116). This topology of visual RFs distinguishes itself from others in that it adds fusion as a visual structure. However, it fails to define a list of individual RFs that may be helpful for their research and design.

Ehses (1984), a representative of the scholars who applied verbal principles to visual RFs, used a taxonomy of verbal RFs in his analysis of visual RFs in graphic design of posters for the play *Macbeth*. The taxonomy features four categories of contrast, resemblance, contiguity and gradation (Ehses 1984, 56–57). In this taxonomy, antithesis is "the juxtaposition of contrasting ideas" (Ehses 1984, 56). It can be found in a verbal sentence like "By the time the wallet is empty, life will be full" (Ehses 1984, 56), or in a visual poster featuring a juxtaposition of a face half white and half black to represent the contrasting combination of Macbeth, the loyal general and Macbeth, the viciously evil king (Ehses 1984, 62).

The taxonomy proposed by Ehses (1984) in fact highlights the semantic-logical relations between the elements and resources of different modes involved in the creative process of constructing RFs. Particularly, the strength of this taxonomy lies in the fact that it includes gradation, a semantic relation frequently neglected by other scholars. Although expressed in different terms, Ehses's resemblance and contrast are two logic-semantic relations, almost equal to Durand's similarity and opposition, respectively.

McQuarrie and Mick (1999, 2003) adapted their taxonomy of verbal RFs proposed earlier (McQuarrie and Mick 1996) to the categorization of visual RFs, believing there is a resonance between verbal and visual rhetoric. They first differentiated visual schemes (repetition and substitution) from tropes (reversal and destabilization). Visual schemes, for instance, alter typical arrangement of lines, shapes, colours, objects, symbols or other formal image characteristics to create repeating or reversed patterns.

2.3 Rhetorical figures in multimodal texts

Unlike the scholars who focused on either verbal or visual RFs, other scholars use a more comprehensive framework in which some verbal, visual and other mode RFs are grouped under the same definition for discussion.

In his study of RFs in TV ads, a type of multimodal text, Rossolatos (2014) proposed a more comprehensive taxonomy of RFs, suggesting that an RF can be verbal, visual or musical under the same title, and that visual RFs may be used solely or in partnership with verbal or musical ones. For instance, he defined hyperbole as "quantitative augmentation of one of the properties of an object, state-of-affairs; may be encountered purely verbally or visually or as the employment of a visual that augments the importance or the argumentative force of a voice-over" (Rossolatos 2014, 73). According to this definition, hyperbole can be purely verbal or purely visual. At the same time, visual hyperbole can be used in partnership with an acoustic one. Another figure, inversion, is similarly defined as (1) verbal, the permutation of the elements of a syntactic construction contrary to expectations; (2) visual, such as the inversion of a sequence of events in a picture; or 3) both music and visual, "the inversion of the role performed by a syntactic element in a multimodal syntax involving music and visuals" (Rossolatos 2014, 73).

In addition to the RFs shared across different modes, there are some newly defined RFs which admit the particularities of certain semiotic modes. These new terms of visual RFs, such as accolorance and reshaption, are "particularly useful for capturing salient aspects of how nuanced anaphorical relationships are structured in the visual rhetoric of ad filmic texts" (Rossolatos 2014, 76) Accolorance means the repetition of the same colour in the majority of visuals in a filmic syntagm or across syntagms, while reshaption involves repetition of the same shape in the majority of visuals in a filmic syntagm or across syntagms. These RFs are only to be found in visual modes.

Rossolatos (2014) listed four rhetorical operation, namely suppression, adjunction, substitution and permutation, which are rather similar to or even identical with the operation dimension proposed by Durand (1987). The number of multimodal RFs defined by Rossolatos reaches 39, being the greatest ever listed by the scholars under review. However, Rossolatos' classification of RFs is not without problem. For instance, hyperbole, an RF involving exaggeration of the quantity or quality of an object, is improperly listed as adjunction operation, since adjunction means adding to a thing something else as a supplementary rather than an essential part.

2.4 A summary

This section summarizes the aforementioned researches on RFs, taking into consideration the strength and the weakness in their definitions and taxonomies. The summary will incorporate the essential elements of RFs into one comprehensive system, trying to be inclusive and exhaustive, so as to offer a clear roadmap for the application and research of RFs in one mode or across multiple modes.

The previous study on RFs has revealed at least three fundamental dimensions: semiotic resource, semantic-logical relation, and deviation operation. They constitute the basis on which RFs can be analysed, classified or designed, and consequently they can facilitate necessary aid to intersemiotic translation researchers as well as practitioners. Semiotic resource reminds people of the semiotic materials at their disposal. Logic-semantic relation between/among semiotic units provides instruction to RF designers that may be helpful in deciding concept formulation, and to audience that can aid their understanding of the arranged semiotic elements. Deviation operation indicates the means by which the semiotic resources or expression units can be physically arranged so as to create the effect of alienation or defamiliarization.

To begin with, semiotic resource forms the first essential dimension for the definition and investigation of RFs. Semiotic resources are raw materials with which RFs are created such as words and phrases from a language, colours and shapers in an image. RFs can be monomodal if they are created with resources from only one mode; they can also be multimodal if they are designed with resources across two or more modes. It shall be noted that an RF may exist in only one particular mode due to its unique quality, such as accolorance, which repeats the same colour.

Under the category of each mode, there are rich and varied semiotic resources that can be used by authors or designers to create RFs. For instance, the resources for visuals RFs may include colour, line, shape, angle, vector, image and texture, while those for musical ones may include rhythm, melodies, harmony, orchestration and dynamics. Semiotic resources can be realized at different ranks. According to O'Halloran (2008, 456), linguistic and visual forms of semiosis can be realized on the expression stratum at different ranks, namely clause complex, clause, word group/phrase and word. Similarly, corresponding units for visual expression stratum include scene, episode, figure and part. These corresponding ranks among linguistic and visual modes lay a foundation for the investigation of RFs in intersemiotic translations.

The second dimension of RFs is the logic-semantic relation(s) between or among the semiotic resources expressed at different ranks. There are five types of relations: identity, similarity, difference, opposition and negation. Identity means that the elements involved in the RF are the same or duplicates. For instance, some verbal RFs reiterate the same words, like anaphora, anadiplosis and epistrophe, and repetition can be a visual RF which reproduce the same images several times in a text.

Similarity suggests that the elements used in an RF share some qualities, but they are not identical. Rhyme, for instance, repeats only sounds at the end of different words or phrases, and metaphor suggest a likeness or analogy between one thing described and another absent.

Difference highlights the feature that distinguishes one expressive unit from another, in order to highlight the impression of a great amount, density, or diversity. Contrast, for instance, is an RF that emphasizes the disparity between semiotic resources.

Opposition indicates an antonymous relation between two or more elements within an RF, such as male/female, black/white and hot/cold. In a visual antithesis, semiotic resources, colours and shades may exist in opposition of black/white, thick and thin.

Negation means that one element or unit is referred to or treated as false while it is actually true, or vice versa. For instance, antiphrasis is the use of a word or phrase to mean something different from its literal sense (e.g. saying on a rainy day, "What a great day for a camping!"); and antanaclasis is the repetition of a similar word in a sentence with different meanings, or a word is repeated in two or more different senses (e.g. Shakespeare's lines, "Put out the light, then put out the light").

The third dimension of RFs is the five deviational operations dealing with semiotic resources: juxtaposition, suppression, substitution, destabilization and fusion. Juxtaposition occurs when two or more semiotic resources are placed side by side in a visual sequence or syntagma to create reoccurring patterns. Parallelism and anaphora, for instance, are the result of juxtaposition.

Suppression means to delete or omit units of expression that are supposed to be there, which are completely substitutable in visual sequence/syntagma. Readers are expected to fill in the missing units. Metaphor is a product of suppressing operation since the tenor is often omitted with the meaning not explicitly expressed.

Substitution replaces one element with another in a sequence or syntagma, to replace a part by a whole, or a whole by a part. Substitution involves a double process of deleting one thing and adding another. Synecdoche and metonymy are created by substituting operations. Substitution also happens when a colour object replaces the same object that supposed to be black and white in a monochrome image.

By means of destabilization, we can (1) put two expressive units in a different order than expected in a syntagma or a sequence, such as the reversed/upside-down order; (2) enlarge elements or deform objects beyond expectation, like exaggeration; or (3) minimize the degree of something, or reduce the size of an object to a great extent, like understatement. Destabilization breaks down the inner balance of an object or an order. Anagram and antimetabole are two instances of destabilization.

Fusion suggests that two expressive units are jointed together in a way that neither of them can be easily recognized or separated. By fusing two elements together, general attributes of the elements are brought to the foreground. Oxymoron, as a compressed paradox, is formed by conjoining two contrasting, contradictory or incongruous terms as in "bitter-sweet memories," "orderly chaos" and "proud humility." Tmesis, such as "abso-bloody-lutely," also involves fusion operation. Two images can also be partially presented and fused together to generate a desired effect. In other cases, verbal characters may be fused into images by creative designers.

The three dimensions of RFs summarized above can provide criteria to define, detect and examine not only monomodal but also multimodal RFs. Further, comparison of individual RFs within a mode or across modes can be made against these dimensions. With such comparison, researchers are easier to find ways to approach intersemiotic translation of RFs.

3 Methodology and data

Our study on intersemiotic translation of RFs is based on a multimodal translation of *The Art of War*. This section gives a description of the data and methods to be used in the present study.

3.1 Data: **The Art of War** *and its multimodal translation*

The Art of War (孙子兵法 Pinyin: *Sunzi Bingfa*) is a classical military text believed to be written by Sun Tzu in China over 2,500 years ago and reputed as the earliest existent military thesis known in human history. Consisting of 13 chapters, the book features a systematic argumentation of military strategy, such as the views on war, military leadership, tactics, terrain and espionage. *The Art of War* (hereinafter *AOW*) has been carefully studied and extensively applied by distinguished Chinese military generals, scholars and politicians. Sun Tzu enjoys a household reputation in China for his military wisdom. Consequently, *AOW* constitutes a prominent and valuable part in the repository of Chinese culture. Among the numerous editions, *The Art of War Commented by Ten Scholars* (孙子十家注) edited by well-reputed scholar Sun Hsing-yen (孙星衍) is generally referred to as the most prestigious edition. It was reprinted by the Commercial Press later (Sun 1940) and we choose this version as the source text (hereinafter ST).

This Chinese military masterpiece has been translated into many major languages around the globe, printed in numerous editions and become a bestselling book. According to statistics, till the end of 2011, its translation can be found in over 34 countries in more than 30 foreign languages, including Japanese, Korean, French, Russian and

English. Particularly, *AOW* boasts multiple English translations. According to my survey, over 60 translators have contributed their English versions and the number of English editions in publication reaches 200. The earliest English version came out in 1905 (Calthrop 1905) and the latest one in 2020 (Nylan 2020).

Among these translations, some are monomodal linguistic renditions from the ST, while others are multimodal with linguistic, visual and acoustic resources employed in coexistence. These multimodal translations are important in disseminating Sun Tzu around the globe, and to investigate RFs among the multimodal translations is a worthwhile undertaking.

This case study focuses on one multimodal translations of *The Art of War*, which is published in the form of picturebook (Wang and Sui 2004). This translation is initially published in 1998 by Asiapac Books under the title *Sunzi's Art of War: World's Most Famous Military Classic* (the translated text, hereinafter "TT") translated into English by Sui Yun (隋云) and illustrated by Wang Xuanming (王宣铭). The translation is so popular among readers that in 2004 the publisher issued its 10th edition. Asiapac Books is Singapore's leading publisher of educational comics and illustrated books designed to enhance lifelong learning, with a focus on Asian culture. The translation is listed in the Asiapac Strategy and Leadership Series, which includes *Strategies from the Three Kingdoms, Sima's Rules of War, Thirty-Six Stratagems*, and *Sun Bin's Art of War* (another book translated by Sui Yun). Sui is a professor at School of Humanities and Social Science (Shenzhen Campus), Chinese University of Hong Kong. She used to work in University of International Business and Economics in China. Wang, the illustrator, is a contemporary cartoonist from the mainland of China who has adapted and converted into cartoons a series of ancient Chinese military classics. His earlier books, such as *Thirty-Six Stratagems, Six Strategies for War* and *Strategies from the Three Kingdoms*, have been warmly received by readers.

The TT is a translation from verbal to verbal-visual mode, constituting an ideal site to investigate the issue of RFs in intersemiotic translation. It includes interlingual translation from Chinese text of about 7,000 Chinese words to English text of about 8,800 words. The intersemiotic translation involves the rendition of over 440 Chinese sentences into more than 540 visual episodes in black and white. On average, there are four half-realistic cartoon pictures on each page of the TT. The verbal to visual translation is done on a one-sentence-for-one-picture basis. Such basis provides researchers a relatively clear view of the corresponding units that is essential and conducive for the analysis of RFs from the small unit to larger ones.

It is important to note that when translating from Chinse verbal sentences to visual episodes, Wang added some linguistic elements in the form of speech bubbles to indicate what the persons in the episodes are thinking or saying. Therefore, episodes in the TT usually consist of verbal translation from the ST by Sui, the verbal-to-visual rendition by Wang, and the verbal translation from Wang's linguistic addition. The focus of the present study is placed on how the verbal RFs are translated into the visual RFs, while some linguistic elements may be referred to in the discussion if they appear in the episodes.

To fully understand what happens when translating rhetorical figures from verbal to multimodal texts, at least three processes are worthy of our attention: (1) interlingual translation from a verbal RF in one language to that in another language, such as the translation of a verbal RF in English to that in Chinese; (2) intersemiotic translation from verbal RFs to non-verbal RFs, or the other way around; and (3) the interaction between the verbal and non-verbal RFs in a target text. Among these processes, the intersemiotic translation of RFs receives the least academic attention and therefore becomes the focus of this study.

3.2 Analytical method and procedure

The study was done with a mixed method of qualitative and quantitative analysis assisted with a self-built corpus. It was carried out through four steps: (1) preparing ST and TT data, (2) detecting ST verbal RFs, (3) detecting TT visual RFs and (4) measuring intersemiotic translation strategies.

In the first step, the ST and TT were transformed into digital text and aligned on a one-sentence-to-one-episode basis for comparison purposes. In a small number of cases, there are several sentences matching with one visual episode, or one sentence matching with several episodes. In such cases, priority is placed on episode in the process of alignment. Consequently, a comparative corpus consisting of ST verbal sentences, TT verbal sentences and TT visual episodes was established for analysis.

At the second step, ST verbal RFs were detected according to the three dimensions of RFs as summarized in section 2.3, which include locating resources, deciding logic-semantic relations and determining deviation operations. At the same time, 39 definitions of RFs by Rossolatos (2014, 73) and those by Durand (1987, 295) were used as reference. Following the pattern in the second step, the third was finished to spot visual RFs.

The fourth step involved comparing the ST verbal RFs with TT visual ones, analysing translation strategies and gathering up statistics for analysis. According to four situations in which the RFs could be translated, we proposed four fundamental strategies: equivalence, replacement, omission and addition. Equivalence means an RF in one mode is translated into its counterpart in another mode; for instance, to translate a verbal hyperbole into a visual one. Replacement suggests that a type of RF is translated into another type in another mode so as to achieve the similar effect; for instance, to translate a verbal antithesis into a visual metaphor. Omission occurs when an RF in the ST is not translated at all. The RF may be simply neglected or interpreted in plain language. Addition arises when no RFs exist in the ST, but new ones are added into the TT to enhance expressiveness; for instance, to add a visual metonymy into the TT.

4 Intersemiotic translation of RFs in *The Art of War*

Our analysis was conducted with the help of the self-built corpus. On the basis of examination of individual RFs, it mapped out the general picture of the verbal RFs in the ST, visual RFs in the TT and the way verbal RFs are translated.

4.1 An overview

Our investigation has found that the ST, though featuring abstract and terse military terms, is rather figurative with a large number of RFs in various kinds. In total, there are approximately 273 cases of RFs among 440 sentences, which suggests about six RFs among every ten sentences. With reference to the definitions of 39 RFs proposed by Rossolatos (2014, 73), we found out that these verbal RFs fall into about 16 types: antithesis, parallelism, metaphor, simile, anaphora, hyperbole, repetition, antimetabole, contrast, allusion, anti-climax, comparison, metonymy, anadiplosis, paradox and synecdoche. Among them, four RFs account for the largest share: antithesis 34%, parallelism 28%, metaphor 10% and simile 7%, as shown in Figure 3.1.

The TT is also rich in visual RFs. In total, there are approximately 167 individual cases of RFs among 540 episodes, which suggests a lower density of RFs than that in the ST. These visual RFs fall into 11 types: antithesis, parallelism, simile, reshaption, metaphor, metonymy, repetition, hyperbole, simile, synecdoche and anticlimax. Among these RFs, the first four take up the largest share; to be specific, antithesis 37%, parallelism 33%, simile 8% and reshaption 7%, as shown in Figure 3.1. There is a decline in the type and number of visual RFs in the TT compared against the ST. This suggests that some verbal RFs are not translated into the visual ones in the TT. However, it has to be noted that reshaption, a unique RF in visual mode, has taken up a considerable proportion among the total.

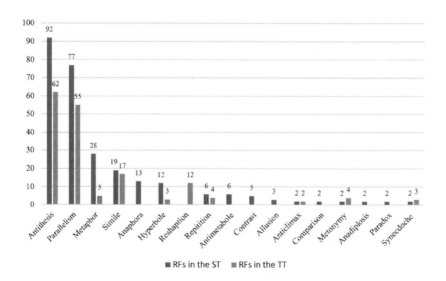

Figure 3.1 RFs in the ST and TT

Intersemiotic translation of rhetorical 77

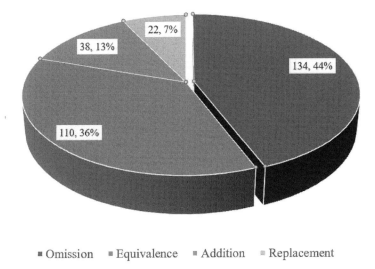

Figure 3.2 RF translation strategies

The survey of the translation strategy suggests that four strategies are employed in the intersemiotic translation of RFs: omission, equivalence, addition and replacement, as shown in Figure 3.2. Among them, cases of omission account for 44% of the total, which suggests infeasibility of intersemiotic translation of RFs since almost a half of the verbal RFs are not translated into visual ones. At the same time, cases of equivalence and replacement add up to 58%, which confirms the intersemiotic translatability of RFs since a majority of verbal RFs are translated into visual ones in one way or another.

The next four subsections will look into more details of each translation strategy with sample analysis. They highlight what resources are mobilized, what logic-semantic relations exist among them and what specific operations are taken in the intersemiotic translation process.

4.2 *Omission*

Omission ranks the first among the four translation strategies most frequently employed. This suggests that intersemiotic translation is by no means an easy task, and in some cases, the cartoonist chooses to give up the idea of literal translation. Those most frequently omitted RFs are antithesis, parallelism and metaphor.

78 *Luo Tian (Kevin)*

Example 1. (omission of metaphor)

ST: 饵兵勿食。
TT verbal: Do not swallow a bait offered by the enemy.
TT visual:

Figure 3.3 Omission of metaphor

Example 1 is a typical instance of omission in intersemiotic translation. The Chinese ST sentence contains a metaphor 食饵兵 (swallow a bait). Metaphor, created by substituting an abstract concept with a concrete word or visual, involves the use of "a word or visual in a different sense to its habitual one, in order to effect a contrived similarity between them" (Rossolatos 2014, 73). In the ST, "饵" (literally, "bait") refers to the soldiers that are sent out to lure and capture enemy, while "食" (literally, "swallow the food") is used to suggest the action of capturing. The metaphor "食饵兵" is translated equivalently in the TT verbal with "swallow a bait." However, no equivalent visual metaphor can be identified in the visual episode as the picture describes several soldiers on foot inviting a fighting from enemy soldiers riding on horses and no visual resources, such as parts and figures, are used to signify something like a bait or a trap. As a result, the TT visual fails to translate the verbal metaphor from the ST.

Example 2. (omission of parallelism and paradox)

ST: 乱生于治，怯生于勇，弱生于强。
TT verbal: Disguise yourself and deceive the enemy by appearing to be weak, cowardly and disorganized.
TT visual:

Intersemiotic translation of rhetorical 79

Figure 3.4 Omission of paradox and parallelism

Example 2 represents an omission of two RFs: paradox and parallelism. Paradox is defined as the "syntactical co-occurrence in the same syntagm of two words or phrases or visuals that appear to be contradictory, but contains a truism or topos" (Rossolatos 2014, 73). In the ST, there are three clauses with the same syntactic structure of the same length in words, each containing two words with contradictory meanings. Therefore, there are two verbal RFs in the ST: paradox and parallelism. They can be literally translated into "Apparent confusion is a product of good order; apparent cowardice is a product of courage; apparent weakness is a product of strength".

However, the visual episode only depicts an army of soldiers in confusion and displays no contradictory elements. No visual resources are employed in parallel or in pairs to signify relations of similarity or opposition that can provide evidence for the existence of a visual paradox or parallelism. Thus, the visual episode fails to translate two verbal RFs from the ST.

4.3 *Equivalence*

Equivalence is the most frequently used translation strategy second only to omission. This suggests that there is great possibility that the verbal RFs can be matched with visual ones of the same kinds. These literal translations are evidence for the intersemiotic translatability of RFs. The most frequently occurring cases of RFs that involve equivalence strategy are antithesis, parallelism and simile.

Example 3. (equivalence of parallelism)

ST: 一曰道，二曰天，三曰地，四曰将，五曰法。

TT verbal: A general may win only if he has a good understanding of five factors: Doctrine, Commander, Terrain, Weather and Moral influence.

TT visual:

Figure 3.5 Equivalence of parallelism

In Example 3, there is an equivalent translation from verbal parallelism to visual one, via the combination of verbal and visual elements. The ST sentence lists five factors that a general must take into earnest consideration. These factors are expressed in a sequence of five minor clauses with the same number of Chinese words (three) and in the same syntactic structure. The verbal resources used here are words and syntactic structure, logic-semantic relation among them is that of similarity and rhetoric operation is juxtaposition. This sentence thus constitutes a figure of parallelism in the ST.

The TT visual episode depicts a general displaying five playing cards. Each card is numbered from 1 to 5, of almost the same shape, size and colour. The visual resources constituting parallelism in this episode are the shape, size and colour of five cards, which are juxtaposed according to the logic semantic relation of similarity. Consequently, this picture constitutes a visual parallelism. Aided by a verbal list of the five factors, the verbal parallelism is equivalently translated into its visual counterpart.

Intersemiotic translation of rhetorical 81

Example 4. (equivalence of parallelism)

ST: 故用兵之法，十则围之，五则攻之，倍则分之。

TT verbal: The art of manoeuvring
Surround the enemy when you outnumber the enemy by ten times.
Attack the enemy when you outnumber the enemy by five times.
Attack the enemy from the front and the flank when you are double the enemy in numbers.

TT visual:

Figure 3.6 Equivalence of parallelism

Example 4 is another case of equivalent intersemiotic translation of parallelism. The ST stipulates Sun Tzu's rule to use tactics in face of enemies of different scales. There are three sentences, each in the same number of Chinese characters, and each with the same syntactic structure. The logic-semantic relation among the clauses is similarity and the rhetorical operation involved is juxtaposition. Therefore, the sentence constitutes a parallelism of clauses.

In the TT, three visual episodes are used to express the meaning of three ST sentences. Each episode describes a scene of fighting between two armies. In the first episode, a large army of fully armed soldiers (estimated to be about 40 since on one side, there are 10) riding on horses surround on four sides a small group of soldiers (only 4). Therefore, the first picture conveys the meaning of the first sentence "surround the enemy when you outnumber the enemy by ten times." The second episode describes an army of about ten soldiers are attacking a group of about three soldiers and roughly represents the meaning of the second sentence in the ST. The third episode depicts four soldiers attacking two from back and front and conveys the meaning of the third sentence in the ST.

These three visual episodes are of the same size, each depicting a scene of two armies fighting each other, with variations in their numbers. The logic-semantic relation among these episodes is that of similarity, while the rhetorical operation is juxtaposition. Set in such a sequence, these episodes form a visual parallelism and consequently an intersemiotic translation of the verbal parallelism occurs.

Example 5. (equivalence of simile)

ST: 兵之所加，如以碫投卵者。

TT verbal: Our troops are so irresistible in attacking the enemy that it is simply like a stone smashing an egg.

TT visual:

Figure 3.7 Equivalence of simile

Intersemiotic translation of rhetorical 83

Example 5 displays an intersemiotic translation from a verbal simile to a visual one. In the ST, there is a comparison between 兵之所加 (irresistible troops defeating small enemy) and 以碫投卵 (smashing an egg with a stone). These two different things (one abstract, the other concrete) are creatively put together and compared because they have one quality in common or resemblance: overwhelming force and superiority. The logic-semantic relation between the two things are of similarity, and the rhetoric operation involved is juxtaposition.

The TT visual episode mainly portrays an army, shrouded in a big stone and smashing an egg. This episode puts two different things side by side, an attacking army and a stone, to highlight their resemblance: the devastating power. The logic-semantic relation between the two is that of similarity, and the rhetoric operation is juxtaposition. Hence, the episode constitutes a visual simile, which adequately translates the meaning of the ST verbal simile.

4.4 Addition

Addition is another extensively used strategy in intersemiotic translation of RFs. This may help heighten the vividness, aesthetic appeal and persuasive power of the TT or compensate for the loss that omission of an original RF may incur. Antithesis and parallelism are among the most frequently added RFs.

Example 6. (addition of antithesis)

ST: 佚而劳之。

TT verbal: When the enemy forces need to have a good rest, try every means to harass them.

TT visual:

Figure 3.8 Addition of antithesis

84 *Luo Tian (Kevin)*

Example 6 shows the addition of RFs in intersemiotic translation. The ST is a simple sentence which means "When the enemy forces need to have a good rest, try every means to harass them" in English. It contains no RFs with artful deviations from normal expressions and expectation.

In the TT visual episode, there is a sharp contrast between two teams of soldiers. One team of two soldiers are beating drum and striking gong very enthusiastically. The darkness in the background suggests this event occurs at night, a time for rest. However, the other team are watching from the high wall of a city, with one complaining "I had another sleepless night," while his companion saying "I ate sleeping pills eight times. But they did not have any effect!" The sharp contrast between the two teams is obvious: one team are energetic, trying to wake the enemy up, while the other team are listless, trying to get some sleep. The picture uses visual lines, colours and figures to express oppositional relation among the expressive units by means of juxtaposition. Consequently, this episode constitutes a visual antithesis, a figure not found in ST but added in TT.

Example 7. (addition of metonymy and parallelism)

ST: 必以全争于天下，故兵不顿，而利可全，此谋攻之法也。

TT Verbal: Therefore, it is necessary to master the strategy of gaining a total victory through stratagems instead of prolonged fighting.

TT Visual:

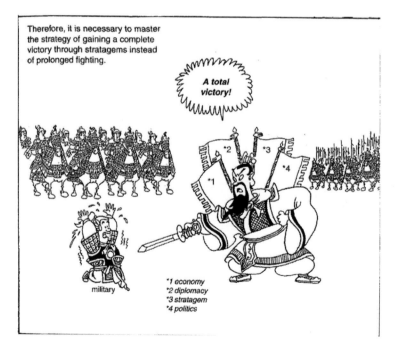

Figure 3.9 Addition of metonymy and parallelism

Intersemiotic translation of rhetorical 85

Example 7 typifies the addition of different RFs in intersemiotic translation. The ST explains that complete victory is to be gained through stratagem rather than prolonged fighting. At most, a verbal antithesis can be identified as two minor clauses, "兵不顿" and "利可全," sharing the same syntactic structure juxtaposed with different meanings.

In the TT episode, there is no case of visual antithesis since it is not possible to spot two visual elements with the same structure but opposite meaning. However, it is easy to identify two different types of visual RFs, metonymy and parallelism. In the picture, a military general bears four banners on his back, numbered from 1 to 4. A list at the bottom of the picture interprets the meaning of each number on the banners: (1) economy, (2) diplomacy, (3) stratagem and (4) politics. Military banners in ancient China were used to give order, show identity or carry slogans. In the visual episode, four concrete banners are used as a metonymy to signify the abstract rules to be followed by the general. They are placed in a sequence, which constitutes a visual parallelism. Therefore, an addition of RF occurs in this episode since there is only one verbal RF (antithesis) in the ST but two different visual RFs (metonymy and parallelism) in the TT.

4.5 Replacement

Replacement is the least used strategy in the intersemiotic translation of RFs. When no relevant visual semiotic resources are found that can be used to translate a certain verbal RF, replacing strategy is resorted to so as to preserve more or less the aesthetic appeal and persuasive power of the ST. In the TT, visual RF reshaption is occasionally used to substitute verbal RF anaphora from the ST.

Example 8. (replacement of antithesis with hyperbole)

ST: 故小敌之坚，大敌之擒也。

TT verbal: Weak troops will eventually fall captive if they engage in desperate fighting against a strong enemy.

TT visual:

Figure 3.10 Replacement of antithesis with hyperbole

86 *Luo Tian (Kevin)*

Example 8 showcases the replacing strategy in intersemiotic translation of RFs. A verbal antithesis is used in the ST, since there are two noun phrases, "小敌之坚" and "大敌之擒," with the same structure but the opposite meanings. These phrases are put side by side, which forms a rhetorical operation of juxtaposition.

However, in the TT visual episode, no instance of RF can be found except for hyperbole. The picture portrays a soldier holding his enemy in hand, while the latter shouts: "I'll fight you to the end." Here, the difference in size between two soldiers is exaggerated to such an extent that the weak soldier is almost the size of the hand of another, which could not be true in the real world or in the normal sense. The visual resource employed here is size, the logic-semantic relation is that of negation in truth value, and the rhetorical operation is that of destabilization. As a result, it can be said that a visual hyperbole exists in the TT to replace the verbal antithesis in the ST.

Example 9. (replacement of anaphora with reshaption)

ST: 孙子曰：兵者，国之大事。(第一章 计篇)
孙子曰：昔之善战者，先为不可胜，以侍敌之可胜。(第四章 形篇)
TT verbal: War is a matter of vital importance to the state. (Chapter 1)

The skilful generals in ancient times first made themselves invulnerable before seeking the chance to defeat the enemy. (Chapter 4)

TT visual:

Figure 3.11 Replacement of anaphora with reshaption

Intersemiotic translation of rhetorical 87

Figure 3.12 Replacement of anaphora with reshaption

Example 9 involves translating verbal anaphoras from the ST into visual reshaptions. According to Rossolatos (2014, 74), anaphora repeats "the same first or middle word or phrase or sound (in the case of sonic markers) or visual marker (e.g. balloon) or setting (in the case of background settings) or object (e.g. beer bottle)" in the same or in various syntagms. In the ST, all 13 chapters begin with the same phrase "孙子曰" (Sun Tzu said) in the first sentence. Example 10 provides two ST sentences (one from Chapter 1 and the other from Chapter 4) and their corresponding visual episodes from the TT. The ST sentences constitute a case of anaphora.

In the TT, no speech bubbles or other linguistic elements are used to reproduce the repeated pattern of "Sun Tzu said." An image of a general, however, is used to stand for Sun Tzu and is reiterated in each chapter, most frequently in the beginning. This constitutes the figure of reshaption, in Rossolatos' (2014, 72) words, the "repetition of the same shape in the majority of visuals in a syntagm or across syntagms." As portrayed in the repetitively appearing figures, Sun Tzu wears the same scarf, moustache, wardrobe and even the same facial expression. The only variation is that he sometimes carries a sword and other times does not. But this does not deny the fact that reshaption of Sun Tzu's image is used throughout the 13 chapters. This replacement of verbal anaphora with visual reshaption is certainly a conscious choice by the cartoonist because of its frequent recurrence in different visual settings.

5 Concluding remarks

Rhetorical figures are important measures to enhance expressiveness in texts and their translations across different genres and modes. With a review of previous studies on RFs, we summarized three essential dimensions for the research and application of RFs in multimodal settings: semiotic resource, logic-semantic relation and deviational operation.

Referring to the three dimensions and focusing on intersemiotic translation, our case study of *The Art of War* has given evidence to both feasibility and infeasibility in verbal-to-visual translation of RFs. On one hand, infeasibility exists since there is a considerable portion of RFs that are not translatable. On the other hand, the translatability of RFs across modes is obvious as more than a half of verbal RFs are rendered visually to retain the expressiveness.

The study also shows that there is a set of strategies for the intersemiotic translation of RFs (equivalence, replacement, addition and omission), and that which strategy is used depends on how the three dimensions of RFs are handled in the TT. If resources in another mode are allocated to process the same deviational operations to signify the same logic-semantic relations as the RF does in the source text, an equivalent translation occurs. If the TT resources are used to process the same operation only, or to convey the same logic-semantic relation only, a replacement of RF surfaces. Replacing strategy is also used when a source text RF is expressed in different resources with different operations in another logic-semantic relation. In some cases, an intersemiotic translator may choose to omit RFs possibly because of the great difficulty in finding matching resources and in accomplishing deviation operations. At last, translators can choose to add new RFs into the TT by allocating new resources, formulating other semantic relations or performing different operations.

Many factors may contribute to translators' (or cartoonists') choice over intersemiotic translation strategies of RFs. One factor is the supply of corresponding semiotic resources across modes. Semiotic resources unique in one mode that are used to create an RF may be extremely difficult in finding their counterparts in another mode. For instance, verbal phonetic RFs such as rhyme and alliteration are hard to find their matches in pictures. Another factor concerns the possibility of deviational operations. An operation easy to be accomplished in one mode may become hazards for cartoonists who attempt to replicate the operation in another mode. For instance, verbal semiotic resources expressing abstract notions and concrete objects can be easily juxtaposed to create a verbal RF like simile, but such operation is not an easy job in visual mode and music mode. Other influential factors may include translator's inability to identify certain RFs, translator's decision to give up, or simply the lack of enough space in the TT.

Much more work is still needed to continue the research on intersemiotic translation of RFs. For instance, we can look into intersemiotic translation of RFs across other modes in other genres. A larger set of corpora would map out more accurately the translation choices with more reliable results. The advancement of research in this issue will gain us more insight into the field of multimodal translation.

Acknowledgement

This work was supported by the National Social Sciences Fund of China under Grant No. 17BYY200.

References

Bigliazzi, S. 2013. *Theatre Translation in Performance*. London & New York: Routledge.
Boria, M., A. Carreres, M. Noriega-Sánchez, and M. Tomalin, eds. 2020. *Translation and Multimodality: Beyond Words*. London & New York: Routledge.
Borodo, M. 2015. "Multimodality, Translation and Comics." *Perspectives* 23(1): 22–41.
Calthrop, E. F. 1905. *Sonshi: The Chinese Military Classic*. Tokyo: Sanseido.
Chen, X. 2018. "Representing Cultures Through Language and Image: A Multimodal Approach to Translations of the Chinese Classic Mulan." *Perspectives* 26(2): 214–231.
Cook, G. 2001. *The Discourse of Advertising*, 2nd ed., The Interface Series. London & New York: Routledge.
Corbett, E. P. J. 1971. *Classical Rhetoric for the Modern Student*, 2nd ed. New York: Oxford University Press.
Durand, J. 1970. "Rhetoric and Advertising Image." *Communications* 15(1): 70–95.
Durand, J. 1987. "Rhetorical Figures in the Advertising Image." In *Marketing and Semiotics: New Directions in the Study of Signs for Sale*. Vol. 77 of *Approaches to Semiotics [AS]*, edited by Jean Umiker-Sebeok. Berlin: de Gruyter.
Dyer, G. 1982. *Advertising as Communication*. London & New York: Routledge.
Ehses, H. H. J. 1984. "Representing Macbeth: A Case Study in Visual Rhetoric." *Design Issues* 1(1): 53.
Feng, D. 2017. "Metonymy and Visual Representation: Towards a Social Semiotic Framework of Visual Metonymy." *Visual Communication* 16(4): 441–466.
Feng, D. 2019. "Analyzing Multimodal Chinese Discourse: Integrating Social Semiotic and Conceptual Metaphor Theories." In *The Routledge Handbook of Chinese Discourse Analysis*, 1st ed., edited by Chris Shei, 65–81. London & New York: Routledge.
Feng, D, and K. L. O'Halloran. 2013. "The Multimodal Representation of Emotion in Film: Integrating Cognitive and Semiotic Approaches." *Semiotica* 2013(197).
Gkiouzepas, L. and M. K. Hogg. 2011. "Articulating a New Framework for Visual Metaphors in Advertising." *Journal of Advertising* 40(1): 103–120.
Huhmann, B. A., and P. A. Albinsson. 2019. "Assessing the Usefulness of Taxonomies of Visual Rhetorical Figures." *Journal of Current Issues & Research in Advertising* 40(2): 171–195.
Hurtado, J. C., and S. S. Gallego. 2013. "Multimodality, Translation and Accessibility: A Corpus-based Study of Audio Description." *Perspectives* 21(4): 577–594.
Kjeldsen, J. E. 2018. "The Rhetoric of Sound, the Sound of Arguments. Three Propositions, Three Questions, and an Afterthought for the Study of Sonic and Multimodal Argumentation." *Argumentation and Advocacy* 54(4): 364–371.
Kress, G R. 2010. *Multimodality: A Social Semiotic Approach to Contemporary Communication*. London & New York: Routledge.
Leigh, J. H. 1994. "The Use of Figures of Speech in Print Ad Headlines." *Journal of Advertising* 23(2): 17–33.
Liao, M. 2018. "Translating Multimodal Texts in Space: A Case Study of St Mungo Museum of Religious Life and Art." *Linguistica Antverpiensia, New Series – Themes in Translation Studies* 17: 84–98.
Maes, A. and J. Schilperoord. 2009. "Schemes and Tropes in Visual Communication: The Case of Object Grouping in Advertisements." In *Discourse, of Course*, edited by Jan Renkema, 67–78. Amsterdam: John Benjamins Publishing Company.
McQuarrie, E. F., and D. G. Mick. 1996. "Figures of Rhetoric in Advertising Language." *Journal of Consumer Research* 22(4): 424.

McQuarrie, E. F., and D. G. Mick. 1999. "Visual Rhetoric in Advertising: Text-Interpretive, Experimental, and Reader-Response Analyses." *Journal of Consumer Research* 26(1): 37–54.

McQuarrie, E. F., and D. G. Mick. 2003. "Visual and Verbal Rhetorical Figures Under Directed Processing Versus Incidental Exposure to Advertising." *Journal of Consumer Research* 29(4): 579–587.

Miller, D. W., and M. Toman. 2016. "An Analysis of Rhetorical Figures and Other Linguistic Devices in Corporation Brand Slogans." *Journal of Marketing Communications* 22(5): 474–493.

Mubenga, K. S. 2009. "Towards a Multimodal Pragmatic Analysis of Film Discourse in Audiovisual Translation." *Meta: Journal des traducteurs* 54(3): 466.

Munday, J. 2004. "Advertising: Some Challenges to Translation Theory." *The Translator* 10(2): 199–219.

Nylan, M. 2020. *The Art of War: A New Translation* [eng]. New York: W. W. Norton & Company.

O'Halloran, K. L. 2008. "Systemic Functional-Multimodal Discourse Analysis (SF-MDA): Constructing Ideational Meaning Using Language and Visual Imagery." *Visual Communication* 7(4): 443–475.

O'Halloran, K. L., Sabine Tan, and Peter Wignell. 2016. "Intersemiotic Translation as Resemiotisation: A Multimodal Perspective." *Signata* (7): 199–229.

Pârlog, A. 2019. *Intersemiotic Translation: Literary and Linguistic Multimodality*. Palgrave Pivot. Cham: Palgrave Macmillan.

Peterson, M. O. 2019. "Aspects of Visual Metaphor: An Operational Typology of Visual Rhetoric for Research in Advertising." *International Journal of Advertising* 38(1): 67–96.

Phillips, B. J., and E. F. McQuarrie. 2004. "Beyond Visual Metaphor: A New Typology of Visual Rhetoric in Advertising." *Marketing Theory* 4(1–2): 113–136.

Rossolatos, G. 2014. "Conducting Multimodal Rhetorical Analysis of TV Ads with Atlas.ti 7." *Multimodal Communication* 3(1).

Sun, T 孙子. 1940. *The Art of War Commented by Ten Scholars* 孙子十家注 *(edited by Sun Hsing-yen* 孙星衍校*)*. Shanghai 上海: The Commercial Press 商务印书馆.

Susam-Saraeva, Ş. 2019. "Interlingual Cover Versions: How Popular Songs Travel Round the World." *The Translator* 25(1): 42–59.

Theodorakis, I. G., Christos Koritos, and Vlasis Stathakopoulos. 2015. "Rhetorical Maneuvers in a Controversial Tide: Assessing the Boundaries of Advertising Rhetoric." *Journal of Advertising* 44(1): 14–24.

van Mulken, M. 2003. "Analyzing Rhetorical Devices in Print Advertisements." *Document Design* 4(2): 114–128.

Wang, X. and Y. Sui. 2004. *Sunzi's Art of War: World's Most Famous Military Classic*, 10th ed. Singapore: Asiapac Books.

Zhang, M. 2015. "Teaching Translation with a Model of Multimodality." *Asia Pacific Translation and Intercultural Studies* 2(1): 30–45.

4 Reshaping the heroic image of Monkey King via multimodality
A hero is back

Wang Hui (Wanda) and Li Xiaowei

1 Introduction

The year 2015 witnessed an extraordinary success of the animated film *Monkey King: Hero Is Back* (hereinafter *MKH*) in China, breaking the single-day box-office records for animated movies and becoming China's animated film box-office champion. It was almost at the same time the film went global and its distribution rights were sold to over 60 countries (Ren 2015). A year later, the dubbed English version of *MKH* made its debut on American streaming sites and then in cinemas. What enchanted the audiences most, home and abroad, in the film is the "humanized" Monkey King (*SUN Wukong* in Chinese Pinyin), quite distinct from its traditional superhero image in the minds of the Chinese people. It is for this reason that the film was widely accepted both in China and the Western world as reported in *Yangcheng Evening News*, in which Xiaopeng Tian, director of the film, concluded, "it [the film] is all about humanity (our translation)" (Li 2015). Our preliminary analysis of the pair of the Chinese and English movies, however, shows that a number of changes have been made to the English lines and the two were dubbed by different actors, although the moving pictures remain the same. It is thus worth a further investigation on how the identical visual and different audio and verbal modes operate simultaneously to create and recreate a "humanized" image of Monkey King to suit the target social contexts.

To achieve this purpose, this chapter adopts a multimodal approach, one of the most applied theoretical frameworks in audiovisual translation studies (e.g. Pérez-González 2014; Xu 2017; Chaume 2014; Bosseaux 2019). To date, the existing literature in multimodality and audiovisual translation has mainly centered on subtitle studies (Xu 2017; Guillot 2018). Although multimodality has been considered effective in gaining a full, or better picture, of the dubbing process and the impact of dubbing for dubbing studies (Bosseaux 2019, 57), scant attention so far has been paid specifically to the impact of differing verbal and vocal modes on the meaning-making of the same moving images and its resulting characteristics of the protagonist for the target cultural context in Chinese-English translation.

This chapter analyzes some Chinese-English excerpts from the animated movie *MKH*, and addresses the following questions: (1) What choices are made by the translator in setting the lines to the same images in the process of transferring

Monkey King to the American market? (2) How does the same image work with differing lines as well as the soundtrack to reshape the image of Monkey King? (3) What are the "humanized" images of Monkey King presented in the two different versions of the movie? (4) What are the underlying factors triggering the changes made to the English movie?

2 Recap the image of Monkey King in China

Monkey King, a magical monkey born from a primeval stone egg, is a Chinese iconic hero produced in a Chinese classical novel *Journey to the West*. With shape-shifting powers and a size-changing magic rod, the monkey rebelled against the heaven. His rebellion came to a halt when he met Buddha and was subjugated and then imprisoned under the mountain. Five hundred years later, Xuanzang, a pilgrimage monk, released him from his curse and the monkey then escorted Xuanzang on his pilgrimage to the West. After conquering 81 tribulations while accompanying Xuanzang in the journey and eventually retrieving the Buddhist sutras, Monkey King successfully ascended to Buddhahood.

The story of Monkey King was repeatedly told in a range of stories developed out of the novel, and his image has undergone changes from a trickster, to a revolutionary hero during the Mao period, and to a post-socialist hero (Sun 2018, 108). To contemporary Chinese, Monkey King has been a role model and his image is "overwhelmingly positive," because he is "not only fearless and willing to challenge authorities but also loyal to his master Tripitaka (Xuanzang) and devoted to the goal of the band of pilgrims" (ibid., 60). The monkey has typical characteristics of a hero, as Goethals and Allison (2012, 186–187) pinpoint, "highly competent," and "of great courage and strength." His unrivalled power and intelligence made him an undefeated hero enjoying popular worship up until now, whereas his fighting spirit, as well as his optimistic and free-standing attitude towards life, has been his universal appeal that enabled his ongoing popularity and adaptability.

3 Towards a multimodal analytical framework

3.1 The theoretical background of the present research

This section sets out to chart the contextual background of the present study. It points out the necessity of multimodal analysis and discusses the strengths and weaknesses of Chaume (2014) so as to pave the way for building an analytical model in the next section.

Compared with the print media, the cinema screen provides a platform for a wider range of semiotic modes, such as spoken language, written texts, visual representations, music and sound, to be orchestrated to make rich and complex meaning, shape characters and create a cinematic story. This prompts the need for the use of a multimodal approach to examine how the individual semiotic mode functions and how these modes add up and interact with each other to make meaning for the film viewers. Chaume (2004, 2014) provides a good point of entry in

Table 4.1 Meaning codes in audiovisual translation (Chaume 2014, 172)

Codes transmitted through the acoustic channel	Codes transmitted through the visual channel
Linguistic code	Iconographic code
Para-linguistic code	Photographic code
Musical code	Mobility code
Special effects code	Shot code
Sound position code	Graphic code
	Editing code (montage)

this regard. He categorized these semiotic modes based on channels of communication through which an audiovisual text is dispatched (i.e. the acoustic channel and the visual channel), as shown in Table 4.1. On this basis, he generalized distinct features of signifying codes in each channel. Given that the focus of the present research is on image construction and reconstruction in the dubbed movies, Chaume's model is especially helpful for us to study characterization through performance by means of acoustic and visual analysis.

Admittedly, Chaume's model is general enough to subsume the features of the semiotic codes and sub-codes on the screen, yet it has limitations in dealing with the relationship between these features and their functions, the reason for which might be that Chaume's focus is on discussing "all major aspects of dubbing and the dubbing profession" (2014, xvi). A case in point is the linguistic code, which has features of both written speech and oral texts, making true-to-life dialogues. However, unfortunately, it was not made clear how these codes, sub-codes and their features generate meaning and shape stories. To remedy these, we will adopt frameworks grounded in the Hallidayan theory of three metafunctions, Kress and van Leeuwen's (2006) visual grammar and van Leeuwen's (1999) audio grammar, and will elaborate on them in the next section.

3.2 A multimodal analytical framework

This section adopts a multimodal approach to examine how the verbal, visual and vocal codes work together to create a characteristic role on the screen and how the polysemiotic whole of the original is reconstructed in translation. Specifically, it intends to build a model adapted from Chaume (2014), as seen in Figure 4.1, and complemented by concepts from Halliday (1994), Kress and van Leeuwen (2006) and van Leeuwen (1999). In line with Chaume (2014), the semiotic modes are categorized on the basis of the channel of communication. In the acoustic channel, the linguistic code and the para-linguistic code are chosen for examination, given the focus of the present research is on the dubbed dialogue, which as an "embedded speech cue" (Li and Kuo 2003, 2) is the key to human's content understanding; whereas in the visual channel, the photographic code, the shot code

Figure 4.1 A multimodal analytical framework (adapted from Chaume 2014, 172)

and the mobility code are most relevant to the present study and are hence taken for investigation. When it comes to the meaning-making of these codes and sub-codes, we will borrow parameters from Halliday's functional grammar, Kress and van Leeuwen's visual grammar and van Leeuwen's sound theory for data analysis.

To describe the features of the linguistic code, we will use three metafunctions of Halliday's systemic functional grammar, which provides an elaborate account of semantic relations in human experience, events and actions. According to Halliday (1994), the ideational function construes the experience of social activities; the interpersonal function enacts social relations; and the textual function organizes these construal and enactments as coherent and meaningful discourse. Among all linguistic representations of these three metafunctions, transitivity includes the processes described by the verb, participants in the process and circumstances associated with the process and so forth; lexis represents patterns of extralinguistic experience; modality, realized by finite modal operators (e.g. *must be, will be*, and *should have*) or modal adjuncts (e.g. *usually, probably* and *always*), is "an expression of the speaker's opinion" (ibid., 89); polarity is a choice between positive and negative, realized through the finite element and the mood adjunct; and theme is "the starting point for the message" (ibid., 38) and functions to connect back to previous stretches of a text and signal the development of later stretches.

According to Chaume (2014, 173), the para-linguistic code includes qualifiers (e.g. nasality, moaning or breathing control), discourse markers that represent para-linguistic signs ("huh," etc.) and primary voice qualities, including pitch, volume, rhythm, and timbre, of which discourse markers, pitch and volume are most relevant to the selected episode and are hence chosen for study. Pitch refers to how high or how low the sound is and can be further described in terms of range and level. Pitch range can be defined as the limits between which the pitch is produced (for instance, between the two extremes of "high" and "low"). A "wide pitch range" can express "excitement," "surprise" or "anger,' while a "narrow pitch range" may convey "boredom" or "misery" (van Leeuwen 1999, 106). Pitch level is closely linked to vocal effort. The higher the pitch level, the greater the vocal effort needed, and the louder the voice is; reversely, the lower the pitch level, the more relaxed, and the softer the voice (ibid., 107). Volume is the loudness of the sound. Semiotically, these voice descriptors not only express meanings, but have emotional power. They are combined in different ways to make their contribution to the realization of sound acts (ibid., 110–111) and will, hence, be analyzed simultaneously.

In line with Chaume (2014), the photographic code includes colors and lighting, and changes of color and lighting might affect the meanings of the linguistic code (113). Similar to the *size of frame* in Kress and van Leeuwen (2006), Chaume's shot code contains camera shots (close-ups, extreme close-ups and medium close-ups) and camera angle (long, knee and medium shots), which are interactive, indicating the social distance between the participants and the viewer, or between the participants on the screen. The extreme close-ups, or the bigger close-up in Kress and van Leeuwen's words, could reveal the subject's feelings (2006, 126); the mobility code is specific to audiovisual texts and includes proxemics, kinesics and mouth articulation. Proxemic signs indicate the distance between on-screen characters and the distance from characters to the camera, or differently put, the distance from the viewer to characters, whereas kinesic signs, referring to the movements of the characters, represent social actions.

In the next section, we will use this model to investigate how the semiotic ensemble of *MKH* is adapted verbally and vocally to target at the American market. It is worthy of note that the "translator" in this paper is an umbrella term for all those contributing to the final translation product, including but not limited to the translator himself/herself, the dialogue writer and the dubbing assistant.

4 Case study of *Monkey King: Hero Is Back*

4.1 Data collection

In *MKH*, the all-powerful Monkey King is imprisoned by Buddha in an ice cage deep buried in Five Elements Mountain after defying and irritating the gods. Five hundred years later, monsters attack a village to abduct children for refining elixirs and Little Tang Monk, a boy monk named Jiang Liu'er, flees into the mountains. Liu'er accidentally sets free Monkey King from the mountains, but unfortunately the monkey's magic power cannot be recovered with a remnant of Buddha's seal. In return for the boy monk's salvation, Monkey King accompanies him and Little One (a little girl) back to the city. On their way back, Monkey King is easily defeated by Evil Lord (*Hundun* in Chinese Pinyin, the monster lord) and Little One is thus taken away. The monkey is then trapped in the struggle for saving the little girl. With the help of Liu'er and Pigsy, he eventually retrieves confidence and determines to save the girl. The story ends with his successful vanquish of Evil Lord and other monsters.

We selected a 4-minute episode out of *MKH* for this study, which marks a turning point for Monkey King to develop from being frustrated to becoming courageous and confident in the movie. Right before the episode, the monkey is knocked down in his fight with Evil Lord and falls into the river. He is blown to the shore and gradually comes to life, together with Little Tang Monk and Pigsy. We will concentrate on how Monkey King comes across at this point by looking at the scenes extracted from the pair of movies, with a particular focus on the lines, voice, gestures and facial expressions of the monkey.

In the English clip, the monkey is dubbed by Jackie Chan, a renowned international and Hollywood star, whose voice is generally at a relatively low pitch level and narrow pitch range, whereas the monkey's voice in the original is, relatively speaking, throaty and with a higher pitch level and wider pitch range.

To overcome the difficulty of "detecting these paralinguistic features" (Chaume 2014, 102), we use Praat, a speech analytic software often used in phonetics, to capture the primary voice quality of the para-linguistic code. Praat offers acoustic features of speech and voice samples for analysis and evaluation and produces quality speech analysis images for demonstration in the field of phonetics. In the present study, it provides features for volume and pitch analysis. Pitch analysis uncovers the pitch level at each point as well as the minimum pitch and the maximum pitch to obtain the pitch range.

4.2 *Analyzing* Monkey King *in the Chinese and English excerpts*

The excerpted episode contains eight scenes in total, with each put in a table in sequence. Each table encompasses three columns, showing visual pictures, verbal lines and soundtrack graphics in the pair of movies respectively for analysis. The Chinese example lines are literally translated into English for the convenience of comparison, and the literal translation is indicated in the examples with "lit."

4.2.1 Analysis of scene 1

Scene 1 in Table 4.2 begins as Liu'er rushes towards the monkey and tries to push him to rescue Little One. In the picture, the monkey is shot in medium close-up with a focus on the oblique rear view of his shoulders and his lowered head. He responds to Little Tang Monk's plea for saving the little girl, with his back to the audience. The photo is shot with a low angle taken from the point of view of Liu'er. In terms of the soundtrack in the Chinese version, when the monkey utters the line, his voice is soft and throaty, with sighing breathiness. It has a low pitch level and narrow pitch range; whereas in the English version, the monkey responds in a soft tone. Likewise, his voice is at a low pitch level and narrow pitch range.

Reshaping the heroic image of Monkey King 97

Table 4.2 Multimodal analysis of scene 1

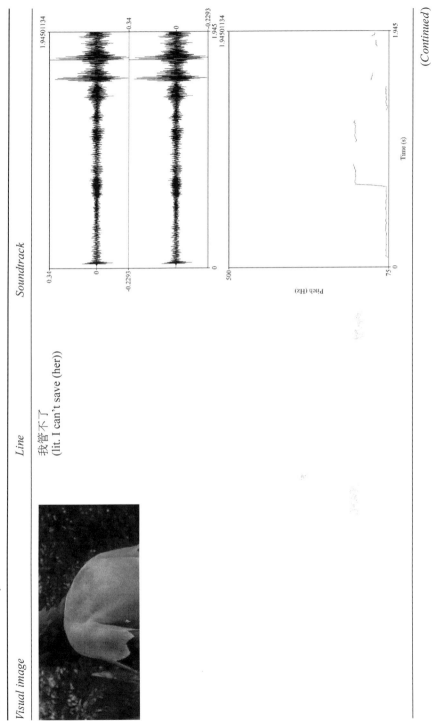

(Continued)

98 *Wang Hui (Wanda) and Li Xiaowei*

Table 4.2 (Continued)

Visual image	Line	Soundtrack
	She's not my problem	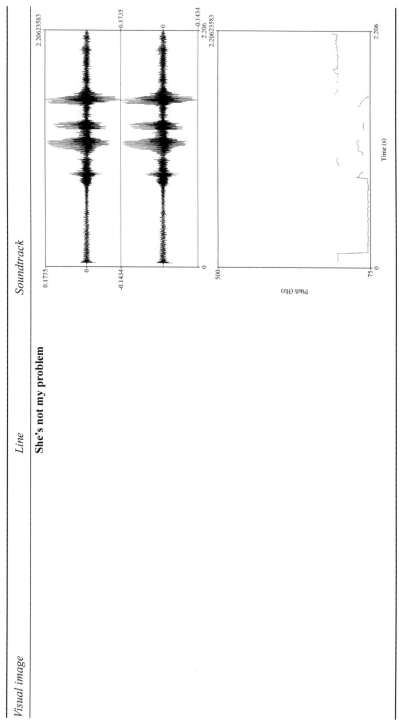

THE CHINESE VERSION

In the first line, "我管不了 (lit. I can't save)," the material process "管(save)," meaning shouldering (the responsibility), and the negative finite "不了(not)," clearly voices out the monkey's inability to save the little girl. Van Leeuwen (1999, 160) contends that the sighing breathiness indicates misery and frustration, and this is fully embodied in the present line. Sadness, misery and frustration could be well sensed when the line is delivered in a low, soft, throaty voice and sighing breathiness.

The low angle highlights Monkey King's superiority as Great Sage in the eyes of the monk. Yet, his lowered head carries a low mood and the rear view indicates how desolate he is when uttering the line.

THE ENGLISH VERSION

Monkey King's response, "*She's not my problem*" is a complete rewrite of its Chinese corresponding part. It is adapted from the idiom "it's not my problem," which is used to say rudely that you are not responsible for dealing with a particular problem and are not willing to help (online Longman Dictionary). When the token *it* is replaced with "she," it is "she (lit. the little girl)" that is identified as a problem, suggesting Monkey King shuffles off his responsibility for saving her and is not willing to help. The Chinese line seems to highlight the monkey's depression and frustration when Liu'er asks him to save the little girl; whereas the English one seems to be rewritten on the basis of the translator's interpretation of the original. Compared with its Chinese corresponding part, it seems to reveal the monkey's real thoughts behind "我管不了 (lit. I can't save)" and thus sets up a cause-effect relationship with the Chinese line, i.e. I cannot save the little girl, as she is not my problem. The identifying process is put in a soft but firm voice and at a narrow pitch range, which, according to van Leeuwen (1999, 106), implies constrained feelings of the monkey. He seems to be sober and firm in his utterance, indicating he is determined not to save the little girl.

The lowered head and the oblique rear view of the monkey suggest his depression and his detachment from the monk. This makes even more obvious Monkey King's coldness and firmness in his decision, as presented in the acoustic analysis of his dialogue with the boy monk.

4.2.2 Analysis of scene 2

Scene 2 in Table 4.3 continues narrating the monkey's response towards Little Tang Monk's persistent plea for rescuing Little One. In the picture, the monkey is shot in a medium close-up with the oblique angle. With quick turning around, abrupt throwing action and suddenly widened eyes, he further responds to the boy monk's plea for saving the little girl. The photo is shot with a high vertical angle. When the monkey repeats the line "我管不了 (lit. I can't save)," he bursts into a loud voice, with a high pitch level and wide pitch range; for the English line, the voice is changed to a loud tone, at a high pitch level and wide pitch range. The extent, however, lessens, compared with that in the Chinese version.

Table 4.3 Multimodal analysis of scene 2

Visual image	Line	Soundtrack
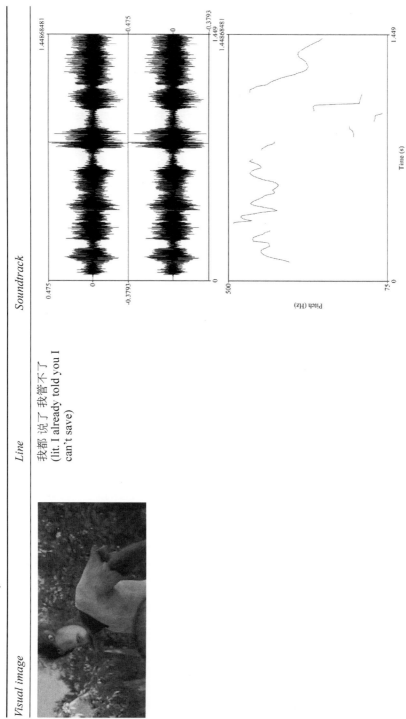	我都 说了 我管不了 (lit. I already told you I can't save)	

Neither are you. I just need to go my own way.

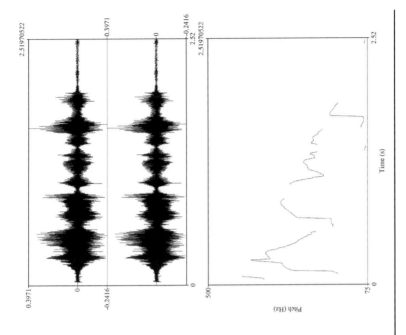

THE CHINESE VERSION

Little Tang Monk keeps appealing Monkey King to save the girl but is quickly refuted. The adjunct "都 (already)" and the repeated shouts of "我管不了 (lit. I can't save)" clearly show Monkey King's impatience in response to the boy monk's further persuasion. The monkey's impatience and agitation explodes through his loud burst of voice at a high pitch level, suddenly widened eyes, and quick turning around towards Little Tang Monk, that is, the monkey's impatience due to the lack of understanding of his companions, and the resulting rage action because of his powerlessness and inability to rescue the little girl. With a high vertical angle in Scene 2, Monkey King looks awesome, whereas Little Tang Monk is, in Kress and van Leeuwen's (2006, 140) words, "small and insignificant."

THE ENGLISH VERSION

With a negative adjunct *no*, Liu'er quickly corrects Monkey King, but is cut off when the monkey snarls, "Neither are you! I just need to go my own way." This scene continues revealing the monkey's true feelings at this point. The English line seems to be derived from what the translator tracks between the lines of the Chinese version. The first sentence is elliptical, omitting the *value*, "my problem." With a negative adjunct "neither," it is closely linked with the above sentence, "she is not my problem," suggesting the little girl is not the monkey's problem either. The modal adjunct "just" and the model verb "need" in the second line emphasize that the monkey "would get an advantage from (minding his own issues)" (online Collins Dictionary). The attribute "my own," forming a sharp contrast with "she" and "you," illustrates the monkey's determination and at the same time strengthens his discarding attitude and resolute refusal towards his fellows. The loud and high-pitched voice very often gives a sense of agitation (van Leeuwen 1999, 106). And this is typically manifested in the monkey's delivery of the line "I just need to go my own way." The emotional voice is complemented by the monkey's widened eyes and throwing action towards the boy monk. Nevertheless, the extent of the loudness of his voice and the width of his pitch range is lesser than that in the Chinese version, which implies the monkey's agitated feeling is relatively constrained, making him calmer and colder.

4.2.3 Analysis of scene 3

Scene 3 in Table 4.4 is a continuation of Monkey King's reaction to Little Tang Monk. In the visual picture, the monkey is shot in a medium close-up with the frontal-oblique angle. He repeats "管不了 (lit. cannot save)" to Little Tang Monk's plea, with his drooping head, downward-looking eyes and mouth squeezed shut. The photo is shot with a high vertical angle. When uttering the Chinese line, "我管不了那孩子 (lit. I can't save that girl)," the monkey's voice changes to soft, with a low pitch level and narrow pitch range, ending with trembling quality; likewise, the English line is delivered in a soft tone, at a low pitch level and narrow pitch range. But the monkey's pitch level is even lower with a narrower pitch range when compared with that in the Chinese version.

Reshaping the heroic image of Monkey King 103

Table 4.4 Multimodal analysis of scene 3

Visual image	Line	Soundtrack
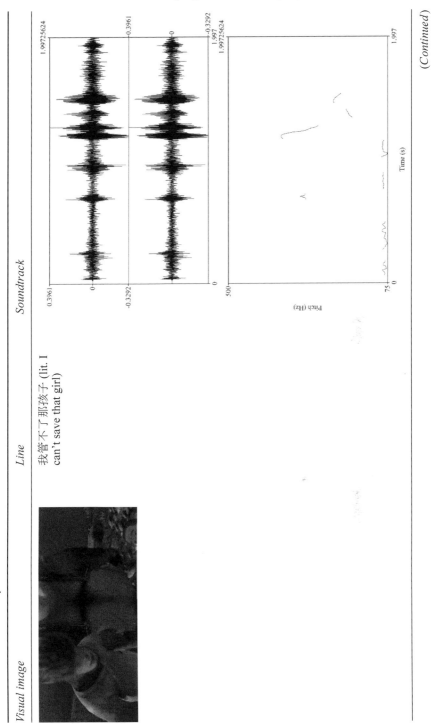	我管不了那孩子 (lit. I can't save that girl)	

(*Continued*)

Table 4.4 (Continued)

Visual image	Line	Soundtrack
	You can take care of her yourself.	

Reshaping the heroic image of Monkey King   105

THE CHINESE VERSION

Monkey King further repeats "我管不了" in the line "我管不了那孩子 (lit. I can't save that kid)." The use of the pet name, "孩子 (kid)," indicates the close relationship between the monkey and the little girl. Nevertheless, Monkey King's soft and low voice suggests his lack of dominance and power, that is, no power to save Little One. On the other hand, his trembling ending with "那孩子 (that kid)" illustrates his strong emotion, that is, his helplessness, unwillingness and sadness in dropping the desire of rescuing the girl despite his superficial refusal.

At the end of the utterance, the monkey has his eyes closed tight, delivering his entangling mood in the rescue issue. The close frontal shot of the monkey at the end of the line invites the viewer's attention and clearly conveys his mood.

THE ENGLISH VERSION

Monkey King turns away from the little boy and further responds with "you can take care of her yourself." Differing from the Chinese line, in which "我 (I, i.e. the monkey)" is *theme* and carries the monkey's sadness and helplessness about his inability to save Little One, the English version takes "you (i.e. the monk)" as *theme* and successfully shuffles off his responsibility onto the boy monk. The reflexive pronoun "yourself" in the sentence, making a striking contrast with "my own" in Scene 2, implies his firmness in shifting the responsibility of protecting Little One to Little Tang monk.

Additionally, the monkey turns down his volume and pitch level with a narrow pitch range. With a lower but clearer voice and narrower pitch range, the monkey is more constrained in the English movie, demonstrating his coldness yet firmness in discharging the responsibility of protecting Little One.

At the end of the utterance, the monkey has his eyes squeezed shut, which seems to hide his true feelings. The close shot and frontal view of the monkey makes his negative and irresponsible attitude clearly conveyed to the audience.

4.2.4 *Analysis of scent 4*

Scene 4 in Table 4.5 shows Monkey King's reaction towards Pigsy when the latter makes a plea for saving Little One. Monkey King and Pigsy are shot in a medium close-up with a frontal-oblique angle. The monkey raises a fist and grasps Pigsy by the collar, with clenching teeth and dilated pupils. The photo is shot with a low angle taken from the view of the audience. When delivering the Chinese lines, the monkey shouts loudly and has a high pitch level and wide pitch range; likewise, the monkey utters the English lines in a loud tone, at a high pitch level and a wide pitch range.

THE CHINESE VERSION

Pigsy tries to placate Monkey King but provokes the monkey's violent reaction in return. In the monkey's response, the negative finite "别 ('don't')" in "别叫我猴子 (don't call me monkey)," the demanding mood in the imperative "给我闭嘴 (you shut up)" and his use of the vulgar expression "蠢猪 (stupid pig)" reveals the monkey's fury towards the Pigsy. "猴子 (Monkey)" is a pet name for Monkey

106 *Wang Hui (Wanda) and Li Xiaowei*

Table 4.5 Multimodal analysis of scene 4

Visual image	Line	Soundtrack
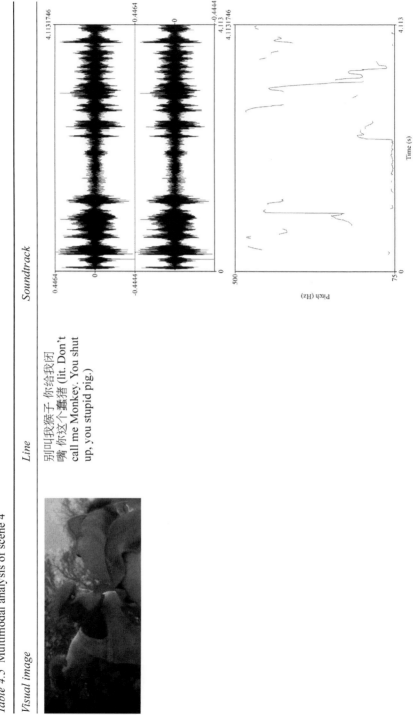	别叫我猴子 你给我闭嘴 你这个蠢猪 (lit. Don't call me Monkey. You shut up, you stupid pig.)	

Reshaping the heroic image of Monkey King 107

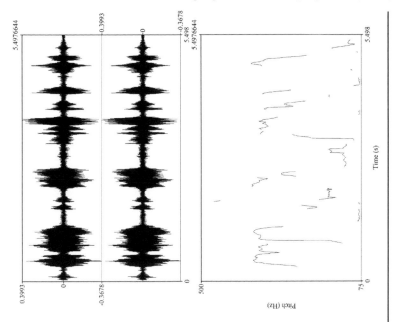

**Huh? You want to be a hero?
Go ahead then, I didn't ask to be saddled with any of you.**

King, indicating Pigsy's emotional intimacy towards the monkey. This is, however, refuted by Monkey King, making clear how irritating the monkey is regardless of their bonds of friendship. The monkey's madness is also evident from his loud voice and wide pitch range.

Monkey King's emotional reprimand is further complemented by his clenching teeth, wide staring eyes, raised fist and firm grasp of Pigsy's collar. Set by the low angle, the implied dominance of the monkey enhances the extent of his anger conveyed to the audience.

THE ENGLISH VERSION

Seeing that Monkey King chooses to give up, Pigsy attempts to talk the monkey into rescuing Little One, but is responded with the monkey's sudden turn with eyes rounded and blazing with fury and a discourse marker "huh" delivered with an emphatic, rushing and deep voice, showing Monkey King's towering disapproval. This is followed by a quick and sarcastic questioning, "You want to be the hero?" From the mental process "want," it is clear that the translator deems "hero" is the real call in the monkey's heart, although he is not able to due to his powerlessness at the moment. His irony towards Pigsy is obvious too, who is never a hero at all but a quitter, as evidenced in Wu's (1988) novel. Immediately after Pigsy's negative response, Monkey King turns to the next line, "Go ahead then, I didn't ask to be saddled with any of you." The demanding imperative "go ahead" is meant to command Pigsy to leave. In the line "I didn't ask to be saddled with any of you," "I" is the *theme*, the starting point of the sentence; the verbiage "saddled," meaning "to burden" (online Collins Dictionary), shows that Little Tang Monk, Little One and Pigsy are all viewed as a burden; whereas the verbal process "ask," meaning requesting, indicates the monkey's initiative in protecting his companions, which is however denied by the negative finite. In other words, deep in his heart, the monkey is eager to be a hero but is restrained because of his powerlessness. Meanwhile, he does not take it as his responsibility to protect his fellows. All lines are delivered with a loud voice and at a high pitch level, which, in van Leeuwen's (1999, 108) words, suggests the monkey's dominance in the relationship with Pigsy.

Simultaneously, Monkey King's widened eyes and flourished clenched fist in the visual mode clearly manifests his aggressiveness and rage towards Pigsy as well as his annoyance with the "burden." Additionally, the low angle shot implies the monkey's dominance in the relationship between him and Pigsy. The conversation between the monkey and Pigsy ends with the latter's being pushed to the ground.

Monkey King's refusal for saving the little girl pushes Little Tang Monk to leave to rescue the comrade himself.

4.2.5 Analysis of scene 5

After Little Tang Monk's departure, Monkey King explodes with extreme despair and frustration about his loss of magic power. After letting out his feelings, the exhausted monkey collapses into the water. In Scene 5 in Table 4.6, the monkey

Reshaping the heroic image of Monkey King 109

Table 4.6 Multimodal analysis of scene 5

Visual image	Line	Soundtrack
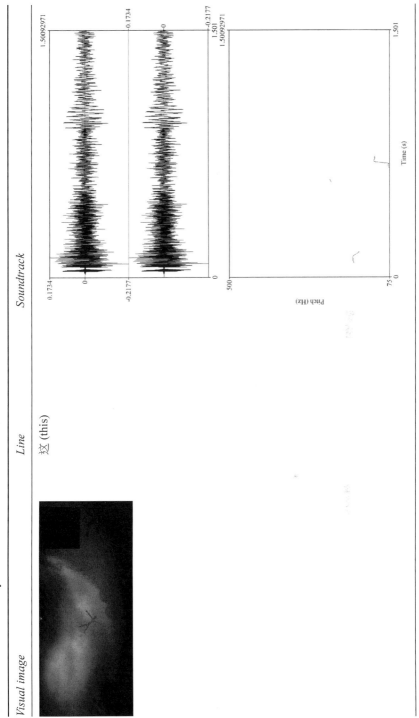	这 (this)	

(*Continued*)

110 *Wang Hui (Wanda) and Li Xiaowei*

Table 4.6 (Continued)

Visual image	Line	Soundtrack
	I didn't ask for this.	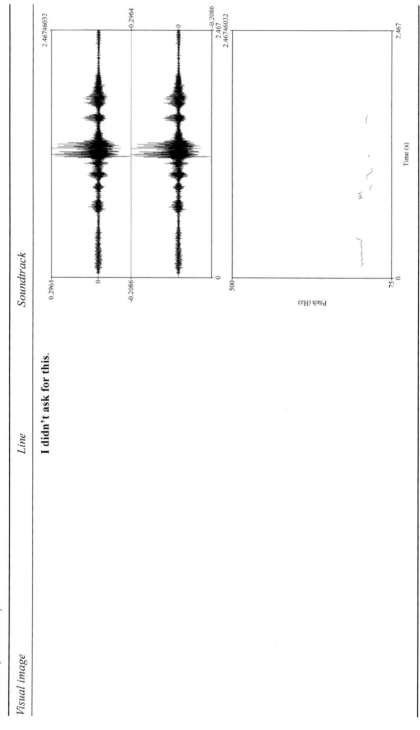

immerses himself completely in water, sprawling and leaving his back to the audience, when Liu'er continues to plead on the bank. The brightness of the water forms a sharp contrast with the darkness around the water. When the monkey mumbles "这 (this, i.e. saving Little One)" in the Chinese movie, his voice is soft with a low pitch level and narrow pitch range; whereas in the English movie, the monkey uses a soft tone in his monologue. It has a low pitch level and narrow pitch range, and a stress is put on the verbal process "ask," where the pitch level is much higher;

THE CHINESE VERSION

In response to the monk, Monkey King murmurs "这" (this, i.e. saving the little girl) as the start of his soliloquy. "这 (This)" serves as the *theme* and topic of the next line, highlighting the significance of rescuing the little girl in the monkey's mind. When "这 (this)" is delivered in a soft and hesitant voice with sighing breathiness and low pitch level, his sadness and hesitation in the face of difficulties is fully manifested.

The monkey's depression is also reflected through the long shot and high angle of the scene. The diminished monkey, along with his detachment from the audience indicated by his back view in the horizontal angle, sets off a lonely, sad and powerless monkey with a sense of despair.

THE ENGLISH VERSION

The monkey says, "I didn't ask for this," in response to Little Tang Monk's pleading. "这" is translated into "this" and inserted in the English line as *verbiage*. In the translation, the monkey's attitude towards "这 (this, i.e. saving the little girl)" is added: "I" serves as *theme* and sayer, the verbal process, "ask for," means to "behave in a provocative manner that is regarded as inviting (trouble)" (online Collins Dictionary), and the verbiage "this" (i.e. saving the little girl) turns to being a trouble in the eyes of the monkey, and is hence denied with a negative finite, "didn't."

Monkey King's voice is soft and firm, at a low pitch level and narrow pitch range, but the word "ask" is stressed with louder and longer voice, highlighting his impatience for the trouble. Compared with the Chinese line, the English version is loosely connected with the visual image, where a very small, detached and powerless monkey immersed in water is projected through the long shot, rear view and high angle.

4.2.6 Analysis of scene 6

Scene 6 in Table 4.7 further narrates Monkey King's soliloquy in a medium close shot, with more facial expressions exposed through the frontal view of his shoulders and left-turned head. He continues the monologue with eyes squeezed tight and mouth closed with muscle tension. The photo is shot in an eye-level angle.

Table 4.7 Multimodal analysis of scene 6

Visual image	Line	Soundtrack
	我管不了 (lit: I can't save (her))	

Reshaping the heroic image of Monkey King 113

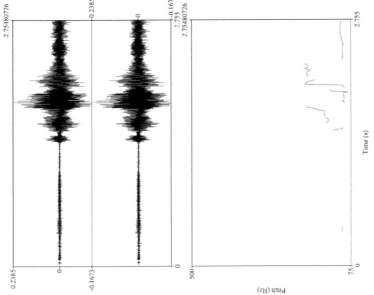

I don't want this.

The Chinese line is uttered in a louder voice, a higher pitch level and wider pitch range, whereas the English line is uttered in a louder tone and at a low pitch level and narrow pitch range.

THE CHINESE VERSION

After a short pause following "这 (this)," Monkey King whispered "我管不了 (lit. I can't save (her))," which has been repeated for the fourth time, reiterating his inability to save the little girl. The increasingly louder voice, higher pitch level and wider pitch range are combined to add increasing agitation and anxiety to the articulation, indicating the monkey's conflicting feelings between his willingness to take the responsibility of rescuing the little girl and his inability and powerlessness to take any real actions. While he speaks, the monkey is shaking his head from left to right with eyes closed tight and mouth compressed into a thin line, revealing his suffering when thinking of this.

THE ENGLISH VERSION

In the translated soliloquy, "I don't want this," the original material process is replaced with a mental process. The negative finite, "don't," and the mental process, "want," suggest the monkey's refusal towards taking the trouble of saving the little girl is deep from his heart. The increasingly louder voice and narrower pitch range implies the monkey's constrained feelings and hence makes even clearer his coldness and firmness in shirking his responsibility of saving the little girl.

Monkey King's negative attitude is further strengthened by his shaking head, which is in congruence with the monkey's firm refusal to rescue.

4.2.7 Analysis of scene 7

Scene 7 in Table 4.8 continues unfolding the monkey's inner world when he is faced with whether or not to save the little girl caught by Evil Lord. The monkey is shot in close-up with a focus on the frontal view of his clasping hands and right-turned lowered head. He further immerses himself in the soliloquy, with eyes squeezed shut and teeth clenched. The photo is shot with a high vertical angle. The repeated "管不了 (lit. can't save)" is delivered in an even louder voice and at a high pitch level and a wide pitch range. The pitch rises on the three words "管 (save)"; the voice quality of the English dubbing is similar to the original, except the extent is less, when compared with the Chinese version.

THE CHINESE VERSION

The repetition of "管不了 (lit. can't save)" in these lines accentuates again the monkey's helplessness and frustration. When the brief line is delivered in a loud and tense voice and the repeated rise on the pitch centered on the word "管 (save)," the recurrent frustrating and annoying phrase is turned into, in the words of van

Reshaping the heroic image of Monkey King 115

Table 4.8 Multimodal analysis of scene 7

Visual image	Line	Soundtrack
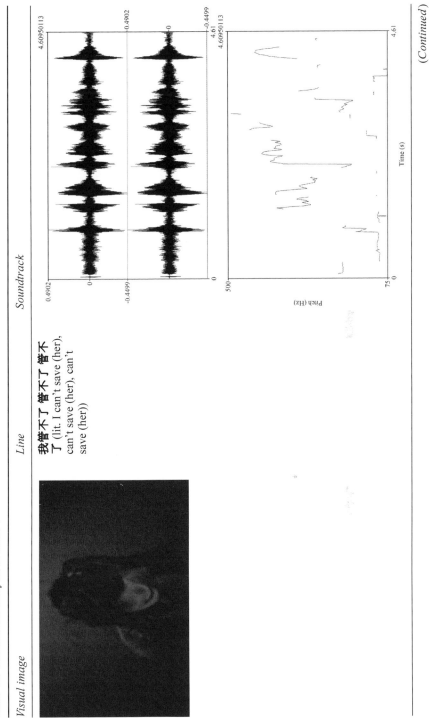	我管不了 管不了 管不了 管不了 (lit. I can't save (her), can't save (her), can't save (her))	

(*Continued*)

Table 4.8 (Continued)

Visual image	Line	Soundtrack
	These people are nothing but trouble.	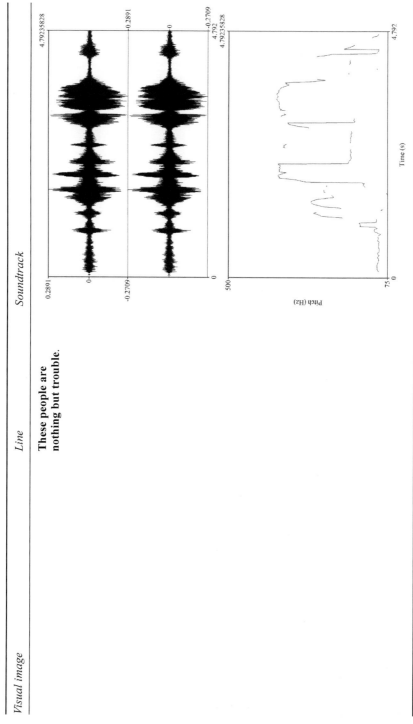

Leeuwen (ibid., 105), "a furious cascading of punches rather than a single blow" on the viewer. Along with these lines, the monkey's shaking head and clenching teeth further increases his mental suffering, which is conveyed to the audience through the frontal view and the close shot.

THE ENGLISH VERSION

The English line is an identifying process, in which these people, including the little girl, are identified as "trouble," and "nothing but" is used as a circumstantial element to emphasize the value. By identifying his companions as "trouble," Monkey King's responsibility of protecting them is reasonably discharged. The rewritten line therefore clears up the audience's doubt about why the monkey is not willing to save them. Meanwhile, his loud and high-pitched voice and his explicit stress on "trouble" highlights the monkey's intense and assertive negative attitude towards these people, thus further stressing his intention of escaping the responsibility of rescuing them.

Nonetheless, the monkey's voice has a narrower pitch range, compared with that in the Chinese movie, showing that he is more constrained in expressing his feeling and in preventing himself from completely discharging the responsibility of saving Little One.

In line with this, his clenching teeth and head clasped in hands make it clear that Monkey King is suffering from thinking of this, forming a contrast with his resolution in dodging the responsibility as presented in the acoustic category. His emotional struggle thus adds some complexity and ambivalence to his irresponsible attitude towards saving the little girl and protecting his fellows. On the other hand, it paves the way for his later attitude change in undertaking the responsibility of protecting the little girl.

4.2.8 Analysis of scene 8

The eyes of the frustrated monkey in the water are gradually drawn to Little Tang Monk's Great Sage. Scene 8 in Table 4.9 is an extreme close-up of Monkey King, with a particular focus on the frontal view of his mouth. The photo is shot with an eye-level angle. When the monkey voices "老猪 跟我走 (Old Pig, come with me)," he uses a loud tone at a low pitch level and wide pitch range; for the English line, the monkey says it in a loud voice at a low pitch level and wide pitch range, with stresses on "kids" and "save."

THE CHINESE VERSION

In the line, 老猪 跟我走 (Old Pig, come with me), the prefix "老 (old)" is often used, as Zhou (2000, 103) contends, in front of the surname of a person you are familiar with, and the use of "老猪 (Old Pig)" hence clearly demonstrates the close relationship between Monkey King and Pigsy, as compared with the filthy words "蠢猪 (lit. stupid pig)" in Scene 4. "跟我走 (Come with me)" is a terse and

118　*Wang Hui (Wanda) and Li Xiaowei*

Table 4.9 Multimodal analysis of scene 8

Visual image	Line	Soundtrack
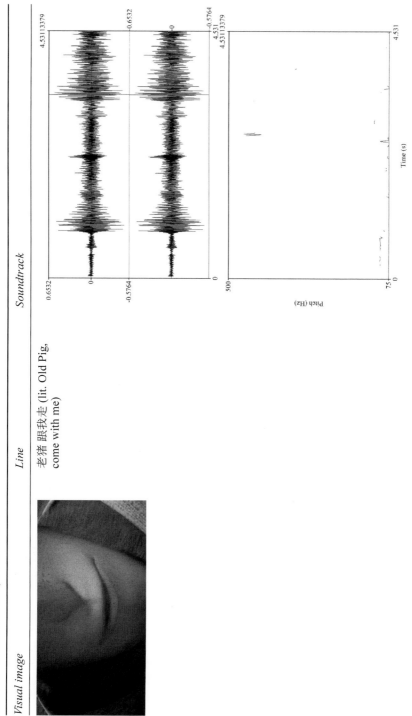	老猪 跟我走 (lit. Old Pig, come with me)	

Reshaping the heroic image of Monkey King 119

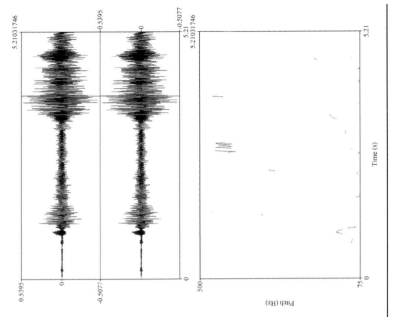

Hey Piggy, we've got kids to save.

forceful imperative, calling on Pigsy to go to rescue Little One. The disjunctive, brief and punchy articulation of the line at a low pitch level and wide pitch range gives a sense of dominance and emphasis to his voice. The extreme close-up shot and frontal and focused view of the monkey's mouth invites viewers' attention to the smile at the corner of his lips, which, along with his voice, indicating the monkey's confidence and courage in saving the kid. In accordance with van Leeuwen (1999, 106), the wide pitch range of this line in this situation indicates the monkey's excitement, which is in line with his confidence conveyed in the visual mode. Apparently, the monk's Great Sage story successfully evokes Monkey King's memory of his own glorious past. He stands up from the water, with his courage and pride fully recovered.

THE ENGLISH VERSION

In the English line, "Hey Piggy, we've got kids to save," the explication strategy is adopted to make clear what Monkey asks Pigsy to do. "老猪 (Old pig)" is replaced with "Piggy," suggesting the monkey's intimacy with Pigsy. The material process "got," goal "kids" and circumstance to "save," in particular the intended stress on "kids" and "save," clearly demonstrate Monkey King's altered intention of undertaking the responsibility of saving comrades. The flicker of smile at the corner of the monkey's lips in the extreme close-up of his mouth successfully catches the viewer's eyes, which works with his stress on "kids" and "save" to highlight a dominant, confident and courageous monkey. Such confidence and courage accords with the potential excitement revealed by Monkey King's wide pitch range at the vocal level.

5 Discussion

As a symbolic figure of Chinese traditional culture, Monkey King's all-powerful superhero image has taken root in the minds of the Chinese people. Differing from its traditional image, the monkey loses all his magical power and is presented as *humanized* in the pair of movies of *MKH*, which is meant to "show that someone has the qualities, weaknesses, etc. that are typical of a human, in a way that makes you more likely to feel sympathy for them" (online Cambridge Dictionary). Nonetheless, our analysis result shows that although being "humanized," it is clear that Monkey King has displayed discrepant characterization in the two movies. In the following section, we are going to discuss the differences and their related social factors.

In the selected Chinese episode, the traditional Chinese superhero has been projected as a responsible and sympathetic yet frustrated monkey. His mental suffering from his strong responsibility for the kids, yet deep frustration and even despair due to his powerlessness is well shown in the combined use of the seven repeated occurrences of the Chinese expression "管不了 (lit. can't save)," the increasingly louder voice, the often lowered head, the distant view of the monkey and so forth. Meanwhile, his squeezed-shut eyes and droopy head when murmuring "我管不了那孩子 (lit. I can't save that girl)," in particular his trembling and soft voice and low pitch level when mentioning "那孩子 ('that girl')," shapes a monkey who has sympathy and cares for the girl yet is incapable of helping her.

By contrast, in the English version, the translator did not maintain the verbal lines of Monkey King but completely rewrote them on the basis of his/her understanding and interpretation of the original, making the monkey more straightforward in revealing his true thoughts; the voice of Monkey King also undergoes considerable changes due to the replacement of the voice actor with Jackie Chan, for his appeal as Hollywood star to a wide range of audiences in the American market. The repetition of the phrase "管不了 (lit. can't save)" in the original script is replaced with the repeated use of the negative finite/complement "not/nothing" in the English lines for the sake of emphasis (e.g. "I do*n't* want this"; these people are "*nothing but trouble*"). As a result, half of the English lines are negative, making the image of Monkey King, his attitude towards saving the little girl in particular, rather negative. Such negative attitude is added with a sense of firmness and coldness conveyed in the monkey's soft and flat voice and detachment through the oblique rear view of the monkey. The icy image of Monkey King thus sets the tone for the whole episode. The selfishness of the monkey is presented through the five occurrences of *I* as Actor/Sayer/Sensor. The repeated use of negative finites, the identification of *these people* as trouble, and the increasingly louder voice and high pitch level, however, forms a sharp contrast with his emotional struggle, as shown in the moving images, such as the monkey's clenched teeth and shaking head in Scene 7, suggesting the ambivalence he is stuck in. In consequence, the rewritten lines and the firm and sober dubbing voice work together with facial expressions and/or gestures to re-project a monkey with more flaws (i.e. selfishness and coldness), although still being frustrated due to his powerlessness.

Noteworthy are the implications of these adapted lines and altered voice to the meaning-making of the visual image in the two versions of the movie; that is, the same image displays differing emotional associations. In Scene 6, for instance, the monkey's shaking head, closed eyes and closely shut mouth reveals his ambivalence and struggle when thinking of rescuing the little girl in the Chinese episode, whereas in the English version, the same image suggests a coldness and firmness in his refusal to save the girl.

For decades, the United States has boasted the dominant film industry in the global market, and American audiences are thus reluctant to watch films in other languages (Rich 2004), which makes it hard for foreign films to "penetrate and succeed" in the US film market (Richard and Newman 2002, 193). To attract American viewers to go to cinemas, one strategy, we deem, might be to camouflage the exotic origin of films from source cultures with a less prestigious role by making these films free of foreign-tongue with rewriting. This is reminiscent of polysystem theory, where the rewritten dialogue lines of Monkey King, according to Cory Edwards, the script writer or translator-editor of the English movie, are to "make the film more understandable for Western audiences" (Hou 2015). This echoes Chaume (2014), who held that over adaptation, or rewriting, frequently appears in the dubbing process so as to make the translated line "sounds realistic, credible and plausible" (16–18). The rewritten lines work together with the dubbed voice and the moving images to add flaws to the hero, which feels more realistic and adds new currency to the film among the American viewers who love flawed heroes (Selbo 2015, 233), although contradictory to his responsible image in the original.

Apparently, rewriting in the English episode of *MKH* and replacement of the dubbed actor have successfully helped the movie find its way into the American market. The charm of the dubbed Monkey King and the flawed hero is evidenced in the review of *Yam* magazine and IMDB.com, the world's most popular and authoritative source for movies, where people commended the movie as "a great Chinese animated picture" with "great characters with real emotions as motivation for character development, great camera-work, great character design, etc." From this, it follows that humanization, as a universal value, is no doubt an effective way to help films go international. Nonetheless, in the dubbing process, further decoding of the universal values is needed, as there might be distinct interpretation of humanization in the source and the target cultures, as indicated in the differing heroic images of Monkey King presented in the two movies.

6 Conclusion

This chapter adopts a multimodal approach to investigating the construction and re-construction of the "humanized" heroic image of Monkey King in the Chinese-English versions of the animated movies of *MKH* and explores its possible underlying sociocultural reasons. The multimodal approach enables us to examine how the dialogue lines, the dubbing voices, the gestures and facial expressions are interwoven into a whole to project the monkey as sympathetic, responsible, yet frustrated in the Chinese movie, and how the rewritten lines and the distinct dubbing voice interact with the same moving images to reproject the "humanized" monkey as frustrated, cold and firm so as to suit the taste of the American film viewers. It appears that the flawed Monkey King is in congruence with the favorite heroic image of American audiences and hence makes the dubbed English movie more acceptable in the American market.

This chapter represents a pioneering effort in investigating the impact of differing dialogue lines and dubbing voices on the meaning-making of the same moving images and the resulting characterization of the protagonist in the Chinese-English dubbed context. Although it is common practice to rewrite the lines to produce target-oriented translations, especially when the target culture occupies a dominant position in the sociocultural polysystem, the translator shall be alert, in the rewriting process, to the possible implications of rewriting in terms of lines and voice quality to the meaning-making of moving images and the characterization of the heroes in the dubbed movie. The use of Praat software from the field of phonetics to capture voice quality helps produce more reliable description of voice qualities and could hence be an effective trial in voice description.

Findings of the study presented in this chapter confirm that multimodal discourses, and the potential performance of various multimodal elements through different interventions and meaning-making selections, are central to purposeful communication with the target audience. Much more research via multimodal approaches is necessary if we wish to get a full picture of translation preferences in the production of original and translated movies. We hope that this study will provide a model that is useful for future research of this kind.

References

Bosseaux, C. 2019. "Investigating Dubbing: Learning from the Past, Looking to the Future." In *Routledge Handbook of Audiovisual Translation*, edited by L. Pérez-González, 48–63. London & New York: Routledge.

Chaume, F. 2004. *Cine y traducción*. Madrid: Cátedra.

Chaume, F. 2014. *Audiovisual Translation: Dubbing*. Manchester: St. Jerome.

Goethals, G.R., and Scott T. Allison. 2012. "Making Heroes: The Construction of Courage, Competence, and Virtue." *Advances in Experimental Social Psychology* 46: 183–235.

Guillot, M-N. 2018. "Subtitling on the Cusp of its Futures." In *Routledge Handbook of Audiovisual Translation*, edited by L. Pérez-González, 31–47. London & New York: Routledge.

Halliday, M. A. K. 1994. *An Introduction to Functional Grammar*, 2nd ed. London: Edward Arnold.

Hou, Q. 2015. "Animation Monkey King to Land in 60 Countries." Available from www.xinhuanet.com/english/entertainment/2015-11/10/c_134802935.htm (Accessed August 4, 2018).

Kress, G., and T. van Leeuwen. 2006. *Reading Images: The Grammar of Visual Design*, 2nd ed. London & New York: Routledge.

Li, L. 2015. "Hero is back: Tang Monk becomes a Boy Monk Wukong is Great Uncle (《大圣归来》唐僧变熊孩子 悟空是酷大叔)." July 16, 2015. Available from http://ent.sina.com.cn/m/c/2015-07-06/doc-ifxesftz6779484.shtml (Accessed August 4, 2018).

Li, Y. and C.-C. Jay Kuo. 2003. *Video Content Analysis Using Multimodal Information: For Movie Content Extraction, Indexing and Representation*. New York: Springer Science+Business Media.

Pérez-González, L. 2014. *Audiovisual Translation: Theories, Methods and Issues*. London & New York: Routledge.

Ren, S. 2015. "Chinese Cartoon is Back with *Great Sage* TIAN Xiaopeng: Chinese Cartoon Needs its Own Hero (国产动画随"大圣"归来 田晓鹏:中国动画需要自己的英雄)." Available from http://culture.people.com.cn/n/2015/0716/c87423-27312382.html (Accessed December 12, 2018).

Rich, B. R. 2004. "To Read or not to Read: Subtitles, Trailers, and Monolingualism." In *Subtitles: On the Foreignness of Film*, edited by Atom Egoyan and Ian Balfour, 153–169. Cambridge, MA & London: MIT Press.

Richard, De Z. and O. Newman. 2002. "Globalization, Soft Power and the Challenge of Hollywood." *Contemporary Politics* 8(3): 185–202.

Selbo, J. 2015. *Film Genre for the Screenwriter*. London & New York: Routledge.

Sun, H. 2018. *Transforming Monkey: Adaptation and Representation of a Chinese Epic*. Washington: The University of Washington Press.

Van Leeuwen, T. 1999. *Speech, Sound and Music*. Basingstoke: Macmillan.

Wu, C (ca. 1500–1582). 1988. *Journey to the West*. Beijing: People's Literature Publishing House.

Xu, M. 2017. "A Review of Multimodal Translation Studies in China (中国多模态翻译研究综述)." *Journal of Guangdong University of Foreign Studies* 28(2): 40–46.

Zhou, Y. 2000. "Study on the Semantic Meaning of Prefix "Lao" and Affix "Lao" (前缀"老"和"老"缀词语义色彩探微)." *Journal of Anhui University* 24(3): 100–103.

5 "Dis"covering *Hamlet* in China

A case analysis of book covers of the Chinese *Hamlet*

Xie Guixia (Rosie)

1 Introduction

Hamlet, first translated by Tian Han and published in 1922, is the first full-text Shakespearean play introduced to Chinese readers. Since then, Shakespearean translation kicked off in China and reached its first peak in the 1930s and its second peak after the 2000s. By 2020, there have already been seven versions of the complete Shakespeare. Each individual Shakespearean play also has more than one version of translations. Among them, *Hamlet*, with 18 Chinese versions in total, is the most retranslated one among all the plays. These 18 versions were produced in a time span of nearly a century with the most recent one produced by Fu Guangming in 2018. With the long time span in the translating history and its relatively numerous retranslated versions, the translations of *Hamlet* have been a topic for diachronic studies (e.g. Chao 1981; Bei 2004; Xie 2011; Wang 2015; Jin and Zhu 2016). Nevertheless, these studies primarily focus on the introduction of the translators, their language styles and the recontextualization of the different versions in the history. The same pattern also exists in the diachronic study of Shakespeare in China (e.g. Meng 1994; Zhang 1996; Levith 2004; Sun 2010). In these studies, however, paratexts have not yet been the focus of the scholars.

Paratexts are regarded as "more flexible, more versatile" compared to the relative immutability of the text inside the book, and are thus regarded as the "instrument of adaptation" (Genette 1997, 408). This adaptability allows paratexts to reflect the changes of the relevant cultural environment as well as possible reception of a book and its later editions in a society over time. The study, therefore, will use book covers from the different types of paratexts as the focus of study and seeks to answer the following three research questions:

1 What type of elements can generally be found on the book covers of the different Chinese versions of *Hamlet*?
2 What are the differences in the book cover designs of these versions over the years?
3 How do these differences reflect the changes in *Hamlet*'s reception in China?

To find answers to the above questions, the study will first present a brief review of the research of book covers and then adopt social semiotic multimodality as the theoretical framework to describe and analyze the changes on book covers.

2 Book covers of translated texts

The book cover plays an important role in presenting the book to the readers and is regarded as the "threshold" (Genette 1997) or "doorway" (Weedon 2007) through which the readers can have a glimpse of the book. Yet, important as they are to books, book covers have not attracted sufficient attention in the existing research. Many earlier studies on book covers are mainly about their developing history and their functions in introducing and positioning the book (e.g. Kratz 1994; Powers 2001; Phillips 2007; Williamson 2007), or about their effect on the readers' interpretation and reception of the book (e.g. Petric and Croatia 1995; Webby 2007). Some early studies and most of the recent researches start to pay attention to the socio-cultural mediating role of book covers between the author and the readers, arguing that book cover "re-presents and re-positions the text across languages, cultures, times and spaces" and "performs a crucial act of socio-cultural mediation, providing a bridge between authors and readers" (Sonzogni 2011, 15). Some other studies also show that book covers represent not just the content of the text but also the culture and history (Drew and Sternberger 2005), and have the potential for exploring the ideology behind the reception of a book (e.g. Held 2005; Machin and van Leeuwen 2016; Li, Li, and Miao 2019).

Some of the above studies also consider the important role of book covers in translation, such as Sonzogni seeing book covers as "visual translation" of the text (2011, 20). However, in the field of translation studies, book covers are mainly found in paratranslation-related studies (Harvey 2003; O'Sullivan 2005; Delistathi 2011; Summers 2013; Hou 2013; Kung 2013), in which book covers are regarded as one type of peritexts, helping to establish the atmosphere or reflecting the theme or ideology of the book. These studies mainly focus on the paratexts in translations in general, and book covers only constitute a small section of the research. Moreover, in previous studies on book covers, only one or two elements such as the photography, the blurb or the color are discussed.

In recent years, with the development of multimodality theories, scholars in the field of journalism, such as Lirola (2006), have started to examine covers of magazines or books from a multimodal perspective. Similarly, some translation scholars have also begun to apply multimodal theories in the analysis of different book covers of translated texts across cultures. For example, Chen (2017) analyzes the covers of two English translations of the Chinese classics *Mulan* and finds that the image of Mulan has been transformed in these translations both visually and verbally. Yu and Song (2017) analyze the different representations of the Zen master in two translations and find out that there is a picture-text congruence in translation; Li et al. (2019) also conduct a multimodal and cross-cultural comparison of book covers of the *Wild Swans*, discovering the intersemiotic relations within a book cover and the ideological congruence between the covers and the translated texts. In these studies, the use of multimodal theoretical frameworks helps to present a more systematic description than the earlier studies on book covers. Yet it is also found that these previous studies on book covers all adopt a synchronic perspective, while no diachronic studies on book covers of the same translated text in one culture or across cultures have yet been found. Judging from the very little existing literature on a multimodal approach to book cover analysis in translation studies and the limited perspectives adopted by these existing studies, we can say that, regardless of their important roles in representing books in a culture and age, the book cover of translated texts is still an area that deserves due scholarly attention. This study, therefore, takes this niche and aims to find how book covers of the translations of the same source text in different periods of time differ from each other and how they could reveal to us information about its reception over time.

3 Coding framework for multimodal analysis

The social-semiotic approach to multimodal analysis is a domain of inquiry that uses "several semiotic modes in the design of a semiotic product or event" (Kress and van Leeuwen 2001, 20). Based on Halliday's (1994) discussion of ideational, interpersonal and textual functions of language in systemic functional linguistics, Kress and van Leeuwen develop a quadruple framework of image analysis, including the narrative and conceptual representational meaning, the interactive meaning and the meaning disclosed by composition. This multimodal approach emphasizes the communication of meaning not just by linguistic signs but also by other modes such as images, colors, layout, postures, gestures and the gaze of figures. Kress and van Leeuwen's social-semiotic approach to multimodal analysis has been frequently referred to in the analysis of different types of discourses (e.g. Baldry and Thibault 2006; Painter, Martin, and Unsworth 2012; Feng 2019) and translated texts (e.g. Taylor 2003, 2016; Torresi 2008; Borodo 2015; Chen 2017; Yu and Song 2017; Li et al. 2019). However, the book cover includes not only images but also verbal texts. Though Kress and van Leeuwen have admitted that a visual sign is "connected with the verbal text, but in no way dependent on it" (2006, 18), they have not discussed the relationship between images and texts.

This niche has been covered by some other scholars (e.g. van Leeuwen 1991; Royce 1998; Lemke 1998; O'Halloran 1999; Unsworth and Cléirigh 2004; Martinec and Salway 2005; Liu and O'Halloran 2009; Painter et al. 2012; Bateman 2014). These scholars share the viewpoint that multimodal analysis should "take into account the functions and meanings of the visual images, together with the meaning arising from the integrated use of the two semiotic resources" (O'Halloran 2004, 1). With these viewpoints about the text-image relationship and combining Halliday's logico-semantics with the discussions of Barthes (1977a, 1977b), Martinec and Salway (2005) develop a more generalized and inclusive system of image-text relation analysis that includes both status and logico-semantics in the analysis of text-image relationships. In the following section, I will supplement

Martinec and Salway's approach to Kress and van Leeuwen's visual grammar to build up a framework to discuss the cross-modal relationship of the verbal and non-verbal units on book covers. However, since the pictorial examples used by these scholars in their research are mainly posters, illustrations in textbooks and advertisements (which, though sharing a few similarities, are different from book covers in some aspects), it is necessary to adapt them into a new framework for the analysis of book covers.

3.1 Coding framework of representational meanings on book covers

Representational meaning by Kress and van Leeuwen refers to the representation of "objects (or "participants," "elements" in their terms) and their relations in a world outside the representational system" (2006, 42). These participants can be presented as "unfolding actions and events, processes of change, transitory spatial arrangements" in a narrative structure interpreted as transactional and non-transactional action (material) process, reaction (behavioral) process, and mental or speech process; or they can be represented in a conceptual structure "in terms of their more generalized and more or less stable and timeless essence, in terms of class, structure or meaning," or in terms of classification process, analytical process and symbolic process (ibid., 79). In this study, representational meaning on book covers includes the verbal elements such as title, name of author, translator or publisher, and blurb; it also includes the non-verbal elements such as images and ornaments. Some of these elements are obligatory to appear on the covers according to the prevailing publishing norms, such as the title, the name of the publisher and the author's name, while the others are more optional. Except for the blurb in which clauses may be found, the other verbal elements are mostly nominal phrases. Moreover, since the translations under study are from the same source text, the meanings of verbal elements are basically unvaried or similar on these book covers. Therefore, I will not include the analysis of the meaning of the verbal elements in the framework but will only refer to them in the discussion.

In contrast to the relatively unvaried verbal elements, the non-verbal elements on book covers are more diversified. There are images in narrative representations (see Figure 5.1) and conceptual representation (see Figure 5.2). To describe these book cover images, I will use Kress and van Leeuwen's framework of representational meanings. Nevertheless, since the case under study is not book covers of comic books, science books or textbooks, no images of mental process, verbal process or conversion can be found, neither are there any classificational image structures and analytical structures in this particular case, I will omit these five processes when analyzing the representational meaning in the analytical framework but will focus on the action process and the symbolic process.

Besides the representational meanings enacted by images, the interplay of verbal elements with non-verbal elements also enacts another type of representational meanings. According to Martinec and Salway (2005), in terms of status, image and text would acquire an equal relationship when they are independent

Figure 5.1 Cover of Zhu Shenghao's translation by Lianhe Press in 2014

"*Dis*"*covering* Hamlet *in China* 129

集全亞比士莎譯曹

36
特萊姆漢
HAMLET

行 發 總 司 公 作 合 化 文

Figure 5.2 Cover of Cao Weifeng's translation by Cultural Cooperation Company in 1946
Source: Public domain image.

of or complementary for each other, and they are unequal when either one subordinates to another. The logico-semantic relationship is realized through expansion and projection. Expansion is further categorized into elaboration, extension and enhancement. Elaboration means the image and text are either the same generality (exposition) or either the text or the image is more general (exemplification); extension means a text-image relationship in which either the text or the image adds new and related information; and enhancement means either the image or the text qualifies the other circumstantially. Among the verbal and non-verbal elements on book covers, the major text-image interaction is between the title and the image, and due to the feature of genre, no projection relation can be depicted in this case.

Yet what deserves our attention is that, in the process of coding, the title of this case also poses a few questions. *Hamlet*, in this case, is both the title designating the whole translated text and the name of the protagonist. Such a difference in interpretation will lead to different logico-semantic coding results. In this study, "Hamlet" on the book cover will only be seen as a title designating the whole text, regardless of the reference meaning of this title to the character. Following this vein, if the image on the book cover is Hamlet the protagonist, it is in an unequal status with the title, and belongs to the category of "text more general" in exemplifying elaboration in logico-semantics, since the image of Hamlet is one specific character in the play indicated by the title. Similarly, the image of Shakespeare is also in an unequal status and belongs to the category of "image more general" in exemplifying elaboration in logico-semantics with the title, since the title indicates one of Shakespeare's plays. However, in some cases, the book titles also have subheadings like "Shakespeare's Complete Works." In such cases, the image of Shakespeare is in an unequal status with the title and belongs to "image subordinate to text" type since it only represents part of the content in the title; its logico-semantics relation with the title falls into the category of exemplification of elaboration, in which the image is more general since it refers to the author while the title only refers to one of this author's play. Yet, since book covers are different from pictures with a caption that a relationship between them is definitely to be found, there are some cases in which no relationship can be depicted between the title and the image. For this reason, I will add a "no relation" category to describe these cases.

Based on these discussions, the analytical framework for describing the representational meanings of book covers is formulated according to Table 5.1.

3.2 Coding framework of interactive meanings on book covers

Representational meaning mainly concerns the relations among the verbal and non-verbal elements and between the people, places and things depicted in the images on the book covers; interactive meaning refers to the relation between the images and the viewers of the book covers. Three types of interactive meanings are identified by Kress and van Leeuwen (i.e. contact, social distance and attitude), and they are realized through gaze, distance of shot and angles. Generally speaking, being with or without gaze from the participants in the image is interpreted as demanding or offering; the close-up, medium shot and long shot are interpreted respectively as intimate, social and impersonal relations between the participants in the image and the image viewer; and different angles are related

Table 5.1 Coding framework of representational meanings

Relations	Structures	Realizations
Relations in images	Narrative	Action (transaction; non-transaction); Circumstances (setting/means/accompaniment)
	Conceptual	Symbolic attributive; Symbolic suggestive;
Relations between title and image	Status	Equal (independent/complementary); Unequal (I subordinate to T; T subordinate to I)
	Logico-semantics	Elaboration (exposition/exemplification); Extension; Enhancement (temporal/spatial/casual)
	No relation	

Table 5.2 Coding framework of interactive meanings

Relations	Interactive meaning	Realizations
Contact	Demand	With gaze
	Offer	Without gaze
Social distance	Intimate/personal	Close shot
	Social	Medium shot
	Impersonal	Long shot
Attitude	Involvement	Frontal angle
	Detachment	Oblique angle
	Viewer power	High angle
	Equality	Eye-level angle
	Representation power	Low angle

with the involvement or detachment of the viewer to the image as well as the power relationship between the participant and the viewer.

In this part, the coding framework is directly borrowed from Kress and van Leeuwen's visual grammar except for the part of objective images, since no charts, diagrams or maps are depicted on the book covers in this case. Moreover, some of the book covers are purely typographic, so I only describe the interactive meanings of those book covers with images. However, unlike images, modality is more social and dependent on the social group (Kress and van Leeuwen 2006, 156), and it is represented in scales instead of more objective variables. I will thus not incorporate it into the coding framework.

With these adjustments, the coding framework of interactive meanings is shown in Table 5.2.

3.3 Coding framework of compositional meanings on book covers

The compositional meaning is about "the way representational and interactive elements are made to relate to each other, the way they are integrated into a meaning whole" (ibid., 176). What integrate them are the systems of information value (i.e. the placement of elements in terms of left or right, top and bottom, and center and margin); salience (i.e. the use of size, color and shape to foreground the element so as to attract the viewer's attention); and framing (i.e. the disconnects and connects of elements through framing devices). I will use the information value system to code compositional meanings. But since salience is closely related to a modality that depends on the beholder's eyes in some sense and can only be measured in scale, and it is also difficult to generate variables of framing, I will, therefore, leave these two aside too.

What needs to be noted is that Kress and van Leeuwen focus more on the "relations" or function of the major images, and barely discuss about what "objects" ("element" in this study) are presented. Nevertheless, what "objects" are present and how many of them are present on book covers may also carry some meanings. For example, the lurid cover was once considered essential for securing mass sales, and cheap reprints are represented in picture covers in America (Wilson 1974, 106), According to Charles Rosner, the design of book covers is related to "the literary style and content of the book." Generally speaking, "most lighter fiction will carry a pictorial design along more popular lines," while "a volume of historical studies will call for a purely typographical jacket" (Rosner in Sonzogni 2011, 23). Based on these discussions, besides placement, the type and the number of objects or elements that appear on the book covers also contain compositional meanings.

These elements can be analyzed by four variables: (1) covers of pure verbal elements, (2) covers of verbal elements with ornaments, (3) covers of verbal elements with images and (4) covers of verbal elements with ornaments and images. Based on Rosner's view, it can be inferred that covers of the first type tend to be covers of the more serious genre, while the latter three tend to be on different scales of popularity. Based on the adjustment and the discussions, Table 5.3 is developed to code the compositional meanings of book covers.

Table 5.3 Coding framework of compositional meanings

Relations	Meanings	Realizations
Information value	Circular	Center and margin
		Triptych
	Given/new	Horizontal polarized
	Ideal/real	Vertical polarized
Types of elements	Serious genre	Pure verbal
	Popular genre	Verbal with ornaments
		Verbal with image
		Verbal with image and ornaments

4 Data analysis

In this section, I will firstly explain how book covers are sampled for coding and then move to the analysis of the data collected manually by using the aforementioned three coding frameworks.

4.1 Data collection

As the most translated Shakespearean play in China, *Hamlet* has been translated into Chinese by 18 different translators. Recent years have also witnessed a surge in the reprints of these translations. Not taking the adapted versions and collections into account, such as the *Hamlet* included into books titled as "Four Tragedies of Shakespeare" or "Complete Works of Shakespeare," there exist a total number of 196 covers of separate edition by 2020 as shown in Table 5.4.

In this study, book covers to be analyzed are sampled by the following criteria: first, I will include all the separate editions published before the 1990s and all the first editions of new translations published separately in later decades in my corpus for analysis. With this criterion in mind, those translations of *Hamlet* published in collection will not be included. For example, Zhu Shenghao's 1947 first version of *Hamlet* was published in the collection with other seven plays with a cover titled "Complete Works of Shakespeare," so it is not included in this study even though it is the first version of the play. Second, due to the great volume of book covers published in the recent two decades, only 20 covers from the 2000s and 30 covers from the 2010s are sampled out randomly from the corpus for analysis. Third, book covers of reprints with the same book cover design of the early version by the same translator will also be excluded from the analysis. One example is Tian Han's several new versions published in the 1930s. They share the same cover design with the earliest version in 1922 and are thus not included in this analysis. Another example is Can Weifeng's 1961 version. The cover of the version is the same as his 1955 version and is also excluded in this case, which results in a lack of samples in the 1960s. By this sampling method, the total number of covers for multimodal analysis is 70 out of the total 196.

Table 5.4 Number of book covers and samples

Periods of time	The 1st stage: The Republic of China Period			The 2nd stage: The New China Period			The 3rd stage: The Reforming Period		The 4th stage: The Contemporary Period		Total
Decades	'20s	'30s	'40s	'50s	'60s	'70s	'80s	'90s	'00s	'10s	
No. of book covers	2	5	1	3	1	4	1	7	66	106	196
No. of samples	2	3	1	2	0	4	1	7	20	30	70

134 Xie Guixia (Rosie)

As shown in Table 5.4, I also divide the decades into four stages based on culture, politics and economics. The first stage (1920s–1940s) includes the three decades in the Republic of China period. It is a period right after the decline of the semi-colonial Qing Dynasty and a time with much political turmoil. It is also a time when Western ideology and culture were abundantly introduced to the Chinese people. The second stage (1950s–1970s) includes the first three decades from the founding of the People's Republic of China. In this stage, the new China was economically backward after years of wars and the whole society was more engaged in political movements. The third stage (1980s–1990s) includes the two decades after China implemented its reform and opening-up policy and became more open in its economic policy. The fourth stage (2000s–2010s) includes the contemporary decades of the new millennium when China is fully engaged in the world economic system. In the next section, I will analyze the data by using the variables in Tables 5.1, 5.2 and 5.3 to depict the tendency of book cover designs in these four periods.

4.2 Data analysis of book covers

In this section, data collected by using Tables 5.1–5.3 are analyzed in terms of representational meaning, interactive meaning and compositional meaning with reference to the four stages.

4.2.1 Representational meanings of book covers

The representational meanings are obtained through the analysis of the relations among the participants in the 51 covers with images and the relations between the titles and the images.

In the 51 images on the covers, four types of participants in the images can be identified: Shakespeare the author (15), Hamlet alone or with other characters (17), other human participants (9) and inanimate images such as a natural scene or architecture (10). Among them, Shakespeare with a total number of 15 and Hamlet with a total number of 17 are the major participants in the images. In the representational meanings of these different types of participants, neither projective processes in narrative representation nor classificational and analytical processes in conceptual representation are identified in these images, which is probably due to the literary nature of this book. Therefore, the description mainly focuses on the transactional or non-transactional reaction in the action processes and the symbolic attributive and symbolic suggestive processes. The data are shown in Figure 5.3. To explore more details about the different processes, a further description of the representational meanings with reference to the types of participants (i.e. Shakespeare, Hamlet, other characters and other human participants) is also conducted and shown in Figure 5.4.

It can be seen in Figure 5.3 that 21 images are of narrative processes, 13 of which are transactional reaction and eight are non-transactional; and that 30 images are of conceptual processes, with five of them being symbolic attributive processes

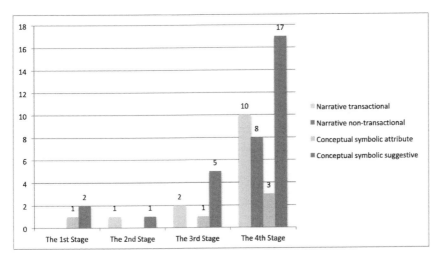

Figure 5.3 Narrative and conceptual representational meanings of images

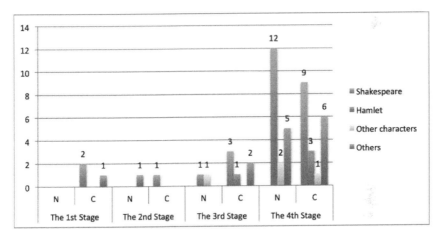

Figure 5.4 Narrative and conceptual representational meanings in images with reference to participants

and 25 being symbolic suggestive processes. Conceptual processes appear on the images of all stages, and narrative processes are mainly found in the third and fourth stages.

Further analysis of the participant types in the narrative and conceptual processes also finds that 15 out of the 51 covers are portraits of Shakespeare, and all of them are represented in symbolic suggestive processes in different stages. Almost all the portraits of Shakespeare used in our data are either the Droeshout portrait or the Chandos portrait (see Figure 5.2). These portraits depict Shakespeare with de-emphasized details and generalized essence rather than in point of genuineness. The other few symbolic suggestive processes are images of natural scenes or architectures, suggesting a general atmosphere or implying the locality of the story.

The images of Hamlet are found on 17 covers. In terms of the representational meanings of images with Hamlet, three differences can be found in comparison to the images with Shakespeare. First, images of Hamlet firstly appear on book covers in the third stage, and this number even exceeds that of Shakespeare in the fourth stage. Second, Hamlet as the participant in the images is mainly represented in narrative processes. Some images depict Hamlet in transactional processes with other human or object participants and others with Hamlet alone in non-transactional processes. Third, unlike Shakespeare's portrait (which is the Droeshout portrait or the Chandos portrait), Hamlet's images are much more diversified on book covers. There are Hamlet images painted specifically for the book, or those taken from famous paintings such as the "Hamlet and Horatio in the Graveyard" by Eugène Delacroix in Figure 5.1, or those from the stage photos of movies or movie posters such as Laurence Olivier's 1948 Hamlet. Similarly, the sources of other characters in the play are diversified, and they are also mostly depicted in a narrative process such as image with Ophelia climbing the willow tree.

From the differences of representing processes of Shakespeare and Hamlet in the images, two types of representational meanings can be implied. The representation of Shakespeare in the conceptual process on the covers tends to emphasize that the book belongs to the serious or famous literary genre; while covers with Hamlet in the narrative processes tend to unfold action and events, and thus highlight more on the dramatic aspect of the book as a story.

One more detail that deserves our attention is that, for the 15 images with other participants appearing in the fourth stage, most of them are difficult to relate either to the characters or to plots of the play. Therefore, these images seem to be independent from the cover and do not help to constitute coherent readings of the book covers as a whole, which can also be interpreted as low quality in book cover design that may be resulted from the mass production.

In terms of the title and image relationship, most of the images are found subordinate to the title in status, which in this study is understood as representing the translated text instead of referring to the protagonist. Thirty-five of the titles and images have an unequal relationship, with 28 of those having images subordinate to the title and seven vice versa. For those 16 covers with titles and images in equal status, they are independent from each other. In their logico-semantic relations, most of them are elaborative to each other, with 20 covers with more general titles and 13 more general images. Extension and spatial enhancement are rare in this case. In the two cases of extension, one cover image shows a silhouette of people performing on the stage, adding new information to the title that it is a play. In enhancement logico-semantics, no other types can be found except for the four spatial ones. For example, images like a castle indicate the place where the story may have taken place.

Besides the above basic information about the logico-semantic relation between the title and the image, another ten covers are identified with images that bear no possible relation with the title. For example, some book cover images depict scenes and figures that are difficult to relate to the plots or characters in *Hamlet*. Moreover, this type of book covers is all found in the fourth stage, with most of them mainly accompanied by relatively more complex book covers or covers with a blurb. This phenomenon can be interpreted as being towards mass sales and popular lines based on Wilson's (1974) and Rosner's (1949 in Sonzogni 2011) viewpoints discussed above.

4.2.2 Interactive meanings of book covers

Interactive meanings refer to the relation between the image and the viewer. In interactive meaning, attitude can be analyzed through the use of different vertical or horizontal angles, the social distance through the different length of shots and contact through the gazes. Similar to the analysis of representational meanings, a combination of the descriptive data with reference to the participants also shows us a few tendencies.

Among the 51 covers with images, 41 covers are with human participants and ten with inanimate participants. In the following, I will only analyze the covers with human participants, which mainly include the portraits of Shakespeare, the figure of Hamlet and other human participants. Since the images with Shakespeare are either the Droeshout or the Chandos portrait of Shakespeare, they are almost the same in interactive meanings but with a variation in social distance resulting from the different size of frames above the waist. In these images, Shakespeare is depicted as confronting the viewers with a calm and peaceful gaze (see Figure 5.2) to demand the viewers to enter into a relation of social affinity with him. These Shakespeare portraits are either with a close-up shot or a frame size above the chest of Shakespeare, suggesting a personal to intimate relationship with the viewers. From the perspective of angles, these portraits are represented in a horizontal angle between frontal and oblique angles and on a vertical eye level, indicating that the viewer is partly involved with the author on an equal power relationship. All these send out the message to the viewers of these book covers that they are invited on an equal basis to the world of Shakespeare, thus suggesting that the text beneath the cover is waiting for the viewers to explore the world of this famous playwright.

The situation of Hamlet and other characters are quite different from Shakespeare's. As it is shown in Figure 5.4, Hamlet and other human participants are only found in the third and fourth stages. A description of their interactive is shown in Table 5.5.

It can be seen from Table 5.5 that most representations of the Hamlet and other human participants are without eye contact with the viewers and with long shot; and in terms of angles, the data of frontal and oblique angles are similar, so is that of the high and eye-level shots; nearly no participants are depicted with low angle. Based on these data, we can say that on most occasions the viewers of these images are not asked to be engaged in any intimate relationship with the

Table 5.5 Interactive meanings of Hamlet and other human participants

Meanings		Contact		Social distance			Attitude				
Realizations		With gaze	Without gaze	Close shot	Medium shot	Long shot	Frontal	Oblique	High	Eye-level	Low
The 3rd stage	Hamlet		2		1	1	1	1		1	
	Other human participants		1		1			1	1	1	
The 4th stage	Hamlet	2	13	2	5	8	7	8	7	7	
	Other human participants	1	7	1		7	5	2	5	3	1

"Dis"covering Hamlet in China 139

participants. Instead, they are invited to keep impersonal with these participants, sometimes involving in their world and sometimes not. In terms of power relationships, viewers are half in equal relationship with the participants and half in a high angle, meaning that the participants are reduced to ground level and overpowered by the viewers. In other words, this can be interpreted that images with Hamlet and other human participants on book covers tend to show the viewers the situations of the participants in a more distant and impersonal way. Instead of establishing any relations with the viewers, the design of these book covers intends to invite the viewers not to be involved in the events but to be onlookers of what is displaying.

4.2.3 Compositional meanings of book covers

Compositional meaning in this case refers to the types of elements and the information value of the book covers. A general description of the types of elements on book covers (see Figure 5.5) shows that the types of elements used on book covers differ in the four different periods. Among the different types, the "verbal + image" (30 covers) type is the most widely used, followed by the "verbal + image + ornament" type (21 covers); on the other hand, the "verbal + ornament" type (nine covers) is least used, yet this type appears in three of the stages except the first one, and the "pure verbal" type (ten covers) is the last but one. What is interesting about the "pure verbal" (i.e. typographical) type is that it is one major type on covers at the first stage, yet it does not appear in the middle two stages until the period after the 2000s. From the perspective of diversity, it is found that

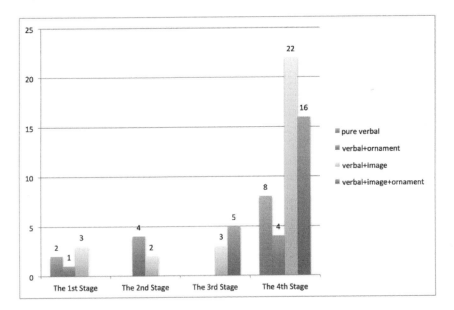

Figure 5.5 Types of elements on book covers over the four stages

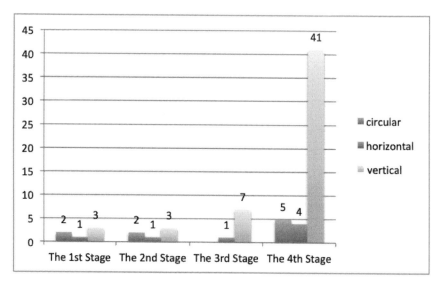

Figure 5.6 Information value on book covers over the four stages

two or three of the types are used at the first three stages, but the four types are all found in the book covers at the fourth stage, with a dramatic increase in the use of the "verbal + image + ornament" type.

As for information value, except for the third stage, all three types of compositional structures (i.e. the circular, horizontal and vertical structures) can be found on the book covers at different times (see Figure 5.6). Among them, the vertical structure (54 covers) is the most commonly used. A closer description of what elements are placed on the Ideal, Mediator and Real positions also shows that the major elements (the most salient) occupying these three slots on the book covers are title, image and blurb. Their distribution is shown in Figure 5.7.

Figure 5.7 shows that titles (31 in Ideal position) are the element most frequently found in the Ideal position on the book covers throughout the four stages and occasionally in the Real position (8); starting from the third stage, they also appear in the Mediator position (21). Forty-one vertical covers are found with images. Compared with titles, no sharp differences can be found about the positions of the images on the cover. For example, book covers such as Figure 5.1 have images occupying the Real positions; and book covers such as Figure 5.2 have images occupying the Mediator and the Real positions, respectively. It is noteworthy that most of the images in the Ideal and Mediator positions are the portraits of Shakespeare; while those in the Real positions are images of other contents. The inclusion of the blurb on *Hamlet*'s book covers is quite a recent phenomenon, and these blurbs generally appear in the Real positions and sometimes even in the Ideal position. For example, the blurb in Figure 5.1 in the red area shows: "the must-read book for primary and middle school students" in the largest size, followed

"Dis"covering Hamlet in China 141

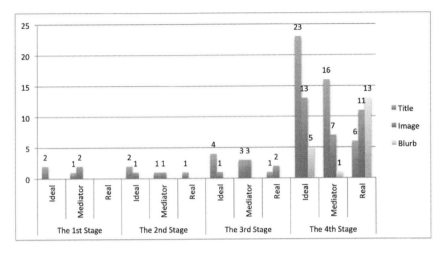

Figure 5.7 Distribution of titles, images, and blurb on vertical covers

Note: Seven of the 54 vertical covers even have both English and Chinese titles. Six of them occupying different slots and are calculated twice, one occupies the same slot (see Figure 5.1) and is calculated as once. Hence, the total number of titles is 60.

by words like "recommended book by the Ministry of Education" and "extra curriculum reading material listed in the new syllabus." In the characters in black and in the smallest size in this area, there are words introducing Shakespeare as the king of drama as well as the introduction of plot and fame of this play. The blurb helps to promote the book to the target readers, who in this case are the middle and primary school students. For book covers of this type, the educational function of the text is highlighted rather than its literary significance.

Circular (9) and horizontal (7) covers are relatively few in this case and no significant increase of these two types can be seen throughout the years in Figure 5.6. Yet we still can see that the circular covers are mainly found in the first two stages with the titles generally placed in the center surrounded with ornaments such as in Figure 5.8. Horizontal covers are also few among the samples. In the few horizontal covers, most have the title and other information on the left Given position and other elements on the right New position, but there are also cases where all the information is placed on the New position. Generally speaking, elements found on both circular and horizontal covers are usually fewer than those on vertical covers. These covers tend to be simple and plain in their design.

From the analysis of the compositional meanings of book covers in this case, we can see that the tendency towards complex design can be seen through the four stages. Particularly at the fourth stage, more types of elements are included in covers in the general trend. Following Wilson's argument that more popular and less expensive books tend to have pictures (1974, 106), we can say that judging from the cover design, *Hamlet* changes from more literary in the early stages to

Figure 5.8 Drawing after the covers of Shao Ting's translation by Commercial Press in 1930
Source: Public domain image.

more popular, and even more commercial with blurbs placing in the Ideal place, in recent decades. Yet in spite of the commercialized tendency found from the book covers, there remain some covers that are typographical or simple in design, which reminds the readers of its serious status in literature.

5 General findings and discussions

Based on the analysis of the data collected by using the theoretical framework of Kress and van Leeuwen's (2006) social semiotic multimodality, we can come to the following summary: in terms of representational meaning, it is found that both narrative and conceptual processes in the representational meaning exist in the images of book covers. On these covers, the portraits of Shakespeare are all depicted in conceptual processes while Hamlet and other characters are always in narrative processes. In the title-image relationship, most of the titles and images are unequal in status with images subordinating to the titles, and their logico-semantic relations are mainly elaborative. However, the fourth stage also witnesses the appearance of "no relation" between the title and the image. When looking into the interactive meaning of book covers with human participants, the study further finds that Shakespeare is always shown with a demanding, personal and equal relation with the viewers, while Hamlet and other characters, who just began to appear in the third and fourth stages, are always in an offering and impersonal style, with the viewers holding more power over them. The covers with Shakespeare's portraits seem to remind the viewers that they are invited by the world famous playwright to read the literary classics, while covers with Hamlet and other characters tend to hint at the viewers that what is waiting for them under the book covers is an exciting story. The types of elements and information value show us the compositional aspect of these covers and indicate that different types of covers coexist at every stage but a tendency towards popularity can be seen at the fourth stage.

When co-relating the above findings of the three types of meanings together, we can come to the conclusion that *Hamlet* in China is received in the following three ways.

First, *Hamlet* is read as serious literature. Covers with this approach to *Hamlet* are mainly pure verbal, or verbal with a few simple ornaments. Such a simple style of design indicates that a group of readers, translators or cover designers approaches the book as a piece of classical and serious literature.

Second, *Hamlet* is read as light fiction. These covers add the verbal elements on the covers images of Shakespeare, which can be interpreted as emphasizing the greatness of the book by borrowing the symbolic power of Shakespeare and presenting him in a way as inviting the readers to join the classical world of the author. Some covers also have the image of Hamlet the protagonist and other characters, and these covers tend to emphasize the narrative side of the play and present the text in a way as a piece of light fiction.

Third, *Hamlet* is read as commercialized reading materials. This approach to the play has covers crowded with different types of elements, highlighting the commercial aspect of the book either by foregrounding the contents in the blurb or using a poster-like style of book cover design with highly contexualized imagery to attract the attention of the viewers. Some of these covers also go so far as to violate the rules of successful covers put forward by Wendell Minor by providing images that do not honor either the story or the writer (Minor 1995, i). For this part of the book, the publication aims at a large-scale sale rather than presenting the story or introducing world classics.

From a diachronic perspective, these three types of reception of *Hamlet* did not exist simultaneously from the very beginning. Judging from the data collected, it can be seen that this play was first received as serious literature at the first stage and gradually developed into light fiction since the second stage. Until the third and the fourth stage, a dramatic increase in the number of books also caused it to become popular. Yet at the fourth stage, the three approaches coexist.

According to theories of social semiotics, the choice of different signs to convey the meanings are socio-culturally motivated. As one of the most flexible instruments of adaptation, the different approaches to this play also reflect the designer's different interpretations of the specific social contexts and the expectations of the readership. By relating the above findings with the developing history of Shakespeare in China, we may be able to reach some explanations about the changes in the approaches to *Hamlet*.

The play was firstly translated by Tian Han in 1922. The cover of this first translation is pure verbal. This may be related to the role attached to this play at the beginning. Tian Han's version was introduced to Chinese readers in the series named "Series of Books by the Young China Association" and "Collection of Shakespeare's Masterpieces." The Young China Association was established in 1919 by the revolutionist Li Dazhao and other scholars with the aim to bring merits to the new China. The association was famous for publishing and introducing books on literature, philosophy, social science and so forth. This set the tone for the early reception of *Hamlet* as a serious masterpiece. This attitude towards *Hamlet* was reinforced during the 1930s, when China started to view Shakespeare as the world literary giant and endeavored to translate his complete works. This trend greatly publicized the works of Shakespeare, and Chinese readers' enthusiasm towards this playwright reached its peak when Zhu Shenghao published his complete translation of Shakespeare in the 1940s. Over a span of six decades, *Hamlet* and other plays of Shakespeare had been read as literary classics.

It is until 1990 when the Ministry of Education in China amended the national curriculum of Chinese language teaching, in which *Hamlet* was listed as one of the 32 recommended books for high school students. This amendment is very important since it can be regarded as the authoritative canonization of *Hamlet* in the literary field in China, and it also brings the book to a larger and more diversified readership group. In turn, the inclusion of a large number of student readers in the existing readership, together with the policies to relate this play with education, pushes it to become commercialized in the contemporary era. As we can see, all the social information about this play is nevertheless reflected in a multimodal way on the book covers.

6 Conclusion

This study aims to investigate the differences of *Hamlet*'s reception in China in different periods of time through the exploration of paratextual elements in the book covers of different *Hamlet* translations. With reference to the visual grammar put forward by Kress and van Leeuwen and the text-image relationship by Martinec and Salway, the study discovers three approaches to this world classic in China. The research results show that book covers are also fruitful resources for the diachronic study of the reception of translated texts.

The study also has two limitations. On the one hand, the sampling method still needs improving. Though I have included all the samples before the 1990s for analysis, there are some covers of the early years that cannot be found at the moment; on the contrary, covers after 2000s are numerous in number, and random sampling might have left out some other possibilities. On the other hand, since the study is mainly quantitative, some multimodal aspects are difficult to become variables in this study and thus are not included in our analysis frameworks, such as the analysis of modality and framing. This has definitely caused the neglect of some other meanings on the book covers.

References

Baldry, A. and P. Thibault. 2006. *Multimodal Transcription and Text Analysis: A Multimedia Toolkit and Coursebook*. London: Equinox.

Barthes, R. 1977a. "The Photographic Message." In *Image-Music-Text*, edited by Roland Barthes, 15–31. London: Fontana.

Barthes, R. 1977b. "Rhetoric of the Image." In *Image-Music-Text*, edited by Roland Barthes, 32–51. London: Fontana.

Bateman, J. 2014. *Text and Image: A Critical Introduction to the Visual/Verbal Divide*. London & New York: Routledge.

Bei, T北塔. 2004.《哈姆雷特》剧本的汉译(The Chinese Versions of Hamlet), 南阳师范学院学报(*Journal of Nanyang Teachers' College*) 3: 36–41.

Borodo, M. 2015. "Multimodality, Translation and Comics." *Perspectives* 23(1): 22–41.

Chao, S周兆祥.1981. 汉译《哈姆雷特》研究(*Studies on Chinese Translations of Hamlet*). Hong Kong: Chinese University of Hong Kong.

Chen, X. 2017. "Representing Cultures through Language and Image: A Multimodal Approach to Translation of Chinese Classic Mulan. *Perspectives* 26(2): 1–18.

Delistathi, C. 2011. "Translation as a Means of Ideological Struggle." In *Translation and Opposition*, edited by Dimitris Asimakoulas and Margaret Rogers, 204–222. Clevedon: Multilingual Matters.

Drew, N. and P. Sternberger. 2005. *By Its Cover: Modern American Book Cover Design*. New York: Princeton Architectural Press.

Feng, D. 2019. "Analyzing Multimodal Chinese Discourse: Integrating Social Semiotic and Conceptual Metaphor Theories." In *The Routledge Handbook of Chinese Discourse Analysis*, edited by Chris Shei, 65–81. London & New York: Routledge.

Genette, G. 1997. *Paratexts: Thresholds of Interpretation*. Translated by J. E. Lewin. Cambridge: Cambridge University Press.

Halliday, M. 1994. *An Introduction to Functional Grammar*, 2nd ed. London: Arnold.

Harvey, K. 2003. "'Events' and 'Horizons': Reading Ideology in the 'Bindings' of Translations." In *Apropos of Ideology, Translation Studies on Ideology – Ideologies in Translation Studies*, edited by María Calzada Pérez, 43–70. Manchester: St. Jerome.

Held, G. 2005. "Magazine Covers – A Multimodal Pretext-Genre." *Folia Linguistica* 39(1–2): 173–196.

Hou, P. 2013. "Paratexts in the English Translation of the Selected Works of Mao Tsetung." In *Text, Extratext, Metatext and Paratext in Translation*, edited by Valerie Pellatt, 33–46. Newcastle upon Tyne: Cambridge Scholars Publishing.

Jin, J 金静, and Zhu, J 朱健平. 2016. 《哈姆雷特》在中国的百年译介与研究 (Chinese Translation of Hamlet over the Past Hundred Years),中国翻译 (*Chinese Translators Journal*) 5: 43–48.

Kratz, C. 1994. "On Telling/Selling a Book by Its Cover." *Cultural Anthropology* 9(2): 179–200.

Kress, G. and T. van Leeuwen. 2001. *Multimodal Discourse – The Modes and Media of Contemporary Communication*. London: Edward Arnold.

Kress, G. and T. van Leeuwen. 2006. *Reading Images: The Grammar of Visual Design*. London & New York: Routledge.

Kung, S. 2013. "Paratext, an Alternative in Boundary Crossing: A Complementary Approach to Translation Analysis." In *Text, Extratext, Metatext and Paratext in Translation*, edited by Valerie Pellatt, 49–68. Newcastle upon Tyne: Cambridge Scholars Publishing.

Lemke, J. 1998. "Multiplying Meaning: Visual and Verbal Semiotics in Scientific Text." In *Reading Science: Critical and Functional Perspective on Discourse of Science*, edited by James Martin and Robert Feel, 87–113. London & New York: Routledge.

Levith, M. 2004. *Shakespeare in China*. London & New York: Continuum.

Li, L., X. Li, and J. Miao. 2019. "A Translated Volume and its Many Covers: A Multimodal Analysis of the Influence of Ideology." *Social Semiotics* 29(2): 261–278.

Lirola, M. M. 2006. "A Systemic Functional Analysis of Two Multimodal Covers." *Revista Alicantina de Estudios Ingleses* 19: 249–260.

Liu, Y. and K. L. O'Halloran. 2009. "Intersemiotic Texture: Analyzing Cohesive Devices between Language and Images." *Social Semiotics* 19(4): 367–388.

Machin, D. and T. van Leeuwen. 2016. "Multimodality, Politics and Ideology." *Journal of Language and Politics* 15(3): 243–258.

Martinec, R. and A. Salway. 2005. "A System for Image-text Relations in New (and Old) Media." *Visual Communication* 4(3): 337–371.

Meng, X 孟宪强. 1994. 中国莎学简史 (*A Historical Survey of Shakespeare in China*). Changchun: Northeast Normal University Press.

Minor, W. 1995. *Art for Written Word: Twenty-Five Years of Book Cover Art*. London & New York: Harcourt Brace.

O'Halloran, K. 1999. "Towards a Systemic Functional Analysis of Multi Semiotic Mathematics Texts." *Semiotica* 124(1/2): 1–29.

O'Halloran, Kay. 2004. "Introduction." In *Multimodal Discourse Analysis: Systemic-Functional Perspectives*, edited by Kay O'Holloran, 1–7. London & New York: Continuum.

O'Sullivan, C. 2005. "Translation, Pseudotranslation and Paratext: The Presentation of Contemporary Crime Fiction Set in Italy." *Enter Text* 4(3): 62–76.

Painter, C., J. Martin, and L. Unsworth. 2012. *Reading Visual Narratives: Image Analysis of Children's Picture Books*. London: Equinox.

Petric, M. and S. Croatia. 1995. "Judging a Book by Its Cover: The Visual Reception of American Literature." In *American Literature for Non-American Readers:*

Cross-Cultural Perspectives on American Literature, edited by Meta Grosman, 177–187. New York: Peter Lang.

Phillips, A. 2007. "How Books Are Positioned in the Market: Reading the Cover." In *Judging a Book by Its Cover: Fans, Publishers, Designers, and the Marketing of Fiction*, edited by Nicole Matthews and Nickianne Moody, 19–30. Hampshire: Ashgate.

Powers, A. 2001. *Front Cover: Great Book Jackets and Cover Design*. London: Mitchell Beazley.

Royce, T. 1998. "Synergy on Page: Exploring Inter Semiotic Complementarity in Page-based Multimodal Text." *JASFL Occasional Papers* 1: 25–50.

Sonzogni, M. 2011. *Re-covered Rose: A Case Study in Book Cover Design as Intersemiotic Translation*. Amsterdam & Philadelphia: Benjamins.

Summer, C. 2013. "What Remains: The Institutional Reframing of Authorship in Translated Peritexts." In *Text, Extratext, Metatext and Paratext in Translation*, edited by Valerie Pellatt, 9–31. Newcastle upon Tyne: Cambridge Scholars Publishing.

Sun, Y. 2010. *Shakespeare in China*. Kaifeng: Henan University Press.

Taylor, C. 2003. "Multimodal Transcription in the Analysis, Translation and Subtitling of Italian Films." *The Translator* 9(2): 191–205.

Taylor, C. 2016. "The Multimodal Approach in Audiovisual Translation." *Target* 28(2): 222–236.

Torresi, I. 2008. "Advertising: a Case for Intersemiotic Translation." *Meta* 53(1): 62–75.

Unsworth, L. and C.s Cléirigh. 2004. "Multimodality and Reading: The Construction of Meaning through Image-text Interaction." In *The Routledge Handbook of Multimodal Analysis*, edited by Carey Jewitt, 151–163. London & New York: Routledge.

van Leeuwen, T. 1991. "Conjunction Structure in Documentary Film and Television." *Continuum: Journal of Media and Cultural Studies* 5: 76–114.

Wang, R 王瑞. 2015. 《哈姆雷特》百年汉译形式演化 (The Chinese Translations of Hamlet: A Century's Evolution), 山东外语教学 (*Shangdong Foreign Language Teaching*) 5: 92–98.

Webby, E. 2007. "Literary Prizes, Production Values and Cover Images." In *Judging a Book by Its Cover: Fans, Publishers, Designers, and the Marketing of Fiction*, edited by Nicole Matthews and Nickianne Moody, 63–70. Hampshire: Ashgate.

Weedon, A. 2007. "In Real Life: Book Covers in the Internet Book Store." In *Judging a Book by Its Cover: Fans, Publishers, Designers, and the Marketing of Fiction*, edited by Nicole Matthews and Nickianne Moody, 117–127. Hampshire: Ashgate.

Williamson, V. 2007. "Relocating Liverpool in the 1990s: Through the Covers of Regional Saga Fiction." In *Judging a Book by Its Cover: Fans, Publishers, Designers, and the Marketing of Fiction*, edited by Nicole Matthews and Nickianne Moody, 31–42. Hampshire: Ashgate.

Wilson, A. 1974. *The Design of Books*. Salt Lake City and Santa Barbara: Peregrine Smith Inc.

Xie, G 谢桂霞.2011.汉译《哈姆雷特》辞格研究 (*A Study of Rhetorical Device Translations of Hamlet*). Ph.D. thesis, Hong Kong Polytechnic University, Hong Kong.

Yu, H. and Z. Song. 2017. "Picture–Text Congruence in Translation: Images of the Zen Master on Book Covers and in Verbal Texts." *Social Semiotics* 27(5): 604–623.

Zhang, X. 1996. *Shakespeare in China: A Comparative Study of Two Traditions and Cultures*. Newark: University of Delaware Press.

6 Belt and Road Initiatives in texts and images

A critical perspective on intersemiotic translation of metaphors

Zhang Xiaoyu (Heather)

Translating metaphors has long been a complicated issue in translation studies. As stated by Peter Newmark (1988), it is "the most significant translation problem" in translation practice (9). Translators have to balance the meaning, rhetorical effect, and potential cognitive impact of metaphors. Apart from these entrenched principles, the proliferation of multimodal materials has brought new challenges to this area. As stated by Gambier (2006), in today's world, "no text is, strictly speaking, monomodal." Scholars begin to reconsider translation theorizing and practice within the framework of multimodality. Early attempts can be dated back to 1959 when Roman Jakobson identified the "transmutation" from verbal signs to other non-verbal symbol systems as one of the three types of translation. He termed this phenomenon "intersemiotic translation" (Jakobson 1959).

While many researchers have acknowledged the link between verbal and non-verbal elements, their "dominant research perspective remains largely linguistic" (Gambier 2006). Some related studies claimed to adopt the multimodal perspective but focused on translation within linguistic mode, such as the bilingual texts in picturebooks (e.g. Joosen 2010) or the translation of verbal subtitles in movies (e.g. Díaz Cintas 2009). Moreover, no particular attention has been given to the translation of multimodal political genres in contemporary political communication.

This chapter proposes a tentative framework for analyzing intersemiotic metaphor translation in the political arena by presenting a case study of the translation of China's Belt and Road Initiatives (BRI) from a series of the President Xi's international speeches to a 6-minute introductory video named "Da Dao Zhi Xing" (大道之行, hereinafter DDZX). Based on Fairclough's three-dimensional framework of critical discourse analysis (CDA) and with a focus on metaphor analysis, the research attempts to (1) identify the methods of translating metaphors in the text-to-image translation practice, (2) compare the different use of metaphors and explain what has been changed in the framing of BRI, and (3) discuss the potential reasons for the decision-making of metaphor translation in this case.

1 Metaphors in political communication

Metaphor is often used in political communication to explain political issues and persuade the audience to take a certain stand or some action. Its role in political rhetoric has been attested to since the times of Aristotle and Plato, but only in relatively recent times has it been related to cognition (Chilton 2004).

One of the most important publications of metaphor studies is *Metaphors We Live* (1980), written by Lakoff and Johnson. The book systematically introduces the conceptual metaphor theory (CMT), which regards the metaphor as a way of conceptualizing the world. The theory provides a brand-new perspective of explaining and analyzing metaphors in the non-literary language, including political language. According to CMT, metaphors, by relating a more concrete source domain to a more abstract target domain, serve as a practical approach to articulate new, professional, and obscure concepts. For this reason, politicians tend to use metaphors as ways of explaining new policies to citizens or voters who are usually laymen of politics (Chilton 2004, 52; Charteris-Black 2011).

What is more important than explaining the complicated terms is metaphor's use as an effective strategy to "frame" the reality. For one thing, using one or more related metaphorical expressions from one source domain can activate the addressee's structural knowledge, including their understandings and attitudes; for another, readers tend to project such knowledge and evaluations on the new domain. This working system makes it possible for politicians to manipulate the audience's emotions and attitudes imperceptibly by strategically using some source domains.

Many studies have demonstrated such power of metaphors in influencing social cognition and political reality. Howe (1988) investigates the use of metaphors in political news from 1980 to 1985. He argues that the pervasive use of those masculine metaphors in political discourse (e.g. WAR metaphors and SPORTS metaphors) may consolidate the male-dominant political culture. In a diachronic study conducted by Musolff (2017), he investigates how the Euroskeptical and pro-Brexit groups attribute negative values to the *heart of Europe* metaphor, and finally deprive the metaphor of its persuasive power in uniting Britain and Europe.

Most early works of CMT focus on verbal data, but in recent years, research on conceptual metaphors represented by non-verbal signs (Forceville and Urios-Aparisi 2009) has proliferated in both quantity and quality. Some of them also touch upon political discourse. Mazid's work (2008) shows that the use of visual metaphors in political cartoons could function as approaches to (de)legitimate political issues, to "make the bad look good" (451). Feng (2019) draws on the publicity posters of the Chinese Dream to investigate how visual metaphors work in the Chinese political context to cultivate patriotism in Chinese people.

This chapter will look at the translational shift of metaphors from political speeches to a publicity video; therefore, both verbal and visual metaphors are to be examined to see if they are shaping BRI differently in the source and target contexts.

2 Metaphors in translation studies

Although metaphors constitute "the most significant translation problem" in translation practice (Newmark 1988, 9), the related research remains underexplored. While abundant works in metaphor studies suggest the cognitive root of metaphors and show a growing attention in multimodal metaphors, metaphors in the translation arena largely remain linguistic and monomodal (e.g. Alvarez 2012; Newmark 1988; van den Broeck 1981).

For a relatively long period of time, metaphors, in the eyes of translation scholars, have represented figurative expressions indicating the resemblance of a tenor and a vehicle. They are further categorized as novel metaphors and dead metaphors by the degree of conventionalization, for the convenience of selecting proper equivalents. As for the strategies or methods of metaphor translation, these works either focus on the vehicle (e.g. translating metaphors by "sensu stricto" that focuses on the figurative form and closer to the source language norms) or the tenor (e.g. translating metaphors with adaptation to comply with the target language norms).

These studies take metaphors as figurative expressions independent of each other. However, as discussed in the previous section, metaphors gain their persuasive power from the cross-domain mappings that can activate the structural knowledge embedded in human cognition. Therefore, the traditional way that takes metaphors as individual cases in translation studies may be inadequate to reproduce the meaning and effect of metaphors, particularly metaphors strategically used in political communication.

Therefore, deciding the unit of translation is an issue in metaphor translation. A conceptual metaphor is a general conceptual mapping from the concrete source domain to the abstract target domain, but it also includes more specific entailments developed from the basic mapping, and finally, these cognitive processes must be realized through concrete metaphorical expressions, verbal or non-verbal. This chapter adopts the "developed conceptual metaphor" (Tebbit and Kinder 2016) as the unit for translation analysis. The term is used to describe the second layer of conceptual metaphors – more specific conceptual mappings developed from a basic mapping. For example, CHINA IS AN OLD MAN is a mapping developed from the basic conceptual metaphor NATIONS ARE PEOPLE. Compared to basic conceptual metaphors, analyzing the developed metaphors provides specific information and knowledge activated by the metaphorical expressions and can help the translators narrow down the possibilities of interpretation while maintaining the cognitive effect of the metaphors.

The second issue for this research is to define the translation of metaphors in a multimodal context. Current works on multimodal translation do not emphasize metaphors. Fortunately, the works of Chen (2018), Sonzogni (2011), and Pereira (2008) show the translatability from verbal to visual signs. In this sense, it is possible to represent the verbal metaphors with visual elements through some techniques.

According to O'Halloran et al. (2016), intersemiotic translation forms "the basis of cultural communication" by constructing and reconstructing the knowledge and conventions through various semiotic resources. Fernández (2011) also points out that "language boundaries are at the same time boundaries of distinct cultural communities, and metaphor interpretation is strongly culturally conditioned." For intersemiotic translation of metaphors, it is more important to consider the cultural and cognitive background of metaphorical expressions than to focus on the "equivalents" of multimodal signs.

Therefore, I bring in the concept of recontextualization from the framework of CDA to analyze the socio-cultural background of metaphor use and translation in the given context of political communication. The notion of "recontextualization" refers to a process in which signs are extracted from one social practice and introduced into another (Bernstein 1990; Fairclough 2003). Particular to this case, metaphor translation is viewed as the relocation of BRI-related discourse elements from the original speech settings to the new practice of mini-documentary. In this sense, the source and target texts can be regarded as the verbal and visual representation of a same social practice, that is, BRI. The chapter, therefore, focuses more on the translation of knowledge and cultural base of metaphors rather than the reproduction of tenor or vehicle.

3   The three-dimensional framework of CDA

To figure out the socio-cultural reasons behind the selections of particular types of metaphors in political communication and their renditions across semiotic systems, the chapter adopts Fairclough's three-dimensional framework (1992) to "bring together linguistically-oriented discourse analysis and social and political thought relevant to discourse and language" (62).

The three-dimensional framework (Fairclough 1992, 72–73) covers the three layers of language and discourse analysis. The first dimension, *description*, focusing on the textual features of communication, lays the foundation for the other two dimensions of analysis. The second dimension is discourse practice, which is concerned with the *interpretation* of how texts are produced and processed with the change of context and other discursive factors. The third dimension goes up to the social practice that may work to explain the choice of linguistic realizations and the processing of language (*explanation*).

This model, like all other approaches in the field of CDA, regards language, language use (context), and society as an inseparable whole for analysis, and "takes a particular interest in the relation between language and power" (Wodak and Meyer 2009, 1). With a solid textual base, it offers a skeletal structure that opens to various interdisciplinary research. In this study, the model is adjusted with concepts for metaphor analysis (Figure 6.1)

To describe the textual features, the chapter presents the verbal and visual realizations of conceptual metaphors in the source and target texts. The interpretation is concerned with the entailments of the developed conceptual metaphors based on the previous identification of metaphorical expressions, and as part of the intersemiotic translation practice it also focuses on things retained and lost in the process of translation. Finally, this study moves on to the explanation of the social and cultural backgrounds where the source and target texts have been produced.

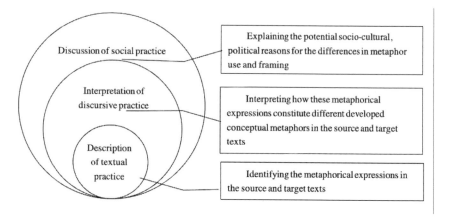

Figure 6.1 Three-dimensional analytical framework for metaphor translation analysis
Source: Based on Fairclough 1995, 98.

4 Data and methodologies

In order to investigate the framing of BRI in the intersemiotic translation, we choose the 6-minute video "Da Dao Zhi Xing" (literal translation provided by the author: "The Prevalence of the Great Way," hereinafter DDZX) as the data for analysis. The video is part of the governmental publicity project *National Album*, which is produced and issued by China's largest state-run media, Xinhua Agency. The project aims to tell stories about China's historical highlights and achievements using old photographs preserved in the National Album. As one of the significant policies of China in the new era on the global stage, the backgrounds, tenets, and achievements of BRI are included in this video.

DDZX is the 37th episode of the whole series. It was first uploaded to the special column of Xinhua Net on 17 May 2017, and then re-uploaded to other major video platforms in China, such as iFeng and Tencent Video, or disseminated through Chinese mainstream SNS like Wechat and Sina Weibo. Although it was posted on YouTube or Facebook by some private users, the video primarily targets Chinese readers and audiences.

The video includes the visual message and verbal narration. The visual data are a mixture of film shooting and photorealistic scenes, and the narration collects the original sound of the speech delivered by Chinese President Xi Jinping at several international conferences. Table 6.1 shows the list of speeches involved and the length of their transcriptions. This video stands out as a case for the intersemiotic translation from text to image, given the fact that the seven speeches are made far earlier than the visual message.

The research data include the verbal part and the visual part. The verbal data are composed of the full texts of the seven speeches, and are saved as individual files

Table 6.1 Source speeches involved in the narration of DDZX

Speeches	No. of characters
Keynote at the UN Office, Geneva (18 January 2017)	6,511
Keynote at the World Economic Forum, Davos (17 January 2017)	6,728
Keynote at the APEC CEO Summit, Lima (19 November 2016)	4,279
Speech at the Senate of the Supreme Assembly of Uzbekistan, Tashkent (22 June 2016)	4,698
Keynote at the Boao Forum for Asia, Boao (28 March 2015)	5,425
General Debate at the UN Assembly, New York (28 September 2015)	3,046
Speech at Nazarbayev University, Astana (7 September 2013)	3,543
Total	**34,230**

and later imported into NVivo 11 for further coding and analysis. Visual data are fragmented into 126 analytical units by "shots" – the result of "a single continuous 'take' delimited by 'cuts' brought about by stopping and restarting the camera," which is a standard way of unit division in film studies (Bateman and Schmidt 2013). For practical reasons, shots are snipped into pictures and saved in NVivo 11.

NVivo is the tool used for qualitative research. Coding the data with "nodes" enables analysts to figure out the relations between the marked elements. In this research, we make two types of nodes: the nodes of metaphorical expressions and the nodes of translation methods.

The coding of metaphorical expressions distinguishes verbal metaphorical expressions from visual expressions. Verbal metaphors are identified according to their meanings: if the contextual meaning of the identified phrase/word has a more basic meaning in the dictionary, it is marked as a metaphorical expression (Cameron and Maslen 2010; Charteris-Black 2014). The identification of visual metaphors follows Bounegru and Forceville's (2011) principles for visual metaphor identification. In their description, if a visual element counts as a metaphorical expression, it should include at least one connotation of the source domain that can be mapped on to the target domain; moreover, such source-to-target mapping should be irreversible.

For translation methods, the research adopts a critical point of view that takes translation as the "recontextualization of source-language texts in new social and cultural contexts" (Ieţcu-Fairclough 2008, 63). There have been several attempts to apply recontextualization to translation studies; for example, Kang (2014) investigates the English-to-Korean translations of three pieces of news on North Korea. Despite the focus on news, her research suggests that translators may "[use] language strategically to convey special meanings and to project certain images deliberately" to make the renditions "manageable and controllable for the purposes of recontextualization." Her identification of recontextualization strategies is based on the linguistic shifts in the discourses, such as omission, addition, and generalization. However, when it comes to the rendition of metaphors, translation works at both the linguistic level and the epistemological levels, given that metaphors may reflect the divergence of conceptualizing the realities and their translational shifts may be constrained by common knowledge within the community as well as some socio-political factors.

To this end, the chapter borrows Bezemer and Kress's (2008) categorization of recontextualization strategies to examine how metaphor translations change the way of conceptualization. Their work focuses on how artifacts and actions can be recontextualized in writings, speeches, and static or moving images for the pedagogical purpose, and analyzes the social consequences of transmodal and transmedial shifts. It identifies four principles of recontextualization, namely, selection, (re)arrangement, foregrounding, and social (re)positioning, which are described as follows:

1. selection, referring to "selection of meaning material" and "modal resources", which means to omit some irrelevant resources of the originating context in the new context;
2. arrangement, concerning the order of representation, namely, "what epistemological frame is best for this audience and this purpose";
3. foregrounding, related to the reassigning of salience – "what may be most significant in the originating environment may not be so in the environment of recontextualization"; and
4. social-positioning, describing the reconstruction of social relations between the participants of the discursive events, e.g. teacher and students, designers of the resource.

(Bezemer and Kress 2008, 184–186)

Particularly to the case study of DDZX, while the change of social relations does exist in the intersemiotic translation, there are no examples directly related to the transformation of metaphorical expressions. Therefore, this type is not shown in the statistical results. Moreover, Bezemer and Kress's work doesn't mention the unchanged elements in the process of recontextualization. Therefore, I borrow the term "literal translation" from translation studies to describe this phenomenon. In this sense, the chapter identifies four methods to the translation of metaphors from verbal system to visual system (i.e. literal translation, selection, foregrounding, and rearrangement). Based on Bezemer and Kress's categorization, the coding schemes of the four types are clarified in the following.

Literal translation refers to renditions that retain both the metaphorical expressions and the developed conceptual mappings of the original metaphors in the target language. *Selection* describes the selective representation of metaphorical frames, that is, what conceptual metaphors regarding BRI are not reproduced in the target image in any form. *Foregrounding* describes the phenomena that the metaphorical expressions in the source text and target text share the same conceptual mapping, but address different "images," components, or properties of the mapping. *Rearrangement* is concerned with translating metaphorical expressions with the representations of another conceptual mapping.

To apply the concepts and methods from the studies of recontextualization to translation studies offers a critical approach to investigate translation decision-making informed by contextual and cultural factors. As Iețcu-Fairclough (2008) puts it, "it is through recontextualizations of texts in new contexts, by agents having specific purposes and goals that the possibility of 'ideological' appropriation arises" (69).

5 Description: the features of metaphor use in the source and target texts

The description stage of the three-dimensional framework deals with the textual features of the research data. This case study pays attention to the use of metaphorical expressions and their translation methods. With the help of NVivo, this section identifies the salient features of metaphor use in the source and target texts.

Both verbal and visual material adapt a wide variety of source domains. The originating verbal text includes 269 verbal metaphorical expressions from 11 semantic groups, while the target visual text contains 59 visual instances from nine groups (Table 6.2). It is worth noticing that the identification of metaphorical expressions and the classification of metaphor types are different from the identification of (developed) conceptual metaphors. The latter needs to take into consideration a group of interrelated metaphorical expressions and requires further interpretation. This annotation gives us an overview of the use of metaphors in the source and target texts and lays the foundation for future analysis.

It can be seen that the use of HUMAN/FAMILY metaphors and JOURNEY metaphors is a striking feature in the selected BRI discourse, although there are some minor differences between the source and the target texts. To be more specific, the verbal speeches prefer HUMAN/FAMILY–related (104) concepts; however, the video includes more JOURNEY-related metaphors (22) and the HUMAN type comes second.

Table 6.2 Metaphorical expressions in the source text and the target text of data

Metaphors in the source text		Metaphors in the target text	
Human/family	104	Journey	22
Journey	86	Human/family	11
Machine	24	Toys/handicrafts	8
Plant	12	Arts and sports	7
Geography	11	Plants	5
Weather	9	War	2
War	9	Geography	2
Food	5	Food	1
Mythologies/culture	3	Weather	1
Arts and sports	3		
Fire/light	3		
Total	269	**Total**	59

Table 6.3 Classifying translation method by metaphor type

Metaphor type	Selection	Foregrounding	Literal translation	Arrangement
Human/family	**69**	15	14	**6**
Machine	23	0	0	0
Journey	13	**28**	**43**	1
Geography	9	0	2	0
War	7	2	0	0
Fire/light	3	0	0	0
Arts and sports	1	1	0	2
Mythologies/culture	1	1	1	0
Food	1	0	5	0
Plants	1	4	2	**5**
Weather	8	1	0	0
Total	137	52	66	14

The second step is to identifies the four translation methods of metaphorical expressions, including literal translation, selection, foregrounding, and rearrangement. Selection appears 137 times and is the most popular method. Literal translation comes second with 66 times; 52 metaphors are rendered by foregrounding and 14 by rearrangement.

With the help of NVivo we generate Table 6.3, which presents the relation between the translation method and the metaphor type, in which the most frequent types have been highlighted. According to the statistical result, literal translation and foregrounding are more frequently used in the translation of JOURNEY metaphors, while selection takes place in the translation of HUMAN-related concepts. Rearrangement seems not to be a popular method in BRI translation, which is more likely to be found in the translation of WEATHER metaphors.

6 Interpretation: the recontextualization of metaphors in the intersemiotic translation of BRI discourse

This section interprets how the video-maker presents a different image of BRI through selecting and recreating the verbal metaphorical expressions into visuals, and demonstrates how CMT can be used in the analysis of metaphor translation. Based on the qualitative results, we emphasize on the intersemiotic transformation of metaphors related to the conceptual domains of HUMAN, JOURNEY, and WEATHER.

6.1 The recontextualization of JOURNEY metaphors by literal translation and foregrounding

Above all, the term BRI itself is a metaphorical expression. "Belt and Road" is, in its literal sense, a geographic term for the range of the ancient trading routes connecting Asia, the Arabian Peninsula, and Southern Europe, in which "belt" stands for the maritime routes and "road" refers to the land routes. Today, by contrast, this phrase is employed as a political term that refers to a broad scope of interstate cooperation in areas such as policy-making, infrastructure projects, free trade, and cultural exchange along the routes. Within the basic conceptual mapping DEVELOPMENT IS A JOURNEY, the name of BRI comes from the developed metaphor BRI IS A JOURNEY that draws on an analogy between the development policy and a physical path. As the domain of JOURNEY contains various types, two developed conceptual mappings can be identified, including BRI IS A VENTURE and DEVELOPMENT IS A WATER JOURNEY.

The first group of verbal metaphors builds up the mapping between BRI and a venture (Table 6.4). This venture is long and arduous – the road is not smooth and straight, but overall the travelers are proceeding to success (moving forward). Table 6.4, Images 1 and 2 are screenshots of two continuous shots; they work as a whole to create the scene that a road extends across forests and rivers, and leads to a beacon in the sea.

Table 6.4 Analysis of the metaphor "BRI IS A VENTURE"

Image no.	Visual representations of BRI IS A VENTURE	Verbal representations of BRI IS A VENTURE
1	 (Visual description: A bunch of colorful strands visualizes the routes of a venture. It moves forward along the road across the forests.)	3年来"一带一路"建设在**探索中前进**. (New York) (BT: In these three years, the construction of BRI **gropes its way** to proceed.) 为世界经济增长**开辟**新道路(Lima) (BT: . . . **opening new ways** for global economic development) 不管**征程**多么**曲折**、多么**漫长**，胜利总是属于那些永不放弃. . . .的人们。(Boao) (BT: However winding and extended the way is, success will belong to those who never give up . . .)
2	(Visual description: The colorful bunched strands extend and reach the destination, that is, a beacon in the middle of the sea.)	

The image of the road is partially retained, including the zigzags and its direction of "forwarding." However, the verbal and visual metaphors focus on different aspects of the venture. The verbal metaphors pay closer attention to the process of the venture, including the duration and distance of the road (long, extended), and the efforts and potential dangers (grope the way). Whereas, the visuals describe a joyful and prosperous journey portrayed with high-saturated green color, and more importantly, by adding the new element, the beacon, to this frame. The importance of the beacon could be demonstrated by its location as well – it lies in the heart of the picture, a place for central elements (Kress and van Leeuwen 1996, 208). Furthermore, BEACON in political discourse is used more as a symbol for moral evaluation due to its associations with FIRE (warmth), LIGHT, and UP, and therefore is powerful in arousing social aspiration and enthusiasm (Charteris-Black 2014, 157). The text-to-image transformation of the VENTURE mapping suggests a focus-shifting from the trials in the past to a bright future blueprint.

In the second category, metaphorical expressions specify this journey of development as a voyage. In this frame, countries are independent travelers racing to the destination. On the other hand, they have to fight together against the storms. In Davos, Xi stated:

> 中国经济要发展，就要敢于到世界市场的汪洋大海中去游泳，如果永远不敢到大海中去经风雨、见世面，总有一天会在大海中溺水而亡。所以，中国勇敢迈向了世界市场。在这个过程中，我们呛过水，遇到过漩涡，遇到过风浪，但我们在游泳中学会了游泳，这是正确的战略抉择。(Xi, Davos)

(LT by the author: If China wants to develop its economy, (it) has to take risks to swim in the ocean of the global market. If (it) dares not to experience the storms in the ocean and see the world, (China) may be drowned in this ocean one day. Therefore, China bravely steps out to the world market. During swimming, we swallowed water and encountered whirlpools and storms, but we have learned how to swim by swimming, which proves to be the right strategic decision.)

This example describes how China overcomes difficulties and swims in the ocean. The WATER JOURNEY frame is not difficult to identify, even without the first sentence. For China, traveling in the sea is a risk to life, due to the lack of experience and mortal dangers from the external – "whirlpools" and "storms." Nevertheless, China is brave enough ("dare to swim") to face these challenges and fight to the end – it has "learned how to swim" and successfully "seen the world." Drawing on the analogy of SEA SWIMMING, development is seen as a very dangerous or even life-risking tour, and China as the brave one who can manage to go through these risks.

Swimming is not the only mode of transportation in this voyage of development. In the verbal data, ships and boats are also common vehicles for travelers. Most of these metaphorical expressions are used as *Cheng'yu*, the four-character idiom in the Chinese language. Table 6.5 is a glimpse of the VOYAGE-based metaphorical Cheng'yu.

Table 6.5 Cheng'yu based on the metaphor "DEVELOPMENT IS A VOYAGE"

Cheng'yu	Literal meaning	Frequency
同舟共济	Staying in the same boat and traveling together	3
共渡难关	Crossing the difficult barrier in a ferry together	3
一帆风顺	Sailing smoothly with the wind	2
千帆竞发	Thousands of sails launching together	1
百舸争流	Hundreds of ships competing for higher classes	1

These metaphorical expressions, although drawn from the same frame, focus on different elements of the conceptual mapping. "一帆风顺" suggests a peaceful and pleasant trip, but in the source text it is often used negatively to address the obstacles in the course of sailing, for example, "前进的道路不会一帆风顺" (LT: the tour of advancement is *not a peaceful voyage*). "同舟共济" and "共渡难关" emphasize how travelers cooperate to live through severe natural disasters. "千帆竞发" and "百舸争流" look at the competitive side of a sea tour in which ships race to reach the destination in less time.

The profound scenes based on DEVELOPMENT IS A VOYAGE in the verbal text have been omitted or foregrounded for the purpose of recontextualization. Visual representations of the VOYAGE put emphasis on the destination of the journey. Images relating to the WATER JOURNEY create a scenario that ships are travelling in full sail, heading for the same bright destination (to the direction of the sun). The sea is calm with no storms or waves. The image of the development voyage seems not so risky as it is framed in the source text. As the originating verbal metaphors foreground the risks of travelling, such as whirlpools, storms, and waves, the target text shifts the focus to the grand prospect of BRI.

6.2 The recontextualization of HUMAN metaphors by selection

Selection is the most frequently used method for the translation of HUMAN metaphors. In the verbal text, HUMAN-related concepts are closely related to Xi's idea of the globe as the "community of common destiny" (人类命运共同体). In the light of the conceptual mapping from HUMAN to COUNTRY, the development plan at state level are interpreted in terms of the destiny of individuals, and interstate relations are articulated by analogy with interpersonal activities and human bodies. Table 6.6 shows the developed conceptual metaphors related to the semantic domains of HUMAN. These metaphors are employed to construe countries and international relations.

Based on these mappings, China is endowed with human identities, for example, a builder and a protector; meanwhile, it co-occurs with words related to human feeling. Interestingly, the emotions involved are often negative, for example, the use of "perturbation/perturbed" and "fear" to describe China's struggle in deciding whether to join the World Trade Organization. "CHINA IS A PERSON"

Table 6.6 Examples of HUMAN-related metaphors in the ST

Developed conceptual metaphors	Verbal metaphorical instances
CHINA IS A PERSON	中国将始终做世界和平的建设者 (literal translation by the author: China will always be the builder of the world peace); 中国将始终做国际秩序的维护者 (LT: China will always be the protector of the global order); 忐忑 (perturbed)
COUNTRIES ARE PEOPLE/ INTERNATIONAL RELATION IS INERPERSONAL COMMUNICATION	坦诚交流 (frank and open communication); 和谐和睦的好邻居 (harmonious good neighbors); 真诚互信的好朋友 (sincere and trustworthy good friends)
THE GLOBE IS A HUMAN BODY	心心相印、亲如手足 (LT: two hearts linked together; as friendly as hands and feet); 唇齿相依 (lips and teeth leaning on each other)

metaphors, on the one hand, legitimate China's critical role in rejuvenating the global economy, and on the other hand, they draw empathy from the audience by projecting the national decision, which is an unfamiliar domain for many people, onto a more familiar domain of human emotions. In this line of thought, China is also portrayed as a person who is brave enough to overcome its fear of potential dangers and face the challenge.

Another group of HUMAN metaphors explains the contemporary international relation and communication in terms of human activities, that is, the exchange between countries is described within the frame of interpersonal relations between friends or neighbors. An example is related to the negotiations between national leaders, which are more likely to be described as "talk" or "brainstorming" in Xi's speeches and tend to co-occur with modifiers like "frank" and "open" to create a casual atmosphere. There is also a sub-group drawing from the COUNTRY–HUMAN mapping, namely, "THE GLOBE IS HUMAN BODY" metaphor. When countries are believed to have a relation which is closer than friendship or neighborship, they will be reframed within the domain of HUMAN BODY, for instance, two adjacent countries are described as "lips and teeth," whilst countries with good relation can be seen as "hands and feet." It is worth noticing that BODY-related metaphorical expressions are closely related to the Chinese culture and often connote deeper meanings. Taking "lips and teeth" as an example, the metaphor describes not only a positional relation, but also a relation of intimately interdependence. The early record of this allusion can be found in *Zuo Zhuan* (《左传》). It describes the relation between two ancient Chinese states, Guo and Yu. The two countries are adjacent to each other like lips and teeth: "without lips, the teeth will feel cold" (唇亡齿寒). In the history of China, Guo was conquered by Jin and Yu died out soon after, which can be seen a vivid example of the lip-and-tooth metaphor.

In the mini-documentary, most HUMAN metaphors have been omitted (selected). China is presented neither as a guardian nor a building worker, nor

Belt and Road Initiatives in texts 161

Table 6.7 Examples of HUMAN-related metaphors in DDZX

Image no.	Visual instances of COUNTRIES ARE PEOPLE	Visual description
1.		A boy is playing soccer.
2.		Five children with different skin and hair colors are running to a same destination in the distance.

as a person trembling with fear; moreover, interstate relations are not presented metaphorically as parts of a human body. Among the HUMAN-related developed conceptual metaphors, the target text only retains the analogy between countries and people and between international relation and interpersonal relation.

Table 6.7 shows two visual instances of the HUMAN metaphors. They blend literal translation with foregrounding to illustrate state-level decisions and activities within the frame of daily exercise of ordinary people. In both scenes, children are standing at the surface of the global; therefore, they can be seen as metaphors of international exchange. Table 6.7, Image 1 shows a boy playing soccer, whilst Table 6.7, Image 2 presents five children who are running towards a same destination. The general mapping is literally represented by the analogy of daily sports (soccer and jogging) and interaction between states. Meanwhile, given the characters in both shots are adolescents, it in effect foregrounds "age" of the PEOPLE domain, a property which is not explicitly represented in the source text.

6.3   *The recontextualization of PLANT metaphors by rearrangement*

Rearrangement is not a frequently used method in this case study. Only 13 metaphorical expressions are rearranged in the visual data. Considering the frequency

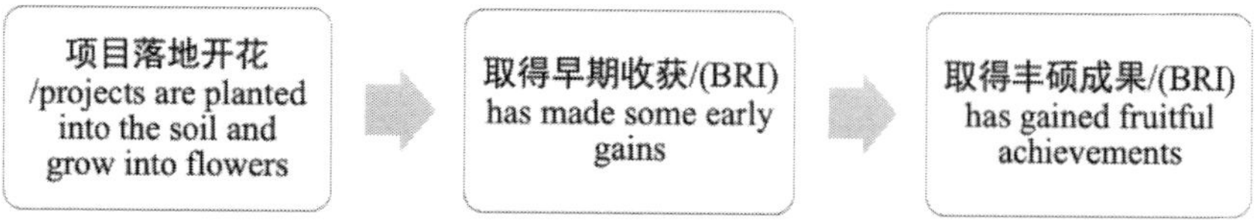

162 Zhang Xiaoyu (Heather)

项目落地开花 /projects are planted into the soil and grow into flowers → 取得早期收获/(BRI) has made some early gains → 取得丰硕成果/(BRI) has gained fruitful achievements

Figure 6.2 Conceptual mapping of the metaphor "BRI IS A PLANT"

Table 6.8 An example of translating metaphor by rearrangement

TOY metaphor in the video	PLANT metaphor in the texts
 (Visual description: A man is inspecting a matryoshka doll, which stands out from the whole picture as it is as large as a building.)	中俄全面战略协作伙伴关系…各领域合作取得丰硕成果。 The China-Russia comprehensive strategic partnership of coordination has gained *fruitful results* in cooperation in many fields.

and the systematicity of metaphorical expressions, this section further analyzes the recontextualization of PLANT metaphors.

In the verbal data, these metaphors entail the conceptual mapping that implementing BRI is growing a plant. The accomplishments of BRI, such as railways, industrial parks, and other related projects, are understood by the analogy of different stages of planting, from putting the seed in the soil to the blossom of flowers, then to early gains and finally, to fruits (Figure 6.2).

Those images, however, have not been fully reproduced in the target texts. With a close look at the video, it is found that some concrete achievements of BRI, such as Puttalam Coal Power Plant and China-Russia cooperative projects, which are originally taken as "early gains" or "fruits" of the plant, are rearranged by the event frame "playing with toys." Table 6.8 is a detailed analysis of rearrangement in intersemiotic metaphor translation. The image in Table 6.8 presents a scene in which a man is inspecting a matryoshka doll located in Red Square. The doll is exceptionally large – it is not the size of a normal toy, but the size of a building like the Kremlin. The text message clarifies the link between the picture and China-Russia cooperative projects. By enlarging the size of the toy, the shot demonstrates to the audience that how surprising the achievements are with the cooperation between China and Russia. In the source speeches, however, the achievements are briefly summarized by an instance from the PLANT metaphor, "fruitful results." The verbal and visual metaphors share a similar source domain but are represented with different target-domain frames.

7 Discussion: potential reasons for the decision-making of political metaphor translation

In the previous section, we took a brief look at the use of metaphors in the source and target texts, and through a case analysis of the JOURNEY metaphors we illustrated how the verbal metaphors are recontextualized into visuals to create the different frames of BRI. In general, while the verbal metaphors legitimate BRI as a solution to the dilemma of global economy and frame China as a capable entity to promote BRI, their visual translations tend to praise BRI, such as showing the achievements made and the promising future of this project. This section discusses the contextual and social factors involved in text production and explains how they influence the recontextualization of metaphors.

7.1 Changes of the contextual factors

As has been mentioned, the chapter takes a critical view of investigating translation in terms of recontextualization. In this sense, translation can be seen as a process in which a source text is de-located from the original context and relocated into a new one so as to fulfill the needs of communication. The decision-making of translation is subjected to the context in which the source and target texts are produced. Following this line of thought, to explain why certain metaphors in the source texted are omitted or recreated in the target text, we should look into the changes of contextual factors.

According to Halliday (1978, 5), context refers to "the total environment in which a text unfolds," the analysis of which can be conducted from three dimensions, namely, Field, Tenor, and Mode. Feng (2019) further explains the application of the notion of context to metaphor analysis. To be more specific, Field explains why certain domains of experience are chosen for metaphorical conceptualization; Tenor deals with the author-reader relations, which "serve to engage readers' attention, construct solidarity, and reinforce intimacy"; and Mode is concerned with the medium and the genre of communication. In the translation practice of the BRI discourse, both the speeches and the video share a BRI theme; therefore, changes in Tenor and Mode are more salient in this case.

Regarding the different channels of communication, the source text is composed of seven speeches delivered by Chinese President Xi Jinping; its target text, by contrast, is a 6-minute mini-documentary of BRI. The medium of communication has been shifted from face-to-face interaction to indirect communication based on mass media and networks; therefore, they employ different strategies to reach the communication goal. This may explain why some HUMAN metaphors, particularly the expressions related to "fate" and "destiny," are more likely to be recreated. In a documentary which is believed to be "a movie about real life" (Aufderheide 2007, 2), these abstract concepts are not easy to be reproduced "literally." They have to be either eliminated, or rearranged within those more concrete frames, such as "the destination" and "light," to make the film more plausible.

The use of recontextualization strategies also demonstrates the change of audience groups. The source speeches were given to people from countries around the world; some were delivered at international forums for political and economic elites. The target text, DDZX, was disseminated through the Chinese websites and SNS platforms, and its audience, limited by the Chinese net users, would be the young and middle-aged between 10 and 49 (CNNIC 2019, 18). Therefore, the differences in metaphor use demonstrate the diverse focuses of publicity.

Targeting the international audience, the speaker puts more emphasis on reducing the potential alienation and the sense of being threatened from the audience. For example, JOURNEY and HUMAN metaphors are used to reframe BRI as a people-centered program that does not have much to do with politics. A fundamental narrative is the STATES ARE PEOPLE/TRAVELERS mapping. Here "state," or nation-state, is a political term that refers to "a convergence between the territorial unit (state) and a plethora of psychological factors resulting in the identification of its people within this territory" (Twardzisz 2013, 18). Drawing on the analogy of PEOPLE, the political and ideological implications of "states" or "nation-states" have mainly been undermined. China is portrayed not as a giant and strong economy but as a pioneer traveler who gives guidance and assistance to partners. Meanwhile, BRI is presented, not as an interstate or investment plan initiated by the Chinese government but as a journey that everyone can join, or a plant that will eventually produce fruits for people. In the respect of revoking emotions, some HUMAN-related metaphors depict difficulties that China has experienced during its journey of development. They communicate negative emotions as well, like perturbation and fear.

As to the mini-documentary for the Chinese audience, metaphors are used to strengthen the patriotism and national pride of the Chinese people. Therefore, the visual metaphorical expressions tend to highlight the achievements brought by the implementation of BRI, and eliminate those parts related to suffering and wavering; for example, the selection of HUMAN metaphors about negative emotions and VOYAGE (JOURNEY) metaphors related to bad weather. Moreover, the color elements of the visual metaphors, for example, the bright colors with high saturation, also contribute to create a pleasant atmosphere and indicate the rosy prospect of BRI.

7.2 Socio-political reasons

Within the scope of critical linguistics, there are always social, historical, or ideological reasons for choosing certain symbols to express meaning (Wodak and Meyer 2009, 10). This is also applicable to explaining the different use of metaphors in the verbal and visual publicity materials of BRI – besides the local contextual factors and persuasive considerations mentioned, political and ideological reasons also play a part.

Proposing and implementing BRI is a process. The seven speeches in the source data cover a time span of five years from 2013 to 2017, and the video was first released online in 2017. Therefore, the backgrounds for the source speeches and the video are different. At the time the first speech was given in September 2013 in Kazakhstan, BRI was barely an embryo that only included the continental trade routes based on the ancient Silk Road. The world was unfamiliar about the new plan and many countries took a wait-and-see attitude. But in 2017, with years of efforts, BRI became a well-developed project and attracted many followers. Therefore, the different metaphor use strategies could reflect the distinction of acceptability to some extent. In the original speeches, some metaphorical expressions involving natural disasters and other dangerous situations are employed to raise "the sense of insecurity" from the audience so as to bring about awareness of the importance of a cooperative plan like BRI. By contrast, the target text was published when BRI had won international support and achieved some results, and thus stressing achievements in a factual manner could be more effective in persuasion, which possibly explains why the video understates the danger and risk of the "journey," but foregrounds the glorious history and the prosperous future.

Culture may also play a part in the recontextualization of BRI. The gap of cultural knowledge between the audience groups of the source and target texts makes intersemiotic transformation of metaphors a problematic issue. To solve the problem, the translator, on the one hand, deletes culture-specific metaphorical expressions in the source texts, and on the other hand adds or foregrounds some elements to fulfill the mental need of the target audience. Metaphors derived from MYTHOLOGIES, such as "Pandora's box" and "Alibaba's cave," are recontextualized by selection. It could be explained by the different cultural backgrounds of the audiences. Most of these metaphors are derived from the foreign mythologies. Xi uses them in his international speeches to fill the cultural gap and close the psychological distance. However, the video targets Chinese audience who shares a similar cultural background with the speaker, and these metaphors seem to be unnecessary in the new context. Targeting the Chinese audience, the film highlights various images of children which are not explicitly presented in the source text. It is presumably a result of the family culture in China, in which children tend to be seen as the hope of the family and attract more attention from the family members. When these images are used in the BRI narratives, the impression of vitality and hope becomes salient.

8 Conclusion

This chapter has investigated the intersemiotic translation of conceptual metaphors in BRI discourse from a critical perspective. Through the case analysis, the research shows how BRI metaphor are translated from the verbal mode into the visual mode to meet the requirement of different communicational contexts. Metaphors in the original speech settings increase the persuasive effect by de-politicizing the framing of BRI and arouse global awareness of the importance of the cooperative plan. They are then relocated into a new communication practice of a mini-documentary through techniques of literal translation, selection, rearrangement, and foregrounding. The chapter discusses the potential reasons for the shift of metaphors, including the change of contextual factors and constraints of socio-political reasons. The study exemplifies the potentials of relating critical discourse analysis and cognitive linguistics with translation studies. It proposes a tentative framework to analyze translations of conceptual metaphors in political discourse and further explore the socio-political significance behind the decisions of the sign-makers.

References

Alvarez, A. 2012. "On Translating Metaphor." *Meta: Journal des traducteurs* 38(3): 479.
Aufderheide, P. 2007. *Documentary Film: A Very Short Introduction*. Oxford University Press.
Bateman, J. A., and K. Schmidt. 2013. *Multimodal Film Analysis: How Films Mean*. London & New York: Routledge.
Bernstein, B. 1990. *The Structuring of Pedagogical Discourse: Class, Codes and Control*. London & New York: Routledge.
Bezemer, J. and G. Kress. 2008. "Writing in Multimodal Texts: A Social Semiotic Account of Designs for Learning." *Written Communication* 25(2): 166–195.
Bounegru, L. and C. Forceville. 2011. "Metaphors in Editorial Cartoons Representing the Global Financial Crisis." *Visual Communication* 10(2): 209–229.
Cameron, L. and R. Maslen, eds. 2010. *Metaphor Analysis: Research Practice in Applied Linguistics, Social Sciences and the Humanities*. London: Equinox.
Charteris-Black, J. 2011. *Politicians and Rhetoric: The Persuasive Power of Metaphor*, 2nd ed. Basingstoke: Palgrave Macmillan.
Charteris-Black, J. 2014. *Analysing Political Speeches: Rhetoric, Discourse and Metaphor*. Basingstoke, Hampshire: Palgrave Macmillan.
Chen, X. 2018. "Representing Cultures through Language and Image: A Multimodal Approach to Translations of the Chinese Classic Mulan." *Perspectives: Studies in Translatology* 26(2): 214–231.
Chilton, P. 2004. *Analysing Political Discourse*. London & New York: Routledge.
CNNIC. 2019. "Statistical Report on Internet Development in China." Available from https://cnnic.com.cn/IDR/ReportDownloads/201911/P020191112539794960687.pdf.
Díaz Cintas, J., ed. 2009. *New Trends in Audio Visual Translation*. Bristol: Multilingual Matters.
Fairclough, N. 1992. *Discourse and Social Change*. Cambridge: Polity Press. Available from www.scopus.com/inward/record.url?eid=2-s2.0-34248847725&partnerID=tZOtx3y1.
Fairclough, N. 1995. *Critical Discourse Analysis: The Critical Study of Language*. London: Longman.
Fairclough, N. 2003. *Analyzing Discourse: Text Analysis for Social Research*. London & New York: Routledge.
Feng, D. 2019. "Analyzing Multimodal Chinese Discourse: Integrating Social Semiotic and Conceptual Metaphor Theories." In *The Routledge Handbook of Chinese Discourse Analysis*, edited by Chris Shei, 65–81. London & New York: Routledge.

Fernández, E. S. 2011. "Translation Studies and the Cognitive Theory of Metaphor." *Review of Cognitive Linguistics* 9(1): 262–279. https://benjamins.com/catalog/rcl.9.1.12sam.

Forceville, C. and E. Urios-Aparisi, eds. 2009. *Multimodal Metaphor*. Berlin & New York: Mouton de Gruyter.

Gambier, Y. 2006. "Multimodality and Audiovisual Translation." In *Audiovisual Translation Scenarios: Proceedings of the Second MuTraConference in Copenhagen 1–5 May*, edited by M. Carroll, H. Gerzymisch-Arbogast, and S. Nauert. Available from www.euroconferences.info/proceedings/2006_Proceedings/2006_Gambier_Yves.pdf.

Halliday, M. A. K. 1978. *Language as Social Semiotic*. London: Edward Arnold.

Howe, N. 1988. "Metaphor in Contemporary American Political Discourse." *Metaphor and Symbolic Activity* 3(2): 87–104. www.tandfonline.com/doi/abs/10.1207/s15327868ms0302_2.

Ieţcu-Fairclough, I. 2008. "Critical Discourse Analysis and Translation Studies: Translation, Recontextualization, Ideology." *Bucharest Working Papers in Linguistics* 2(2): 67–73. www.ceeol.com/search/article-detail?id=61189.

Jakobson, R. 1959. "On Linguistic Aspects of Translation." In *On Translation*, edited by Brower, 232–239. Cambridge, MA: Harvard University Press.

Joosen, V. 2010. "True Love or Just Friends? Flemish Picture Books in English Translation." *Children's Literature in Education* 41(2): 105–117.

Kang, J. 2014. "Recontextualization of News Discourse Recontextualization of News Discourse." *The Translator* 6509(2007).

Kress, G. and T. van Leeuwen. 1996. *Reading Images: The Grammar of Visual Design*. London & New York: Routledge.

Lakoff, G. and M. Johnson. 1980. *Metaphors We Live By*. Chicago: University of Chicago Press.

Mazid, B. E. M. 2008. "Cowboy and Misanthrope: A Critical (Discourse) Analysis of Bush and Bin Laden Cartoons." *Discourse and Communication* 2(4): 433–457. https://doi.org/10.1177/1750481308095939.

Musolff, A. 2017. "Truths, Lies and Figurative Scenarios." *Journal of Language and Politics* 16(5): 641–657. www.jbe-platform.com/content/journals/10.1075/jlp.16033.mus.

Newmark, P. 1988. *A Textbook of Translation*. Harlow: Longman.

O'Halloran, K. L., S. Tan, and P. Wignell. 2016. Signata *Intersemiotic Translation as Resemiotisation: A Multimodal Perspective*.

Pereira, N. M. 2008. "Book Illustration as (Intersemiotic) Translation: Pictures Translating Words." *Meta: Journal des traducteurs* 53(1): 104. http://id.erudit.org/iderudit/017977ar.

Sonzogni, M. 2011. *Re-Covered Rose: A Case Study in Book Cover Design as Intersemiotic Translation*. Amsterdam & Philadelphia: John Benjamins Publishing.

Tebbit, S. and John J. Kinder. 2016. "Translating Developed Metaphors." *Babel* 62(3): 402–422. www.jbe-platform.com/content/journals/10.1075/babel.62.3.03teb.

Twardzisz, Piotr. 2013. *The Language of Interstate Relations*. New York: Palgrave Macmillan.

van den Broeck, Raymond. 1981. "The Limits of Translatability Exemplified by Metaphor Translation." *Poetics Today* 2(4): 73–87.

Wodak, R., and M. Meyer. 2009. *Methods of Critical Discourse Analysis*, 2nd ed. London, Thousand Oaks, New Delhi & Singapore: SAGE Publications.

7 A corpus-assisted multimodal approach to tourism promotional materials of Macao

A case study of three signature events

Lam Sut I (Michelle) and Lei Sao San (Susann)

1 Introduction

Corpus analysis, which refers to a methodology of identifying linguistic patterns of variation automatically generated by using interactive computer programs in a collection of texts of the target language variety, has been a fruitful research method in translation studies (see Baker 1993, 2000; Laviosa 1996, 2002; Tymoczko 1998). This study is a corpus-assisted study of official promotional materials of Macao tourism. In Latin, *corpus* means "body." A corpus-assisted investigation of language could be understood as studying the body of language which refers to "the quantity and representativeness of data being of paramount importance in data collection" (Tuominen, Hurtado, and Ketola 2018). However, the approach focusing only on verbal resources may result in discounting codes from other semiotic resources in the meaning-making process (Rocío Baños 2013, 488). In this case, acknowledging the need for the analysis to consider both linguistic elements and other non-verbal aids, the study of "the use of several semiotic modes in the design of a semiotic product or event," termed *multimodality* (Kress and van Leeuwen 2001, 20), was hence developed. After years of development, challenges remain in how to integrate multimodality into corpus investigations. A few research attempts to solve this problem by building up multimodal corpora and resources, such as Baldry and O'Halloran's (2010) MCA Web Browser, Adolphs and Carter's (2013) Nottingham Multi-Modal Corpus and Jimenez Hurtado and Soler Gallego's (2013) multimodal annotation software Taggetti. Nevertheless, these multimodal resources are often unachievable due to their complex design and construction, which requires constant support from specialist technical expertise (Baños, Bruti, and Zanotti 2013).

Since multimodal corpora are not yet widespread, there are other ways of integrating multimodal analysis into corpus-linguistic research. For example, Salway and Graham (2003) and Salway (2007) used information presented in scripts, transcripts or audio descriptions for insights into the representation of gaze directions, locations, actions and so on. Multimodality is considered a resource and meanwhile a challenge for translation scholars (O'Sullivan 2013). When incorporating multimodal analysis into translation studies, the notion is embraced by some scholars such as Pérez-González (2007), Borodo (2015) and Ketola (2018) in their researches. However, the interplay between verbal and non-verbal resources in translations still seem to be the area to awaiting exploration (Yu and Song 2016). Other scholars hesitate for the reasons that "multimodality oriented corpus-based translation research still has some open questions related to the alignment of modes, the segmentation of units of analysis and the need for a tagging system that takes account of the different modes" (Tuominen et al. 2018).

Recognizing the high threshold of the multimodal corpora and with reference to the existing alternative approaches to multimodal translated discourse studies, the present study hence attempts to present an applicable framework, which has the potential to make up for the aforementioned deficiencies under the limitation of accessing multimodal corpora. First, to ensure the alignment of modes, we draw on the same theoretical basis across different modes, that is, systematic functional grammar (SFG; Halliday 1985, 1994, 2000). Specific steps include an initial corpus-assisted analysis with the verbal resources to offer insights into a subsequent multimodal analysis towards the visual resources and to uncover how the information of verbal resources is translated to different modes for creating meanings and to explore the interplay between modes. Secondly, to systemize the tagging system, types of processes from the SFG (based on Halliday 1985, 1994, 2000) are used in the analysis of the verbal mode, and the systemic transcriptions and analysis towards videos are based on Baldry and Thibault's (2005) methodological tools and Kress and van Leeuwen's (1996/2006) visual grammar, evolved from SFG.

With this chapter, we intend to elucidate our ideas with a case study to probe the representations of Macao's tourism image created by the Macao SAR government with the aforementioned corpus-assisted multimodal approach. The current study is expected to answer the following questions: (1) What are the functions of linguistic and visual configurations in creating meanings in the selected tourism promotional narratives? (2) How is the interplay between the verbal and visual modes carried out? (3) How do the verbal and non-verbal realizations contribute to the tourism image of Macao?

2 Relevant theoretical concepts

This section starts with the core concept of the study, namely, tourism image, followed by the concepts to build up the theoretical framework of this research, which includes systemic functional approach to discourse analysis, multimodal discourse analysis and intersemiotic translation.

2.1 Tourism image

The term "image" in tourism studies is generally defined as a set of beliefs and senses based on information processing from various sources (Choi, Lehto, and

Morrison 2007). "Destination image" is the term widely used in tourism studies, which refers to a combination of impressions, beliefs, ideals, expectations and feelings accumulated about a place over time. By collecting different kinds of information of a place and engaging in the process of interpreting the information, consumers create a mental portrayal or prototype of what the experience will be when traveling the place (Tapachai and Waryszak 2000). This is the "induced image" of a destination, as Gunn (1972/1988, 24) suggests. The induced image is claimed to be shaped by the influence of tourism promotions directed by the market, such as advertising materials and information delivered by tourism organizations. Those who contribute to the induced destination image formation are known as induced agents.

Existing literature demonstrates that various information sources serve as the induced agents to shape the destination image. Information sources include professional advice from tour operators, travel agents and airlines; word of mouth from friends, relatives and social clubs; printed advertisement and ads from broadcast media; and books, movies and news (Baloglu and McCleary 1999; Beerli and Martín 2004; Hanlan and Kelly 2005; Mercille 2005; Stern and Krakover 1993; Woodside and Lysonski 1989). With the support from the aforementioned literature, the current study considers the tourism image of Macao under investigation as the tourists' expectations of the experience when traveling to the destination, which can be shaped by the tourism promotional narratives with both verbal and non-verbal resources.

2.2 Systemic functional approach to discourse analysis

"Language is as it is because of its function in the social structure, and the organisation of behavioural meanings should give some insight into its social foundations" (Halliday 1973, 65). With the thoughts of discourse correlating to social context, systemic functional linguistics provides a systemic scheme for the study of discourse. According to Halliday (1985, 1994, 2000), language plays three functions: ideational, interpersonal and textual. When language is used, it is always, at the same time, representing the world with language to describe events, states and entities involved (ideational); creating, ratifying or negotiating the relationships of the communicators (interpersonal); and connecting sentences and ideas in particular ways to form cohesive and coherent texts (textual). These three metafunctions of language are further realized by lexico-grammar. For representing the world, which is termed as ideational function, it is our experience of reality which is captured in terms of word denotation at word level and transitivity at clause level. The configurations of a process and participants are the grammatical resources for construing experience of the world provided by the transitivity system. The processes are the types of contents as the representation of happening, doing, sensing, meaning, being and becoming, which are termed differently and with different participants in SFG as listed in Table 7.1.

Table 7.1 Types of processes (based on Halliday 1985, 1994, 2000)

Process	Representation	Participant
Material	doing an action or actions	actor, goal
Mental	desiderating or thinking	sensor, phenomenon
Verbal	the content of what is said or indicated	sayer
Relational	being, possessing, or becoming	carrier/token, attribute/value
Existential	existential constructions	existent
Behavioural	material and mental process	behaver

2.3 Multimodal discourse analysis

Extended from the lexico-grammar in Halliday's system of language, Kress and van Leeuwen have developed the *visual grammar* for analyzing how visual resources contribute to the metafunctions of discourse (Kress and van Leeuwen 1996/2006). With the ideational function, visual resources are able to represent aspects of the world as it is experienced by humans. With the interpersonal function, visual resources are able to reflect particular social relations between the participants, including the producer and the viewer of the object represented and the object itself. With textual function, visual resources have the capacity to form texts, complexes of signs which cohere both internally with each other and externally with the context in and for which they are produced (Kress and van Leeuwen 1996/2006, 42–43). Kress and van Leeuwen term these three metafunctions *representation, interaction* and *composition*, respectively.

Representation is realized with two types of processes: *narrative processes* and *conceptual processes*. The former depicts what participants are doing or performing an action or actions, while the latter depicts participants in terms of their class, structure or meaning, which are their generalized and stable and timeless essence. Under narrative processes, there is the *action process* which is similar to Halliday's material process; the *mental process*, which refers to a "thought bubble" or a similar conventional device in connecting two participants; and *verbal processes* formed by the arrow-like protrusion of a "dialogue balloon" or similar device connecting two participants (Kress and van Leeuwen 1996/2006, 59–63). See Table 7.2.

Different from *narrative representations* for actions, *conceptual representations* represent the world in terms of permanent state of affairs and general truths, which include the following three types: classification process, analytical process and symbolic process. *Classification process* relates participants to each other in terms of a taxonomy to present hierarchical structures with participants who will play the role of subordinates with respect to the other participant(s) as the superordinate; *analytical process* relates participants in terms of a part-whole structure involving carriers as the whole and a number of possessive attributes as the parts; and *symbolic processes* represent visually what a participant means or is, with a carrier whose meaning or identity is established in the relation (Kress and van Leeuwen 1996/2006, 80–109). See Table 7.2. All these three types of processes correlate with Halliday's relational and existential processes. With all these processes, the *representation* dimension is concerned with the relationships that exist between things in the world and in the semiotic modes. In *visual grammar*, the people, places and things (including abstract things) represented in semiotic systems are termed *represented participants* (RP; Kress and van Leeuwen 1996/2006, 47).

Aside from participants and processes, representations may contain a secondary participant, the *circumstance*, which "could be left out without affecting the basic proposition realized by the narrative pattern even though their deletion would of course entail a loss of information" (Kress and Leeuwen 1996/2006, 72). There are three types of circumstances, namely setting, means and accompaniments. *Setting* refers to the elements which are drawn or painted in less detail or photographed with a softer focus, recognizable by the contrasts in color saturation and overall darkness or lightness between foreground and background. *Means* are the tools with which the action is executed, and *accompaniments* refer to the participants having no vectorial relation with other participants and cannot be interpreted as a *symbolic attribute* (see Table 7.2).

Connecting to Kress and van Leeuwen's work, while not looking into merely static visual resources, Baldry and Thibault (2005) developed methodological tools in the transcription and analysis of videos as a multimodal text type. The semiotic modalities, such as the duration of shots, the visual frame and so forth, which encompass the visual, verbal, and textual elements of a frame/shot/phrase, are recorded, arranged in sequence and then analyzed. Their approach to transcribing dynamic audiovisual text has inspired scholars from different disciplines to develop a multimodality research design to fit their research context (e.g. Halverson 2010; Halverson, Bass, and Woods 2012; Rose 2012). Table 7.3 summarizes the core elements of different modalities transcribed with Baldry and Thibault's (2005) tools which are related to the current study.

Table 7.2 Representations in visual grammar (based on Kress and van Leeuwen 1996/2006)

Function	Representation		
Ideational function	Narrative	**Process**	**Participant**
		Action	Actor, goal
		Reaction	Reactor, goal
		Mental	Sensor, phenomenon
		Verbal	Sayer, utterance
	Conceptual	**Circumstance**	
		Setting, means, accompaniment	
		Classification	Superordinate, subordinate, inter-ordinate
		Analytical	Carrier, possessive attribute
		Symbolizing	Carrier, symbolic attribute, symbolic suggestive

Table 7.3 Elements of different modalities

Visual modes			Verbal modes
Filming and editing	Kinesics actions	Other visual elements	• Subtitles • Voice-over • On-screen text • Speech
• Visual salience • Social distance • Angle/perspective of camera • Sequence of shots • Transition	• Action and movement • Gesture • Gaze • Facial expression	• Costume • Makeup • Lighting • Set design • Props • Color	–

2.4 Intersemiotic translation

According to Jakobson (1956/1966/2004, 232), there are three types of translation, namely, interlingual, intralingual and intersemiotic. Interlingual translation refers to an interpretation of verbal signs by means of some other languages. Intralingual translation refers to an interpretation of verbal signs by means of other signs of the same language. Intersemiotic translation is defined as an interpretation of verbal signs by means of signs of non-verbal sign systems. Among these three types of translation, intersemiotic translation is quite different from other two types and information loss is at its highest (Gorlée 1994, 168). While both intralingual and interlingual translations are at least potentially reversible, intersemiotic translation is a one-way process (Sturrock 1991, 310). With these distinctive features, intersemiotic translation is also an area which is less explored in the field of translation studies compared with the other two types.

3 Data

To represent the official conducted discourse of Macao's tourism image, the selected data of the study consists of advertising narratives released by Macao Government Tourism Office (MGTO). To efficiently handle the large volume of data, subsequent criteria for selecting the advertising narratives are used: (1) content covers the events hosted or organized by MGTO; and (2) only events highlighted in the policy address of the Macao SAR government between the year 2016 and 2018 are covered. With the mentioned criteria, the advertising narratives extracted cover three major events, namely, the Macao Light Festival, the Parade for Celebration of Chinese New Year, and the International Film Festival and Awards Macao (IFFAM).

Taking into consideration the contributions from both verbal and non-verbal modes in the tourism promotional narratives, the selected data are from two sources, namely, (1) the official news releases of the press conferences of the events in Chinese, which are accessible on the Macao SAR Government portal website;

and (2) the official promotional online videos (with both Chinese and English subtitles) available at the MGTO official channel on YouTube.

3.1 Official news releases

Adhering to the inclusion criteria mentioned above, the sample of the study comprises nine press releases, all in Chinese; a total of 12,970 Chinese characters are analyzed. The selected news releases are characterized by the detailed descriptions of the events. They are reassembled with the whole design of event programs, which are deemed to be the pre-existed verbal resources for the promotional videos to base on. Hence, the present study considers the verbal descriptions of the selected news release as the source texts in the intersemiotic translation process to the promotional videos.

3.2 Online promotional videos

Respecting the promotional videos, the samples of the study are the 22 videos extracted in April 2019 from MGTO's official YouTube channel using a free video downloader. The selected data consists of ten videos in Chinese, ten in English and two without voice-over or subtitles. The total duration of the extracted video is 16 minutes and 16 seconds, including the main content of the video and the closing credits.

Table 7.4 Selected data of present study

Corpus	Lemma types	Lemma token	News releases	Words
C2016	1204	4436	International Film Festival and Awards Macao 2016 Press Conference	1,516
			Macao Light Festival 2016 Press Conference	1,385
			Parade for Celebration of Chinese New Year 2016 Press Conference	1,535
C2017	1094	3911	International Film Festival and Awards Macao 2017 Press Conference	968
			Macao Light Festival 2017 Press Conference	1,526
			Parade for Celebration of Chinese New Year 2017 Press Conference	1,435
C2018	1236	4578	International Film Festival and Awards Macao 2018 Press Conference	1,486
			Macao Light Festival 2018 Press Conference	1,775
			Parade for Celebration of Chinese New Year 2018 Press Conference	1,344

4 Methodology

Data analysis in the present study can be divided into two parts: the analysis of the verbal text and the analysis of the non-verbal text. The analysis of the verbal text is conducted with the corpus tools to investigate Halliday's ideational structure first at word level, with denotation and connotation of words, and second at clause level, with transitivity. With Kress and van Leeuwen's visual grammar, the analysis of the non-verbal text is conducted to examine the ideational structure and interpersonal structure of the text by the investigation of processes contributing to the representation of the text, as well as other visual resources contributing to the interaction of the text.

4.1 Analysis of the verbal text

The verbal texts are the news reports of the press conference for the selected signatures events. With the research tools provided by a corpus-assisted software AntConc, version 3.5.7 (Anthony 2018), a corpus-assisted analysis of the textual resources is conducted and starts from the analysis at word level with the corpus tool, Word List, which is followed by the analysis of transitivity with the corpus tool, Concordance Search. The concordance lines attained by the corpus tool are coded in accordance with the verbal realization at clause level as listed in Table 7.1 with NVivo 12 Plus, another research software to conduct a quantitative comparison with the frequency of varieties of processes and participants.

4.2 Analysis of the non-verbal text

The analysis of videos starts at the outset of the transcribing process of the videos in this study. To ensure that the videos are explored and transcribed systematically, Kress and Leeuwen's visual grammar (1996/2006) is adopted as the backbone approach and is supplemented with Baldry and Thibault's framework (2005) in transcribing and analyzing the videos; as the former is scarcely elucidated in dynamic images, to adopt it alone could hardly suffice to provide a full picture of the inherently complex multi-semiotic resources in the videos. After several times of viewing by the researchers, all retrieved videos are transcribed at two levels (Baldry and Thibault 2005): at a micro level, the researchers aim to retain the information of semiotic modalities in the videos as detailed as possible, to avoid the loss of information or the introduction of discrepancies; at a macro level, the researchers attempt to capture the meaning-making process, and the interplay between elements which made up the artifacts (i.e. the videos per se).

In the technical perspective, Video Ant, a web-based video annotation tool developed by the University of Minnesota, is used to facilitate the transcribing process (https://ant.umac.edu/). Time stamps and annotations of the video clips are then exported in plain text format for further analysis in NVivo 12 Plus and in the MS Excel spreadsheets.

5 Findings and sample analysis

This section presents the examination of the ideational structures of the verbal text and how it is translated into the non-verbal text, and how the interaction of the text is enhanced in the non-verbal text.

5.1 Representation of verbal resources in news releases (ST of intersemiotic translation)

With the mentioned corpus tools, a corpus-assisted analysis towards the verbal text is first conducted at word level and later at clause level.

5.1.1 Analysis at word level

Comparing the word lists of all three corpora, the common frequent lexical words within the top 30 in C2016, C2017 and C2018 are with the words representing the city, the three selected events as well as the organizers of the events, such as 澳門 (Macao),[1] 電影 (movie), 光影 (light), 旅遊局 (MGTO), 巡遊 (parade), 活動 (event) and 花車 (float). However, we can see distinctive words representing the particular theme of the event as 愛 (love) and qualities of the events as 創作 (invention), 本地 (local) in C2017 and 美食 (food), and 新 (new) in C2018, as shown in Table 7.5. The result reveals the common and distinct foci in materials of the years under investigation. It is found that *art and cultural elements* and *joy and*

Table 7.5 Lexical words in top 30 of word lists of C2016, C2017 and C2018

Common frequent words in C2016, C2017, C2018

Region and organizer	澳門、旅遊局 (Macao, MGTO)		
Art and cultural events and elements	影展、電影、光影、表演、花車、巡遊 (movie show, movie, light, show, float, parade)		
Joy and vitality	節、活動 (festival, activity)		

	C2016	C2017	C2018
Love and caring		愛 (love)	
Art and cultural events, elements and qualities	文化 (culture)	匯演、創作 (show, creation)	美食 (gastronomy)
Commercial	國際、典禮、旅遊、頒獎 (international, ceremony, travel, award)	國際、市民、旅客、本地 (international, citizen, traveler, local)	市民、旅客、新 (citizen, traveler, new)

vitality have salience throughout the years. In terms of art and cultural elements, the specific foci vary in the three years.

5.1.2 Analysis at clause level

The analysis is further conducted at clause level. All the verbal resources of the selected new release are coded with Halliday's transitivity. It shows that the most common processes in the selected verbal resources are material processes in all three corpora, with more than 50% of all lines, followed by relational processes (nearly 20%) in the three corpora, and mental processes with only 6% in C2016, but 13% in C2017 and 11% in C2018 (see Figure 7.1).

When looking into the material processes, the word groups representing the activities or activity elements are the most frequent actors identified in all three corpora (Figure 7.2). While there is a noticeable decrease in having the audience as the actors, there is a considerable increase in the use of activity organizer as the actors. As in Example 1, 今年的澳門光影節 (Macao light festival this year), 多位影壇國際巨星新星和導演 (a few international great, new stars and directors in cinema) and澳門旅遊吉祥物"麥麥" (Macao Tourism Mascot "MAK MAK"), the word groups representing the activity itself or other elements of the activity act as the agents of the action processes, as 引入 (introduce), 加盟 (join) and "出沒" (hang around), to show what the activities offer to the public. One more point to be noted is that all these word groups denoting the activities and the related elements are referring to art and cultural elements. In Example 2, 觀眾 (audience) acts as the agent of the action 塗鴉 (draw graffiti) to tell what the audience can do in the

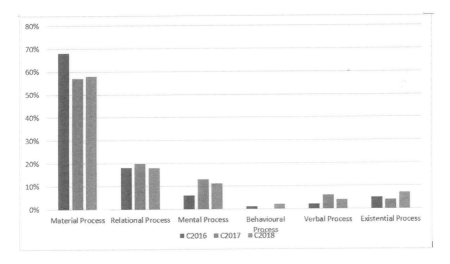

Figure 7.1 Processes in verbal resources of selected news releases

178 *Lam Sut I (Michelle) and Lei Sao San (Susann)*

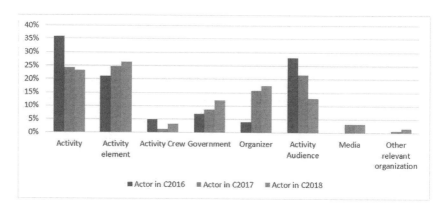

Figure 7.2 Actors of material processes in verbal resources of selected news releases

activity. In Example 3, 影展籌委會 (film festival organizing committee) acts as the agent of the action 邀請 (invite) to show what the organizers of the activity have done in coordinating the event.

Example 1
Corpus: C2016
今年的澳門光影節引入創新光影技術。
Corpus: C2017
多位影壇國際巨星新星和導演加盟影展。
Corpus: C2018
澳門旅遊吉祥物"麥麥"將以聖誕、廚師及美食形象合共14款造型, 分別於3條光影路線"出沒"。

Example 2
Corpus: C2016
觀眾塗鴉屬於自己的光影作品。

Example 3
Corpus: C2018
影展籌委會邀請了幾位國際影壇。

Example 4
Corpus: C2016
花車巡遊已成為 澳門具代表性的節慶活動之一 。
Corpus: C2017
第三年舉行的澳門光影節 內容創新豐富
Corpus: C2018
美食夜市將設於北帝廟前地。

Example 5
Corpus: C2016
華語微電影比賽-鼓勵有興趣投身電影業界的年青人創作澳門元素的作品
Corpus: C2017
主辦單位期待電影同業、媒體、市民及旅客於12月一起共享這次豐富的銀幕盛宴 觀眾於日間也可欣賞光影藝術
Corpus: C2018
觀眾體驗澳門人的童年樂趣

Tourism promotional materials of Macao 179

When looking into the relational processes, we find that the word groups representing activity elements are considerably more frequent than all the others as the participants, which are named as carrier and token in relational processes in all three corpora (Figure 7.3). As shown in Example 4, word groups such as 花車巡遊 (float parade), 第三年舉行的澳門光影節內容 (the content of the third Macao Light Festival) and 美食夜市 (food night market) denote different activity elements acting as the participants of the processes of becoming and being to show the qualities of the activities. To categorize the carrier and token represented, most of them which are denoting to activities and related elements are with reference to cultural elements as well as innovative entertainment.

When looking into the mental processes, more diverse use of participants is found. As presented in Figure 7.4, in C2016, activity itself is the most frequent sensor in the processes; in C2017, the organizer and the audience are the most frequent ones, while the audience is the most frequent one in C2018. As in Example 5, 華語微電影比賽, the word group denoting the activity itself acts as the agent of

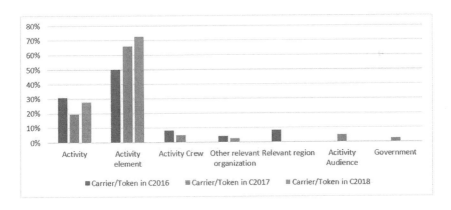

Figure 7.3 Carrier/token in verbal resources of selected news releases

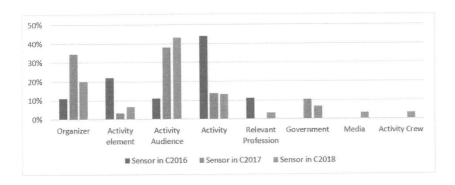

Figure 7.4 Sensor in verbal resources of selected news releases

the thinking process of 鼓勵 (encourage); 主辦單位 (organizer) acts as the agent of the mental process introduced by the vector 期待 (look forward to); and 觀眾 (audience) acts as the agent of the mental process introduced by the vector 欣賞 (appreciate).

To summarize, most of the participants represented in the discourse are with reference to the themes *art and cultural elements* and *innovative entertainment*. With the participants referring to the activity audience, most of them are the word groups denoting *general audience* as the word group 觀眾 (audience), 市民 (citizens), 旅客 (tourists) and just with very few examples as the one with specific denotation as 年輕人 (the young).

This section provides an analysis of the verbal resources of the selected news releases, which reveals that the verbal configurations represent a destination with salience on art and cultural elements, joy and vitality as well as innovative entertainment for the general audience overall. What follows next is how the representation of the verbal resources under investigation are translated intersemiotically into non-verbal resources.

5.2 Representation and interaction in resources of the videos (TT of intersemiotic translation)

With reference to the findings in the corpus-assisted textual analysis of the selected news releases, an investigation of the ideational and interpersonal structures exhibited in the non-verbal (visual) resources has been done with Kress and van Leeuwen's visual grammar (1996/2006) to examine the information transferred in the intersemiotic translation process.

5.2.1 Ideational structure of video

For as much as the ideational structure of the videos is realized basically by the participants and circumstances captured, as well as the types of processes utilized in visual grammar, this section will firstly describe the major findings of the three with some typical examples to assist our elaboration, followed with the major themes generated from the findings.

NARRATIVE REPRESENTATION

Narrative processes refer to the depictions of "actions and events, processes of change, and transitory spatial arrangements" (Kress and van Leeuwen 1996/2006, 59). In the promotional videos, action processes and reaction processes are among the most frequently adopted types of narrative processes.

For action processes, noticeably we found in the videos that vectors stemmed from the actors often do not point to the other participants on-screen, but rather to the viewers of the videos off-screen. Prominent examples can be found in several shots of the mascots or dancers across different promotional videos of the Chinese New Year Parade (e.g. Figure 7.5). On other occasions, invisible vectors are coming out from the actors to the visualized goals. The goal can be either a participant

Figure 7.5 Shot addressing viewers off-screen

Figure 7.6 Shot addressing vector formed from actors to visualized goal

or an object to indicate the interaction between participants or other visual elements in the image. Figure 7.6 showcases the narrative representation of this sort, in which vectors are formed from the actors to the screen, to the bulb, to the cell phones or to some other visualized goals on screen.

For the reaction processes shown in the videos, the vectors are usually formed by an eyeline or the direction of a glance from the reactors to the phenomena (i.e. the passive participant). The phenomenon is not necessary for another participant, but sometimes an object or an event happening on-screen. In the current examples, vectors can be found from the shot with the lady (reactor) to the animated triangles (phenomenon) (Macao Government Tourism 2017a, 00:05), or from the shot with the glance of the two ladies (reactors) in response to the man's greeting (phenomenon) (Macao Government Tourism Office 2018b, 00:10).

It is also witnessed in the promotional videos that reaction processes in which a vector emanates from participants without pointing at the phenomenon in a single shot (i.e. non-transactional reaction with the term in visual grammar). The reaction process is instead achieved through the use of visual cuts of multiple shots or shot-reverse shots in cinematic terminology. For instance, in the promotional video of the 2nd IFFAM, the shots with the interactions between the little girl with braids and the dog are indeed a series of reaction processes (Macao Government Tourism Office 2017b, 01:04). In a series of shot-reverse shots, the vector firstly departs from the girl (reactor) to the dog (phenomenon). This shot is immediately followed by a non-transactional process. Subsequent close-up shots are then given only to the two reactors, the girl and the dog, while the phenomena are left out in the shots. Viewers can still perceive the reaction process realized by the shot of the dog looking at the little girl (off-screen) and the counter-shot of the little girl looking at the dog (off-screen) as a response.

Mental and verbal processes are rarely seen in the selected promotional videos. The only exceptions are the verbal invitations to the 2nd and 3rd IFFAM by the events' talent ambassadors, Jeremy Renner (internationally renowned actor; Macao Government Tourism Office 2017b, 01:53), Aaron Kwok (Hong Kong-based artist; Macao Government Tourism Office 2018a, 01:47) and Nicolas Cage

(American actor, director and producer, and Academy Award and Golden Globe Awards winner; Macao Government Tourism Office 2018a, 01:52).

CONCEPTUAL REPRESENTATION

Conceptual processes represent participants in terms of their more generalized and more or less stable and timeless essence, in terms of class, structure or meaning (Kress and van Leeuwen 1996/2006, 59). In other words, they deal with images where participants are classified, analyzed or defined (Ly and Jung 2015). Unlike our analysis of the verbal resources where activities information is told plainly, activities details are often extracted through the use of conceptual processes such as showing only some features of the events or embroidered with symbolic elements.

On the one hand, under the conceptual structure, analytical processes that captures the visual elements in a part-whole structure are oftentimes found in the promotional videos. Macao's city image as historic, cultural and commercial is weaved through the use of a cluster of images of signature buildings, such as Senado Square (Figure 7.7), the Ruins of Saint Paul's, the Mandarin's House and Galaxy Macau on the Cotai Strip in Macau (Figure 7.8). Analytical processes, by amplifying the distinctive parts or features of the buildings (the possessive attributes), portray the induced tourism image of the city (the carrier).

On the other hand, the adoption of the symbolic process is also found in the promotional videos. For example, the close-up of hands holding a small green plant in a metallic frame-like light installation in a dark place in the promotional video of the Light Festival in 2018 can be treated as a symbolic process (Macao Government Tourism Office 2018b, 00:01). The retro details of the polyhedron light installation symbolize a hypothetical time machine with which one could see through the different dimensions of the city, and the green plant implies the city's vigor and vitality. Moreover, the action to turn on the light installation may suggest to activate the time machine to set off on a time travel in the city. This symbolic process hence aids in sculpting the event's theme, "Time Travel." Other symbolic processes are established through highlighting the conventional association with symbolic values, such as the animated thread in the video of the Light Festival in

Figure 7.7 Example of analytical process (Senado Square – historic and cultural building)

Figure 7.8 Example of analytical process (Galaxy Macau on the Cotai Strip – commercial building)

2017 to symbolize the bond between people to echoes with the theme of the annual event, "Love" (Macao Government Tourism Office 2017a, 00:10).

Furthermore, on some occasions we found in the videos, the shots contain both the conceptual and narrative structures. Take the shots in the promotional video of the 2nd IFFAM again as an example (Macao Government Tourism Office 2017b, 01:00). Narrative processes are realized by depicting the little girl, who leans towards the dog to feed him a bowl of water which she previously got from the fountain. These actions reinforce the notion of caring and impersonal love in the city. With conceptual terms, these shots represent the stereotypes concerning economic status, race and family composition. The nuclear family is made up of two parents and a child with Chinese ancestry; all are kind, healthy, well-dressed and perfectly harmonious with the Western environment (i.e. they are standing before a Portuguese azulejos wall). All these suggest the representation of the characteristics belonging to a common middle-class family and the fusion of Chinese and Western culture in Macao.

5.2.2 Interaction structure of video

As the audience's participation is underscored in the verbal resources practically through the use of direct invitation from the organizers, more diverse use of techniques to form the interaction structure is seen in the video data. This section hence serves to delineate the relationship between the represented participants and the viewers suggested in the promotional videos. The illustration will focus on the following aspects: the kinesics action, gaze, camera angles, social distance and modality.

GAZE AND KINESICS ACTIONS

One prominent indicator to reveal the interaction structure of the videos is the participants' direct gaze at the viewers. It is common in the videos that vectors are formed from the eyelines of the mascots, zodiac characters, performers, dancers in the Chinese New Year Parade and from talented ambassadors of the IFFAM to the viewers, so as to establish an imaginary contact between the participants and the viewers. Furthermore, the participants' facial expressions and kinetics actions, such as performers smiling, waving hands, approaching, leaning towards the camera or even sending a blow kiss towards to the viewers (Figure 7.9), imply the participants' invitation the viewers to establish a sense of social affinity with them.

SOCIAL DISTANCE

Another indicator to show the interactions between the participants and viewers are the "size of frame" through the choice of close-up, medium shot or long shot while producing the image in visual grammar (Kress and van Leeuwen 1996/2006, 141). The shorter distance between the represented and the viewers expresses the more intimate and personalized relations between the two (Baldry and Thibault 2005). Not surprisingly, 55% out of the 268 analyzed shots of the promotional videos are made up of medium to very close shots to encourage the viewers' engagement in the events depicted. Figures 7.5 and 7.9 are the cases in point.

ANGLE

Camera angles of videos are transcribed in two dimensions in the current study, namely, horizontal and vertical. Horizontal perspectives indicate the viewers' idea of the involvement of or empathy with the actions or events depicted in the videos (Kress and van Leeuwen 1996/2006). In this perspective, the frontal/direct angle suggests viewers' involvement; on the contrary, oblique angles indicate detachment with the represented world (Baldry and Thibault 2005). In the current study, many frontal angle shots that place the viewers directly in front of the depicted world are used to amplify viewers' sense of involvement in the events (as shown in Figures 7.5 and 7.9).

Vertical perspective is associated with the power relations between viewers and the depicted world (Baldry and Thibault 2005). Participants are mostly depicted with a median angle (i.e. shots at eye level), indicating no power difference between the viewers and the represented participants (e.g. Figure 7.9). Intriguingly, buildings are shot with low angles to show the solemnity or to emphasize the magnificence of the architecture (e.g. Figure 7.10).

MODALITY

In visual grammar, modality signals the degree of truth or reliability by the viewers towards the depicted world in visual semiosis. A few modality markers are summarized by Kress and van Leeuwen to indicate how true an image is by the beholders (color, brightness, depth, representation, etc.). What should also be noted is that the concept of realism varies across different contexts and by different social groups, and thus the interpretation of the markers needs to be changed accordingly (Kress and van Leeuwen 1996/2006). Therefore, the notion of coding orientation is embraced in visual grammar to help distinguish the orientation to "reality." Since the promotional videos are advertising artifacts in essence, the analysis of images in this study follows the sensory coding orientation.

With the sensory coding orientation, it is revealed that images in the promotional videos have a high modality for the Chinese New Year events and the Light

Figure 7.9 Example shot of creating social affinity (with kiss)

Figure 7.10 Example shot of low angles to show the solemnity of architecture

Figure 7.11 Example shot of high modality (with sensory coding orientation)   *Figure 7.12* Example shot of low modality (with sensory coding orientation)

Festival (Figure 7.11) and a lower modality for IFFAM (Figure 7.12). Images in the videos of the Chinese New Year and Light Festival are usually bright, maintaining details of the participants and the context (e.g. setting or background), and shots are usually with deep perspective and a high degree of illumination. Videos of IFFAM, on the contrary, contain many shots that are blurry, filtered, with a low degree of illumination and brightness. Under the sensory coding orientation, colors play a significant role in terms of the sensually and emotive meaning. The tone of the IFFAM videos is bluish, implying the expertise, seriousness and professionalism of the event; yet the videos of the other two events are usually red-orange, representing energy, vitality and happiness.

5.3 Summary of the findings

To better elucidate our findings, a summation is given with an emphasis to exhibit the similarities and differences between the verbal and non-verbal realizations to identify the shifts in the intersemiotic translation process.

In terms of the ideational structure of the text, with reference to the verbal realizations, we found from the corpus analysis and the close examination of the participants, circumstances and the processes of the videos, we are convinced that a few themes can be identified and categorized. Table 7.6 summarizes the visual realizations with the representations of the major themes identified.

Both the verbal resources and the translated visual realizations function to build up the induced tourism image of Macao. They shared themes identified in the two modes are the following: *art and culture* (with both verbal and visual realizations referring to related events, elements and professions, and addressing the historic and cultural significance of the city), *joy and vitality* (with both verbal and visual realizations denoting the festive atmosphere), *love and caring* (with both verbal and visual resources representing the related theme but elaborated in visual realizations), *commercialization* (with both verbal and visual resources denoting commercial elements of the city, though only in the IFFAM events).

Despite that the major themes extracted in the verbal and non-verbal realizations are broadly consistent with each other, subtle differences are found in the choice of

Table 7.6 Visual realizations of representations

Themes	Participants (actor/reactor/carrier)	Circumstances (setting/means/accompaniment)
Integration of East and West	Samba dancers, performers in green kimonos, performers in Chinese folk costumes, God of Fortune, zodiac characters, women doing taijiquan, dancing lions and dragons, etc.	Ruins of St Paul's, A-Ma Temple, Freguesia de São Lourenço church, Quartel dos Mouros, Taipa House Museum, Travessa da Paixão, Rua da Alfândega, Rua de Cinco de Outubro, sky lanterns, animated confetti, etc.
History and culture	Performers in white and green Canton Opera costumes, women doing taijiquan, dancing lions and dragons.	Ruins of St Paul's, A-Ma Temple, Freguesia de São Lourenço church, Quartel dos Mouros, Taipa House Museum, Travessa da Paixão, Rua da Alfândega, Rua de Cinco de Outubro, etc.
Commercials	Jang Keun Suk, Jeremy Renner, Aaron Kwok.	Galaxy Macao, Venetian Macao, Wynn Palace Macao, Avenida do Infante D. Henrique, Avenida do Almirante Lacerda, Casino Lisboa, etc.
Professionals	Ambassadors of IFFA, Jeremy Renner, Aaron Kwok, Man holding a professional video camera, a crew shooting, man holding an audio pole.	dark room, editing room, aisle of cinema, audio pole, professional camera, editing device, films, row of seats of cinema, etc.
Joy and vitality	A girl in white dress with a wreath on her head, performers in parades, dancers of the duo dance, samba dancers blow kisses, etc.	Animated flash radiated from ground to sky before Ruins of St. Paul, small green plant in a metallic frame-like container, animated confetti, etc.
Bonds, love and caring (between family members, friends, and couples, etc.)	Middle-aged man and the little girl, the couple in suit and bridal dress, man and girl on motorcycle, family before the food van, little girl and the dog, etc.	Travessa da Paixão, Rua de Cinco de Outubro, dining table, animated threads, water bowl, etc.

participants and the processes adopted between the two modes. In verbal realization, the "activity" itself, "activity elements" (i.e. details about the activity, such as time, venues, or performers of the activity) or "activity organizers" are the most frequently actors or carriers to provide the readers with unvarnished information about the events. For the visual resources, except for the videos of the Chinese New Year event where the documentary images of "performers" play a dominant role, major participants in the other two events are the meticulously selected fictional actors or spokespersons. These participants are mostly stereotypic actors or given identities while interacting with the carrier or the symbolic attribute, often contain certain symbolic meanings. Taken also the use of filters, animation, and other post-production techniques, it is convinced that the function of visual realization is to create an atmosphere than disseminating information regarding the events. Another prominent difference between the two modes in the ideational structure is the representation of the "audience." In the verbal resources, "audience," though with several denotations, such as "tourists," "travelers" or "viewers," is mentioned literally and is welcomed and invited to the events forthrightly. However, in visual resources, the audience is almost "invisible" with only very few shots capturing the audience. The encouragement of the involvement by the almost "invisible" audience, is expressed more covertly through creating vectors, such as gazes or kinesics actions, from the performers or characters in the videos, or through the use of shooting or editing techniques.

In terms of interpersonal structure, the audience's participation is underscored in the verbal resources practically through the use of direct invitation from the organizers, while more diverse use of techniques is applied in the video to form the interaction structure. For instance, the extensive use of shots at eye level, frontal shots and direct gazes, smiles and inviting gestures from the performers to the viewers all suggest a more equal relationship between the producers and the viewers. Without the power difference between the viewers and the represented participants, traces of the producers' effort in using the videos to ask the viewers to enter in a relation of social affinity are obvious. The visual resources, meanwhile, also work together to enhance the operative function of the video. With the use of the direct gaze and the inviting kinesics actions, the medium to very close shots, the frontal angle shots to place the viewers directly in front of the depicted world and so forth, the video represents the invitation to viewers' involvement.

The analysis shows that the two modes work together to frame the image of Macao with common themes represented. However, the variations in between are somewhat stable. While verbal semiosis is basically informative in nature, the visual semiosis, on the contrary, is more operative in essence.

6 Discussion and conclusion

The current study draws on Halliday's systemic functional grammar (1985, 1994, 2000) and Kress and van Leeuwen's visual grammar (1996/2006) to offer an insight into and the possible explanations to how resources from different modes work to frame Macao's tourism image from the government's perspective. With the findings above, while common representation is found in the texts in the two modes, there are distinct features contributing to the representation of the texts disclosed in each. In what follows, we discuss the possible factors behind.

In terms of the ideational structure in the promotional materials, the common themes of art and culture, joy and vitality, love and caring, and innovation as well as Chinese tradition are significantly represented in the selected data. These common themes are even elaborated in the process of intersemiotic translation from verbal resources of news releases to the non-verbal resources in the videos. In the videos, with the represented participants and circumstances, the integration of East and West in the city as well as the history and culture of the destination are represented in the non-verbal mode. This shift in the translation process enhances the art and cultural qualities of the destination presented in the non-verbal modes. With both verbal and non-verbal modes, the destination is framed as an art and cultural city with history and integration of East and West culture in particular, which is filled with joy and vitality, love and caring to welcome general tourists worldwide.

As mentioned, rather than a gaming city due to the long history of legalization of gambling activities as well as the rapid development of gaming industry under the name "Monte Carlo of the East" as the largest gambling hub in the world, the city is framed as a healthy destination with profound culture. Referring to "Macao Tourism Industry Development Master Plan," which is a blueprint plan for tourism development of the city drafted by Macao SAR government in 2015 and released to the public in 2017, the blueprint plan is with the principles as elaborating "the uniqueness of Macao's history and culture, as well as create a culturally diverse destination with rich content" and "fostering the development of the creative industries of the city" to develop cultural tourism, introducing "a variety of entertainment facilities and leisure activities" to develop tourism and leisure industries. It is found that the discursive construction goes in line with the government's strategic scheme for the tourism development of the city. As the official conducted discourse of Macao's tourism image, the selected data is with the official voice to create meaning to the public. The official tourism promotional materials hence, as a particular discourse type, not only are the materials reflecting the featured qualities of the city, but also are empowered as a political practice to define or shape the city as to how the authority would like it to be, which is to create knowledge as to how the city is to the particular audience and how the city should be to the outside world.

While the two modes work together to deliver common representation in terms of the city's image, heterogenous text types are found to be utilized across the discourse of different modes. As mentioned above, the analysis reveals that verbal semiosis is intrinsically informative in nature, which serves to provide facts and details related to the events, such as signature activities, guests or performers, venues and locations and so forth. However, visual semiosis, on the contrary, is more operative in essence, which contains more than the concise facts of the events, but also incorporates many shots or even stories with emotional appeals that are wrapped in aesthetic forms to create social affinity and to invite viewers to join the events. This approach to using contrasted communication materials by the government is apprehensible, as the verbal materials target narrow audience, who are mostly press or journalists. Whereas the visual materials are basically advertisements that aim presumably at the general public, tourists, or potential tourists whose willingness and behavior to travel or involve in tourist events, are likely to be influenced by promotion materials with emotional appeals. (Li 2014)

Despite the important insights into Macao's tourism image, this study risked discounting the contributions from other stakeholders by focusing merely on the government's promotional materials in shaping Macao's tourism image. Therefore, extending the sample to promotional materials or even reviews from other stakeholders is highly recommended for future studies to have a more holistic understanding of shaping and negotiating the discourse. Positioning the study per se as a tryout to integrate corpus into multimodality studies, we are in the hope of eliciting better ideas to propose a potential corpus-assisted multimodal approach to translation-oriented discourse analysis.

Note

1 The English translation in parentheses is the literal translation offered by the authors. All other English translations in parentheses in the rest of the chapter are the literal translation offered by the authors.

References

Adolphs, S., and R. Carter. 2013. *Spoken Corpus Linguistics. From Monomodal to Multimodal*. London & New York: Routledge.

Anthony, L. 2018. *AntConc (3.5.7)*. Tokyo, Japan: Waseda University. Available from http://www.laurenceanthony.net/software.

Baker, M. 1993. "Corpus Linguistics and Translation Studies: Implications and Application." In *Text and Technology: In Honour of John Sinclair*, edited by Mona Baker, Gill Francis, and Elena Tognini-Bonelli, 233–250. Amsterdam & Philadelphia: John Benjamins.

Baker, M. 2000. "Towards a Methodology for Investigating the Style of a Literary Translator." *Target* 12(2): 241–266.

Baldry, A. and K. O'Halloran. 2010. "Research into the Annotation of a Multimodal Corpus of University Websites: An Illustration of Multimodal Corpus Linguistics." In *Corpus Linguistics in Language Teaching*, edited by T. Harris, 177–210. Bern: Peter Lang.

Baldry, A. and P. Thibault. 2005. *Multimodal Transcription and Text Analysis*. London: Equinox.

Baloglu, S. and K. W. McCleary. 1999. "A Model of Destination Image Formation." *Annals of Tourism Research* 26(1): 868–897.

Baños, R. 2013. "'That is so Cool': Investigating the Translation of Adverbial Intensifiers in English-Spanish Dubbing through a Parallel Corpus of Sitcoms." *Perspectives: Studies in Translation Theory and Practice* 21(4): 526–542.

Baños, R., S. Bruti, and S. Zanotti. 2013. "Corpus Linguistics and Audiovisual Translation: in Search of an Integrated Approach." *Perspectives: Studies in Translatology* 21(4): 483–490.

Beerli, A. and J. D. Martín. 2004. "Factors Influencing Destination Image." *Annals of Tourism Research* 31(3): 657–681.
Borodo, M. 2015. "Multimodality, Translation and Comics." *Perspectives* 23(1): 22–41. https://doi.org/10.1080/0907676X.2013.876057.
Choi, S., X. Y. Lehto, and A. M. Morrison. 2007. "Destination image representation on the web: Content analysis of Macau travel related websites." *Tourism Management* 28(1): 118–129. https://doi.org/10.1016/j.tourman.2006.03.002.
Gorlée, D. L. 1994. *Semiotics and the Problem of Translation: With Special Reference to the Semiotics of Charles S. Peirce*. Amsterdam: Rodopi.
Gunn, C. A. 1972/1988. *Vacationscape: Designing Tourist Regions*, 2nd ed. Austin, TX: Bureau of Business Research, University of Texas.
Halliday, M. 1973. *Explorations in the Functions of Language*. London: Edward Arnold.
Halliday, M. 1985, 1994, 2000. *An Introduction to Functional Grammar*. London: Edward Arnold.
Halverson, E. R. 2010. "Film as Identity Exploration: A Multimodal Analysis of Youth-Produced Films." *Teachers College Record* 112(9).
Halverson, E. R., M. Bass, and D. Woods. 2012. "The Process of Creation: A Novel Methodology for Analyzing Multimodal Data." *The Qualitative Report* 17(11): 1–27.
Hanlan, J. and S. Kelly. 2005. "Image Formation, Information Sources and an Iconic Australian Tourist Destination." *Journal of Vacation Marketing* 11(2): 163–177.
Jakobson, R. 1956/1966/2004. "On Linguistic Aspects of Translation." In *The Translation Studies Reader*, edited by L. Venuti. London & New York: Routledge.
Jimenez Hurtado, C., and S. Soler Gallego. 2013. "Multimodality, Translation and Accessibility: A Corpus-based Study of Audio Description." *Perspectives: Studies in Translatology* 21(3): 577–594.
Ketola, A. 2018. *Word-image Interaction in Technical Translation: Students Translating an Illustrated Text*. Acta Universitatis Tamperensis 2364. Tampere: Tampere University Press.
Kress, G. and T. van Leeuwen. 1996/2006. *Reading Images: The Grammar of Visual Design*, 2nd ed. London & New York: Routledge.
Kress, G. and T. van Leeuwen. 2001. *Multimodal Discourse: The Modes and Media of Contemporary Communication*. London: Arnold.
Laviosa, S. 1996. *The English Comparable Corpus (ECC): A Resources and a Methodology for the Empirical Study of Translation*. Manchester: The University of Manchester.
Laviosa, S. 2002. *Corpus-based Translation Studies: Theory, Findings, Application*. Amsterdam: Rodopi.
Li, Y. M. 2014. "Effects of Story Marketing and Travel Involvement on Tourist Behavioural Intention in the Tourism Industry." *Sustainability* 6(12): 9378–9397.
Ly, T. H. and C. K. Jung. 2015. "Multimodal Discourse: A Visual Design Analysis of Two Advertising Images." *International Journal of Contents* 11(2): 50–56.
Macao Government Tourism Office. 2017a. "Macao Light Festival 2017." *YouTube*. Available from www.youtube.com/watch?v=ZmWy__c-mH8
Macao Government Tourism Office. 2017b. "2nd International Film Festival & Awards. Macao." *YouTube*. Available from www.youtube.com/watch?v=Q7IG-bEpkqw
Macao Government Tourism Office. 2018a. "3rd International Film Festival & Awards. Macao." *YouTube*. Available from www.youtube.com/watch?v=Ex38M1KDKCE
Macao Government Tourism Office. 2018b. "Macao Light Festival 2018." *YouTube*. Available from www.youtube.com/watch?v=ZmWy__c-mH8

Mercille, J. 2005. "Media Effects on Image: The Case of Tibet." *Annals of Tourism Research* 32(4): 1039–1055.

O'Sullivan, C. 2013. "Introduction: Multimodality as Challenge and Resource for Translation." *The Journal of Specialized Translation* 20: 2–14.

Pérez-González, L. 2007. "Intervention in New Amateur Subtitling Cultures: A Multimodal Account." *Linguistica Antverpiensia* 6: 67–80.

Rose, T. L. 2012. "Digital Media Storis through Multimodal Analysis: A Case Study of Erahoneybee's Song about a Child Welfare Agency." *Journal of Technology in Human Services* 30(3–4): 299–311. https://doi.org/10.1080/15228835.2012.745356.

Salway, A. 2007. "A Corpus-based Analysis of Audio Description." In *Media for All: Subtitling for the Deaf, Audio Description and Sign Language*, edited by J. Díaz-Cintas, P. Orero, and A. Remael, 151–174. Amsterdam & New York: Rodopi.

Salway, A. and M. Graham. 2003. "Extracting Information about Emotions in Films." Proceedings of the Eleventh ACM Conference on Multimedia.

Stern, E., and S. Krakover. 1993. "The Foundation of a Composite Urban Image." *Geographical Analysis* 25(2): 130–146.

Sturrock, J. 1991. "On Jakobson on Translation." In *On Jakobson and Translation*, edited by Thomas A. Sebeok and Jean Umiker-Sebeok. Berlin & New York: Mouton de Gruyter.

Tapachai, N. and R. Waryszak. 2000. "An Examination of the Role of Beneficial Image in Tourist Destination Selection." *Journal of Travel Research* 39(1): 37–44.

Tuominen, T., C. Jiménez Hurtado, and A. Ketola. 2018. "Why Methods Matter: Approaching Multimodality in Translation Research." *Linguistica Antverpiensia, New Series: Themes in Translation Studies* 17: 1–21.

Tymoczko, M. 1998. "Computerized Corpora and the Future of Translation Studies." *Meta: Journal des traducteurs* 43(4). https://doi.org/10.7202/004515ar.

Woodside, A. G., and S. Lysonski. 1989. "A General Model of Traveller Destination Choice." *Journal of Travel Research* 27(1).

Yu, H. and Z. Song. 2016. "Picture–Text Congruence in Translation: Images of the Zen Master on Book Covers and in Verbal Texts." *Social Semiotics* 27(5): 604–623. https://doi.org/10.1080/10350330.2016.1251104.

8 Effects of non-verbal paralanguage capturing on meaning transfer in consecutive interpreting

Ouyang Qianhua (Tasha) and Fu Ai (Ivy)

1 Introduction

Interpreting is a cognitively demanding translational activity taking place in real-time context with the co-presence of speakers, interpreters, and the audience (Kade 1968; Pöchhacker 2016). Interpreters process received information from various channels and then reproduce in near immediacy. Presence in the event and visual access to the communicative parties enable interpreters to leverage different semiotic entities in the reception and reproduction of meaning. Various process models of interpreting thus explicitly recognize multimodal input from either verbal or non-verbal channels as sources of message reception (Kirchhoff 2002; Stenzl 1983; Cokely 1992; Setton 1999). Stenzl's model, for instance, highlights the reception of para- and extra-linguistic input ranging from intonation, facial expressions, and gestures to other visual means. Her model also suggests that interpreters need to process acoustic and visual signs together for an output that can accurately transfer meaning intended by the speaker (ibid., 45).

This coincides with a wide range of intellectual endeavors that address meaning creation from a multimodal perspective. As multimodality "approaches representation, communication and integration as something more than language" (Jewitt 2008, 1), it involves the complex interweaving of textual, aural, linguistic, spatial, and visual resources, which are defined as modes. Meaning is thus orchestrated through a selection and configuration of modes in text, interactions, and events (Jewitt 2009). Existing research has explored the manifold interrelations between different modes (Royce 1999), and the ways in which various modes can offer different aspects in the construction of meaning (Crystal 2001). A special focus has been put on how different types of meaning relations occur across visual and verbal modes (Royce 2002), with the latter accounting for both written and oral language. Goodwin's (2001) work, for example, accounts multimodality as a means to investigate meaning made through actions in oral speech. To sum up, existing literature has proven multimodal approach to meaning-making an important and productive research strand.

As highlighted at the outset, interpreters receive information from multiple channels. Interpreting is thus a multimodal event where meaning is elicited from not only language but also other para- or extra-linguistic resources. However, despite calls to a greater focus on non-verbal resources in interpreting (Wadensjö 2001; Pasquandrea 2011), multimodal research that addresses "non-verbal meaning-making and its impact on the theorization of translation and interpreting remains largely unaddressed" (Pérez-González 2014, 119–120). The limited body of empirical study focuses primarily on dialogue interpreting, for instance, the investigation of gaze in courtroom interpreting (Lang 1978), gaze and gestures in relation to turn organization in therapeutic scenarios (Bot 2005), and Wadensjö's (2001) probe into interpreters' proxemics. Some other notable examples include Mason's examinations (2012) of the intricate relations between body positioning and identities in interpreter-mediated asylum seeker interviews and Davitti's (2012, 2013, 2015) multiple investigations on the role of gaze and body orientations in community settings like the parent-and-teacher meetings.

Given the importance of multimodal resources in meaning-making and motivated by the fruitful multimodal research on dialogue interpreting, this research attempts to extend this research interest into other interpreting modes and settings. Consecutive interpreting, an often-adopted mode in conference interpreting, is investigated in this research. We explored the relationship between the reception of multimodal elements and the quality of meaning transfer in consecutive interpreting. Following the research interest in dialogue interpreting, this research focuses on one specific strand of multimodality in interpreting, that is, speakers' paralanguage, which is defined as the multimodal elements that accompany verbal language and give shades of meaning to what the speakers say. In the context of consecutive interpreting, the most notable paralinguistic resources are facial expressions and gestures.

The research adopts a straightforward dialectical logic. It starts from the intellectual stance of systemic functional linguistics (SFL) that verbal language is only "one among a number of systems of meaning" (Halliday and Hason 1989, 4). This theoretical starting point presumes a general complementarity between the non-verbal and verbal resources used by the speakers in the construing of meaning. Then an ensuing assumption is: interpreters who look at the speakers receive para-linguistic input better and hence may present meaning more accurately in the output. This research substantiates these theoretical assumptions with empirical data collected from a videotaped mock conference. Three research questions explored are as follows: (1) How non-verbal para-linguistic resources complement meaning construed through verbal language in the speaker's speech? (2) Do interpreters who have more frequent eye contact with the speaker during the input stage present meaning more accurately and more completely in their output than those who do not? (3) How does the capturing of non-verbal para-linguistic elements relate to the recapping of meaning in interpreters' output?

It is hoped that this research will contribute to the growing body of empirical and descriptive research on multimodality in interpreting. Research results are discussed in the context of interpreting training as well as professional practices of conference interpreting. We aim at eliciting reflections on how such a research endeavor could shed light on interpreting training and meliorate professional guidelines on conference interpreting.

2 Theoretical background

This section sets out the theoretical background of this research and explains how shades of different theories can correlate together to address the research questions that were proposed in the previous section. This section will be structured as follows. Firstly, the SFL perspective on meaning and vectors of meaning in interpreting activity will be reviewed. Secondly, SFL inspired work on multimodalities, especially Martin and Zappavigna's (2019) social semiotic framework for analyzing paralanguage which underpins the present research, will be introduced. Thirdly, realizations of interpersonal meaning, which is the focus of this research, in the verbal language and non-verbal paralanguage will be systematically explained.

2.1 SFL perspective on meaning

The theoretical underpinning of this research originates from systemic functional linguistics (SFL). Investigation and discussion anchor on SFL's philosophy that language is "social semiotic" and is "a shared meaning potential" construed by various resource systems (Halliday 1978, 1–2). SFL conceptualizes "two main kinds of meaning, the "ideational" and the "interpersonal." They are the "manifestations in the linguistic system of the two very general purposes which underlie all uses of language." The former manifests how we "understand the environment" and the latter embodies how we use language "to act on the others." Combined with these two is a third component, textual meaning, which "breathes relevance into the other two" (Halliday 1994/2000, 39). Owing its existence to anthropologist Bronislaw Malinowski's theory of context, SFL argues that the study of meaning, ideational, interpersonal, and textual alike, should be placed in context. The notion of context or what is "with the text," "goes beyond what is said and written" to include "other non-verbal going-on – the total environment in which a text unfolds" (Halliday and Hasan 1989, 5).

Defined in this light, context is omnipresent in all language activities. Yet, not surprisingly, interpreting research proposes a particular relevance of context to the activity of interpreting (Hatim and Mason 1990/2002; Pym 2008; Baker 2006; Eraslan 2008; McKee and Davis 2010). Setton and Dawrant, for example, argue that interpreters must take advantage of "more direct experience of the context" since the evanescent nature of interpreting only give them "fleeting access to the discourse" (2016, 6). Contextual elements accompanying verbal texts in interpreting take on many forms, ranging from the broader cultural and situational environment to texts and paralanguage that goes with instances of verbal text production. This research scrutinizes the closest element that is "with" the verbal text in speech delivery, that is, the para-linguistic resources employed by the speaker. They have been recognized as integral parts of human social interaction as well as important vectors of meaning (Goodwin 1981; Kendon 1990; Rossano 2013). They can create additional meaning beyond words or accentuate meaning.

2.2 SFL inspired multimodal research

Different paradigms of discourse analysis, conversation analysis, pragmatics, and SFL alike have increasingly recognized the need to more formally integrate multimodal elements into their analytical methods. As one of the mainstream approaches, SFL has seen an explosion of academic work on modalities other than language. Relevant work includes "grammars" of specific modes such as visual images (Kress and van Leeuwen 2006; O'Toole 1994), body action (Martinec 2000, 2001), music (van Leeuwen 1999), and film (Bateman and Schmidt 2012). The essential message here is that modes other than language also work together to communicate a message. Alongside these, the literature is extended to analyzing the integration of different modes in multimodal texts (Bateman 2008; van Leeuwen 2005) and intermodal relations (Liu and O'Halloran 2009; Martinec 2005; Royce 1998; Unsworth and Cléirigh 2009), and their applications in education (Jewitt 2006; Kress 2003) and public as well as media discourse (Bednarek and Caple 2012; Knox 2007).

On a micro level, SFL has also been developed to the study of paralanguage such as gestures and phonology (Zappavigna, Cléirigh, Dwyer, and Martin 2010), which suggests ready applicability to interpreting research. A particular source of inspiration for the present research has been Martin and Zappavigna's (2019) social semiotic framework for analyzing paralanguage. Similar to the textual analysis in SFL, this framework deals with paralanguage also from the three metafunctions of ideational, interpersonal, and textual meaning. In analyzing the manifold intermodal relations among language, paralanguage, and other modalities, this framework draws a clear distinction between non-semiotic behaviour (somasis) and meaning (semiosis). Semiosis is then divided into language and paralanguage. In this framework, the term paralanguage refers to semiosis dependent on language and realized through both sound quality and body language, the latter includes facial expression, gesture, posture, and movement (ibid., 3). Within paralanguage, sonovergent and semovergent resources are identified. The former represents paralanguage that is "in sync with or in tune with the prosodic phonology of spoken language" (ibid., 1), while the latter represents paralanguage that is convergent with the lexico-grammar and discourse semantics of the spoken language, or resources that "support the ideational, interpersonal and textual meaning resources of spoken language's content plane" (ibid., 1). More specifically, ideational paralanguage is "mimetic," concurring with ideation and connection systems; interpersonal paralanguage is "expressive," resonating with negotiation and appraisal systems; and textual body language is "deictic," syncing with identification and periodicity systems (ibid., 11).

2.3 Interpersonal meaning

We reviewed at the beginning of this section that SFL perceives three strands of meaning. Regarding the exploratory nature of this research and restricting it to a manageable scope, we focus on interpersonal meaning in the analysis. This strand of meaning is named interpersonal, as it reflects how the "interaction" and "transaction" between speakers and listeners are going on (Halliday 1994, 34). Realizations of interpersonal meaning in the verbal language include lexico-grammatical resources of mood and modality and semantic resources of appraisal. Mood is the "subject" and "finite" combination in a clause. Subject is interpersonal as it is "something by reference to which the proposition can be affirmed or denied." Finite is interpersonal in two ways: first, finite modal operator (may, can, would, etc.) relates to "the speaker's judgment of the probabilities, or the obligations, involved in what he is saying"; second, polarity, the "choice between positive and negative," makes a clause arguable between the speaker and the listener (ibid., 75–76). Modality, on the other hand, shows the attitude of the speaker and is carried by modal adjuncts (certainly, probably, usually, etc). Speaker's attitude is also reflected by the semantic system of appraisal, which is an extension and development of SFL by James Martin and Peter White (Martin 1992; Martin and White 2005). There are three semantic categories of appraisal: ATTITUDE, GRADUATION, and ENGAGEMENT. ATTITUDE relates to ways of feeling in three dimensions: affect, appreciation, and judgment. Affect relates to emotions like happiness, sadness, and pain; appreciation relates to the aesthetic quality of entities; judgment relates to the moral evaluation of good and bad. GRADUATION concerns with the gradable interpersonal force of discourse. ENGAGEMENT is the degree of the arguability of what the speaker is saying (Martin and White 2005).

Non-verbal paralanguage, on the other hand, enacts emotion or makes attitudes in a more implicit or subtle way. Under Martin and Zappavigna's framework, realizations of interpersonal meaning in paralanguage include facial expressions, bodily stance, muscle tension, hand/arm position and motion (Hood 2011; Ngo 2018), and voice quality. These combined face and body commitments potentially resonate with verbal speech to express attitudes or inscribe qualities.

3 Method

3.1 Analytical framework

The analytical framework of this research draws on SFL (Halliday 1994; Halliday and Matthiessen 2004) and the Appraisal Theory to analyze interpersonal meaning in the verbal text and the social semiotic analysis model (Martin and Zappavigna 2019) to study the speaker's paralanguage that carries interpersonal meaning.

Multimodality attends to all the resources of communication and representation that people use to express themselves and make meaning, such as images, videos, facial expressions, gestures, posture, gaze, and even the interactions between them. Nonetheless, when multiple resources display themselves simultaneously, the immediacy in interpreting activities, coupled with the invisible cognitive load on interpreters, makes it very difficult to fully observe and understand the effect of individual resources on the interpreters' output. Therefore, in the present research, which is situated in a consecutive interpreting context, the focus is narrowed down to facial expressions and gestures of interpersonal paralanguage. Although prosodic features also carry interpersonal meaning, this research assumes an unbiased reception of prosodic features as they are embedded in the auditory channel, the essential source of information reception for interpreters. In the present research, reception or non-reception of para-linguistic resources is operationalized by interpreters' choices of looking or not looking at the speaker during the input stage of consecutive interpreting. The correlation between the non-reception of para-linguistic resources and the loss of meaning in interpreters' reproduction is explored through intertextual interpreting quality assessment.

Data of the research was collected in an interpreted mock conference. Treating of the collected data starts with the analysis of interpersonal meaning in the verbal speech and the social semiotic analysis of the speaker's paralanguage. Following the tradition of SFL, both verbal and para-lingual analyses are carried out primarily at the clause level. For the analysis of verbal speech, instantiations of interpersonal resources examined are (1) Subject and Finite combination that realizes the speech function of question; 2) Subject choices with interactive orientation, e.g. "you" and "I"; 3) Modality, including modal verbs and modal adjuncts; and 4) words of Appraisal. This categorization of interpersonal resources aims not at inclusivity but its applicability to textual analysis for interpreting quality assessment (Ouyang 2018). Instantiations of the interpersonal meaning are tagged at the clause level and counted. The interpersonal meaning profile of each segment is also presented based on these instantiations. Segments in consecutive interpreting are treated as independent texts because of length, meaning autonomy, and structural completeness (Hatim and Mason 2002; Gile 2004). In this sense, the interpersonal meaning profile of each segment captures the speaker's intended interaction and transaction at the discourse level.

For the analysis of paralanguage, though a non-discriminating approach is taken to tag both sonovergent and semovergent para-linguistic resources, the primary focus is on the specific strand of interpersonal semovergent paralanguage. Therefore, sonovergent paralanguage such as hands or head beating in sync with the periodicity of speech, ideational semovergent paralanguage such as hand shapes concurring with entities, and textual sonovergent paralanguage are excluded from this analysis. Interpersonal resources examined are those used by the speaker to share attitudes, grade qualities and position voices other than the speaker's own (Appraisal) (Martin and Zappavigna 2019), such as facial expressions, bodily stance, muscle tension, and hand/arm position and motion (Hood 2011; Ngo 2018), but a special focus is on facial expressions and gestures. Subsequently, the interpersonal implications of these resources are specified. For example, lopsided mouth expression may indicate the speaker's negative attitude.

These two tracks of analyses are then aligned for locating instances of multimodal complementarity, that is, when interpersonal resources in the verbal speech and the interpersonal paralanguage displayed by the speaker are observed at a clause concurrently, there is a relationship of complementarity. Research question 1 is supposed to be answered at this stage. For speech stretches where meaning in verbal and non-verbal modes converges, interpreters' choices of looking or not looking at the speaker are counted and categorized into three different frequency groups: high frequency group, medium frequency group, and low frequency group. Student interpreters' verbal output is then assessed against the source speech in terms of interpersonal meaning transfer. The meaning transfer quality of the different frequency groups is compared to answer research questions 2 and 3.

3.2 Data collection

To answer the proposed research questions and attest to the theoretical assumptions, a mock conference was organized and videotaped. This section is to describe the details of the empirical data gathered from it.

3.2.1 Overview

The materials collected for analysis are from an authentic mock conference that took place in a full-function interpreting lab. The mock conference lasted for about 30 minutes. One speaker was giving a monologic speech in a round-table multimedia classroom. The speaker stood inside the round table and nine student interpreters sat right in front of him in a semicircle, having full visual access to the speaker. Three stand cameras were placed to video-record the performances of both the speaker and the nine interpreters in the encounter. The output of the nine interpreters was also recorded individually by the built-in recording devices on their tables. The interpreters worked in a consecutive mode, where the speaker paused at the end of a complete thought to allow the interpreters time to step up and deliver the same speech in the target language.

3.2.2 Participants

Among the ten participants, the speaker is a native English speaker from the United States. He has years of experience in public speaking and a keen interest in environmental protection, especially plastic pollution. The nine student interpreters are selected from senior classes of the MTI (master of translation and interpreting) program in a university of Guangdong province in China, with Chinese as their A language and English their B language. By the time the mock conference was organized, the nine interpreters had all passed CATTI 2 (China Accreditation Test for Translators and Interpreters), which suggests that they are comparable in terms of interpreting skills and competence. All subjects have also provided liaison and consecutive interpreting services on several occasions and thus are evaluated as ready-for-the-market interpreters. Subjects were coded according to their seat numbers in the interpreting lab.

3.2.3 Material

The material is a speech on plastic pollution. In the mock conference, the speaker shared his thoughts on this particular issue through stories and interactive scenarios. The speech lasted for about 12 minutes, delivered at a rate of 130 words/

min, and was divided into six 2-minute segments. Generally speaking, the material largely resembles average segment length, speed, and manner of delivery of speeches in real-life consecutive interpreting scenarios.

3.2.4 Transcribing and tagging

After the mock conference, the speaker's verbal speech and the nine interpreters' output were transcribed automatically by a speech recognition app and then proofread by the authors. Alongside the speaker's verbal speech, the speaker's paralanguage, such as gestures and facial expressions, gaze, and bodily stance, was tagged manually clause by clause. Apart from the interpreters' verbal output, their choices of looking at the speaker at the input stage were also tagged manually. It should be noted that although a non-discriminating tagging approach was taken, the focus for analysis was still facial expressions and gestures.

4 Analysis

4.1 Quantitative analysis

The quantitative analysis focuses on clause-level results. Based on the tagging of interpreters' gaze and the tagged instantiations of interpersonal meaning realization in both the source speech and the speaker's paralanguage, three sets of data are presented. The presentation of quantitative data in this section does not aim at any statistical significance. What we strive to do is portray a bigger picture so that the qualitative results can be better understood in a context.

- Number and percentage of multimodal complementarity. The source speech has 119 process-carrying clauses. Selected types of interpersonal resources (see section 3.1) stretch over 80 clauses, among which 66 are complemented by the speaker's interpersonal paralanguage, presenting 83% of multimodal complementarity at the clause level.
- Numbers of short gaze of interpreters from different frequency groups. All the nine interpreters' short gazes at the speaker are counted and they are categorized into three frequency groups (Table 8.1). Three interpreters, who looked at the speaker more than 100 times, are categorized into the high frequency group. Four interpreters, who looked at the speaker for fewer than 50 times, are categorized into the low frequency group. The rest of the subjects are categorized into the medium frequency group. One interpreter is randomly selected from each group. The selected high-frequency subject (HFS) looked at the speaker for 117 times, the medium-frequency subject (MFS) 68 times, and the low-frequency subject (LFS) only once. The numbers of short gaze from HSF, MFS, and LFS when multimodal complementarity was observed are 71, 39, and 1, respectively (Table 8.2).

- A comparison of interpreters' performance in terms of recapped instantiations of interpersonal meaning (Table 8.3). Notwithstanding a fairly complete and accurate rendition of the ideational meaning, the student interpreters' performance at transferring interpersonal meaning varied. To recap, 120 interpersonal meaning instantiations were observed in the verbal speech. HFS recapped 58 instantiations (48%), followed by MFS 36 (30%) and LFS 40 (32%), a difference of 18% and 16%, although LFS somehow outperformed MFS by a small vantage. However, the situation was complicated by the interpreters' choices of looking or not looking at the speaker at interpersonal meaning-laden clauses. Even when the interpreters looked at the speaker, results differed depending on whether multimodal complementarity was achieved. When there was multimodal complementarity, HFS recapped 38 out of the 58 (66%) interpersonal meaning instantiations, followed by MFS 36% and LFS 0%. A note should be given here that as LFS only looked at the speaker once, this figure 0% should thus be deemed as of no statistical significance. But still, an even wider gap of 30% was noticed between HFS and MFS in the interpersonal meaning transfer.

Table 8.1 Interpreters' gaze and the resulted grouping

Interpreter	Instances of short gaze at the speaker	Grouping
A5	101	High frequency
A6	110	High frequency
A7 (LFS)	1	Low frequency
A8	42	Low frequency
A9	31	Low frequency
B7 (HFS)	117	High frequency
B8	75	Medium frequency
B9	3	Low frequency
B10 (MFS)	68	Medium frequency

Table 8.2 Short gaze of three selected interpreters of different frequency groups

	Gazes at clauses with multimodal complementarity	Gazes at clauses without multimodal complementarity	Total
HFS	71 (61%)	46 (39%)	117
MFS	39 (57%)	29 (43%)	68
LFS	1 (100%)	0 (0%)	1

Table 8.3 Recapped instantiations of interpersonal meaning

	Total (/120)	Looking at the speaker		Not looking at the speaker
		Clauses with multimodal complementarity	Clauses without multimodal complementarity	
HFS	58 (48%)	38/58 (66%)	9/58 (16%)	11/58 (19%)
MFS	36 (30%)	13/36 (36%)	3/36 (8%)	20/36 (56%)
LFS	40 (32%)	0/40 (0%)	0/40 (0%)	40/40 (100%)

4.2 Qualitative analysis

As introduced in the previous section that the speech is primarily an exposition on plastic pollution, the speaker expressed his attitude on this particular issue through stories and interactive scenarios that appeal to the audience's emotion and judgment. This effort weaved through his speech and resulted in a more or less balanced utilization of ideational and interpersonal resources across segments.

We chose segment 1 and segment 4 as Case 1 and Case 2 for qualitative analysis. These two cases epitomize the speaker's effort to interact and embed his attitude in informative exposition. The qualitative analysis incorporates both discourse-level and clause-level assessment of interpersonal meaning transfer. It starts by comparing the discourse-level interpersonal meaning profile of the source text and the interpreters' output. Then it delves into clause-level intertextual analysis for a detailed account of how the reception of paralanguage may influence the transfer of interpersonal meaning.

CASE 1

In Case 1, the speaker used an imagined scenario to involve the audience and introduce his topic. Following are the transcript and discourse-level interpersonal meaning profile of the source text:

> *ST*: Have you ever found yourself sat on the beach, staring off into the horizon, and wondering just how far the vast ocean stretches, then only to be distracted by the hot sun beating down on your skin which has caused a small bead of sweat to come trickling down your face? What did you do? Chances are you probably did the same as what I've always done– which is to reach over into the cooler box, grab a nice bottle of some chilled drink, to sip on and cool you down. Cooled off a bit, you probably return to your carefree, relaxed state. If it wasn't for that bottle of Sprite, Fanta, or the classic Coca-Cola, you probably would have left that beautiful beach and gone off to some confined space to escape the heat. Thank goodness for cooler boxes and plastic bottles, right? Well, let me tell you something about plastic bottles.

Interpersonal meaning profile

1. The primary function is to interact. There are three instances of questions, six instances of "you" and "I" as Subjects.
2. The speaker invited the audience to an imagined scenario that contrasts the unpleasant feeling caused by the heat on a beach and the positive feeling of drinking a bottled drink. Semantic resources representing the two contrasting feelings weaved through the text.
3. The speaker also invited empathy without over-assertiveness as manifested by medium/low-probability modality resources in clauses with "you" as the subject.

Transcripts and discourse-level assessment of the interpreters' output from the high, medium, and low frequency groups are as follows (Table 8.4).

The discourse level assessment is backed by the clause-level analysis. Table 8.5 lists the speech function, modality and appraisal resources to show the clause-level analysis of interpersonal meaning in segment 1. It shows that semantic resources expressing the two contrasting feelings of discomfort and comfort demonstrate a high level of consistency.

Table 8.4 Transcripts and discourse assessment of the three interpreters' output in case 1

Interpreter	Target text	Discourse-level assessment
HFS	你曾经有过这样的经历吗？你是否在海滩上望着海岸线，想象广阔的海洋到底有多远？但突然这个时候，太阳越来越大，汗水从你的脸颊上流下来，这个时候你会怎么做呢？也许你会选择和我一样，从一个盒子中拿出一瓶饮料来给自己解暑降温。喝完饮料以后，你就在可以继续享受这美好的一天了。如果说没有这瓶饮料的话，你可能就会当即离开海滩，到一个比较密闭的空间里去防暑降温。所以一瓶饮料还是挺重要的。今天我想谈一谈塑料瓶的问题。	1. Speech function of question was mostly recapped and interactive subject choices were recapped. 2. Negative feeling caused by the heat was partly recapped; positive feeling of drinking bottled drink was recapped. 3. Probability level kept.
MFS	你曾经有过这样的经历吗？当你坐在沙滩上，望着远处的天边，想像这一切的场景都非常美，但是这个时候你就会被太阳打扰了。因为太阳很热，打在你的身上，你不停地流汗，你可能会到冰柜里拿一瓶冷饮，比方说可口乐或者雪碧。然后喝了之后，你就能够恢复你原来的放松的状态。如果没有这些冷饮的话，你有可能会离开沙滩，然后去到一些有空调的地方去。那么现在我想跟大家说一说塑料瓶。	1. Speech function of question was mostly recapped and interactive subject choices were mostly recapped. 2. Negative feeling caused by the heat was partly recapped; positive feeling of drinking bottled drink was partly recapped. 3. Probability level kept.

Effects of non-verbal paralanguage 203

Interpreter	Target text	Discourse-level assessment
LFS	大家有没有曾经在海滩上坐着望向远方的地平线，然后想着一些事情的精力。但是你却因为太阳照射在你的脸上分心了，你的脸上一直在流汗。大家在沙滩上往往都会有这种经历，那你会怎么办？你可能会跟我一样，从冷饮箱中拿出一瓶冷冻饮料，可能是芬达、雪碧，或是可口可乐。喝瓶饮料能够让你迅速冷静下来。如果你没有这些饮料，可能就会回去室内逃避沙滩上的热浪。当然，这些饮料是装在塑料瓶中的，我今天来讲一下塑料瓶。	1. Speech function of question was partly recapped and interactive subject choices were mostly recapped. 2. Negative feeling caused by the heat was partly recapped; positive feeling of drinking bottled drink was not recapped. 3. Probability level kept.

Table 8.5 Clause-level realizations of the interpersonal meaning in case 1

Clause	Speech function	Modality			Appraisal		
		Resource	Type	Value	Resource	Type	Value
1 have you ever found yourself...	question	ever	Probability	low	N/A		
4 then only to be distracted by the hot sun beating down on your skin		only	Probability	high	distract hot beat down	affect affect affect	negative negative negative
5 what did you do	question	N/A			N/A		
8 you probably did the same as	statement	probably	Probability	medium	N/A		
9 what I've always done		always	Probability	high	N/A		
11 grab a nice bottle of some chilled drink to sip on and cool you down	statement	N/A			nice cool down	judgment affect	positive positive
12 cooled off a bit you probably return to your carefree relaxed state	statement	probably	Probability	medium	cooled off carefree relaxed	affect affect affect	positive positive positive

(*Continued*)

Table 8.5 (Continued)

Clause	Speech function	Modality			Appraisal		
		Resource	Type	Value	Resource	Type	Value
14 you probably would have left that beautiful beach	statement	probably would	Probability Probability	medium low	beautiful	appreciation	positive
15 and gone off to some confined space to escape the heat	statement	N/A			confined escape	affect affect	negative negative

We then picked up three clauses (clauses 4, 12 and 15) from segment 1 to analyze the speaker's paralanguage. Screenshots (Figures 8.1–8.6) and their corresponding description are provided.

Clause 4: then only to be distracted by the hot sun beating down on your skin
Description: By leaning backward and holding his hand upright, with the back of his palm facing inwards, the speaker showed his resistance attitude (see Figure 8.1). The speaker slightly frowned and pull down his lips, indicating his negative attitude (see Figure 8.2).

Clause 12: cooled off a bit you probably return to your carefree, relaxed state
Description: Corners of the lips were drawn back and up. The mouth was parted and teeth exposed (see Figure 8.3). These, coupled with relaxing and expressive hand gestures, proved him in a relaxed state (see Figure 8.4).

Figure 8.1 Paralanguage at clause 4–1

Figure 8.2 Paralanguage at clause 4–2

Clause 15: and gone off to some confined space to escape the heat
Description: The speaker frowned, looking downward (see Figure 8.5) and then upward. His lips were pressed firmly together, with corners down, showing that he was upset (see Figure 8.6).

As observed, the speaker used facial expressions such as frowning, pulling down lips and pressing lips firmly together, gestures such as leaning backwards and the "stop" sign to show the unpleasant feeling caused by the heat. His positive feeling, on the contrary, was made evident through smiling expressions and relaxing hand gestures. Apart from the three chosen clauses, most instantiations of interpersonal meaning in Case 1 are complemented by the speaker's paralanguage.

Three interpreters attend to this multimodal complementarity differently since they looked at the speaker at different frequencies. We now look at how the capturing of non-verbal para-linguistic elements may relate to the transfer of interpersonal meaning. As discourse-level assessment has shown comparable performance

Figure 8.3 Paralanguage at clause 12–1   *Figure 8.4* Paralanguage at clause 12–2

Figure 8.5 Paralanguage at clause 15–1   *Figure 8.6* Paralanguage at clause 15–2

Table 8.6 Interpreters' recapping of appraisal resources in case 1

Clause	Type of attitude	ST resources	Resource recapped by HFS	Resource recapped by MFS	Resource recapped by LFS
4–5	negative affect	hot distract beat down	越来越大 (more and more fierce)	很热 (very hot)	分心 (distracted)
7–12	positive affect	cool down carefree relaxed	解暑降温 (relieve the heat and cool down) 享受 (enjoy) 美好 (nice)	放松 (relaxed)	none
13–16	negative affect	confined escape	密闭 (confined) 防暑 (escape the heat)	none	逃避 (escape)

of the three interpreters in terms of recapping the speech functions, interactive Subject choices, and modality words, clause-level assessment zooms in on the recapping of appraisal resources to explore the relation between capturing of paralanguage and transfer of interpersonal meaning.

Table 8.6 shows that HFS partly recapped the uncomfortable feeling caused by the "more fierce" sun, well delivered the comfort of drinking something cool using words like "relieve," "cool down," and "enjoy." He also fairly appraised the not so comfortable alternative of going to a "confined" room to "escape the heat." These evidences substantiate our discourse-level assessment that "negative feeling caused by the heat partly recapped" and "a positive feeling of drinking bottled drink mostly recapped." MFS and LFS, on the other hand, left out more appraisal resources as compared to HFS. For instance, MFS's output lost the negative affect of the uncomfortable alternative of going to a room, and LFS did not recap the physiological comfort brought by a cool drink. For the latter, the only appraisal resource used was the phrase "冷静下来" (calm down). Yet "calm down" refers to one's mental state and cannot be regarded as the equivalent to the positive affect or physical pleasure of "cool(ing) down" in the ST.

A rough correlation between gaze and interpersonal meaning delivery can be observed in this case. HFS, who looked at the speaker 21 times throughout segment 1, recapped the interpersonal meaning more adequately as compared to MFS and LFS, whose numbers of short gaze are 13 and 0, respectively. The correlation will be further discussed at the end of this section where more data is presented from the analysis of segment 4 in Case 2.

CASE 2

In Case 2 (i.e. segment 4 of the speech), the speaker mainly talked about actions taken by different stakeholders to tackle plastic pollution. Yet, tactful as the speaker was, he started with a story to contextualize the actions being taken and ended with

Effects of non-verbal paralanguage 207

an imaginary debate to involve the audience. Following are the transcript and interpersonal meaning profile of the source speech:

> *ST*: (part 1) For example, on a surfing trip to Bali, Andrew Cooper and Alex Schulze were absolutely mortified seeing the amount of trash that accumulated among the coastlines. They recalled, one evening in particular, when they stumbled an old fishing village where they saw fishermen struggling to pull their boats through heaps of garbage that had amassed on the water as they were trying to haul their boats to shore. For Andrew and Alex, the sight of this devastated coastline crossed their bottom-line. (part 2) So, they started a company, which operates by collecting garbage and plastic waste from the oceans and coastal areas, and converts that plastic into limited edition bracelets, which then goes on to sell them. They are helping. And along with Andrew and Alex, other concerned individuals, charities, NGOs, and Nations are all rallying to reduce this plastic problem. Some governments are even passing legislation to entirely limit the amount of single-use plastics that are available, right down to fining businesses for providing plastic straws to customers. This issue is even on the discussion table, as we speak, at the UN level, where they are trying to ratify an international treaty to significantly reduce the amount of plastic found in the world's oceans. (part 3) With all this work that is going to eliminate the proliferating plastic issue, one may argue that the plastic problem is getting smaller. I say there is a subtle irony in the phrase, "the plastic problem is getting smaller" because that can have bigger problems associated with it.

Interpersonal meaning profile

The primary function is to represent. But the facts are presented with the speaker's opinions. Based on the change of the speaker's attitude, the segment can be divided into three parts.

Part 1 highlights negative emotion embedded in an individual encounter, which is realized by semantic resources of negative judgment and affect.

Part 2 describes efforts being made and actions being taken where five instances of accentuated interpersonal force are found.

Part 3 ends the segment with a personal opinion disguised in an imaginary debate where the speaker tactfully toned down assertiveness with modality resources of low to medium probability.

Initial assessment of the output sees a more varied performance of the interpreters in part 1 of segment 4. Part 1 is hence selected to illustrate the discourse and clause-level assessment. The transcripts and assessment of the interpreters' output from the three groups at the discourse level are given in Table 8.7.

Table 8.8 lists the clause-level realizations of the interpersonal meaning in part 1. It can be observed that interpersonal meaning resources in this part all point to the negative attitude of the speaker. Examples include the negative feeling (affect)

208　*Ouyang Qianhua (Tasha) and Fu Ai (Ivy)*

Table 8.7 Discourse assessment of the three interpreters' output in part 1 of case 2

Interpreter	Target text	Discourse-level assessment
HFS	有两个人有一次在一个地方冲浪，他们被海洋里边的垃圾吓到了。他们也去到了附近的一个渔村，他们发现了渔村里的渔民基本上不可能把这个船从水里边拉上来，因为水里边的垃圾太多了，这些对他们来说是难以接受的。	Negative attitude embedded in the story was generally recapped.
MFS	曾经就有公司在一个小渔村进行垃圾的收集。他们从水上收集了很多的塑料瓶子。	Negative attitude embedded in the story was lost.
LFS	举个例子，Andrew和Alex他们两个人就在海岸线上收集垃圾，他们有一天晚上在小渔村中，他们打算把自己的小船拖回岸上，但是他们发现当地的海岸线有诸多的垃圾，所以很难把自己的小船拽回海岸线上。因此Andrew和Alex他们非常愤怒。	Negative attitude embedded in the story was mostly lost.

Table 8.8 Clause-level realizations of the interpersonal meaning in part 1 of case 2

Clause	Modality			Appraisal		
	Resource	Type	Value	Resource	Type	Value
42 for example, on a surfing trip to Bali, Andrew Cooper and Alex Schulze were absolutely mortified seeing the amount of trash ...	absolutely	Probability	high	mortified	affect	negative

Effects of non-verbal paralanguage 209

Clause	Modality			Appraisal		
	Resource	Type	Value	Resource	Type	Value
45 when they stumbled an old fishing village	N/A			stumble	affect	negative
46 where they saw fishermen struggling to pull their boats through heaps of garbage	N/A			struggle heaps of garbage	affect appreciation	negative negative
47 that had amassed on the water . . .	N/A			amassed on water	appreciation	negative
49 for Andrew and Alex, the sight of this devastated coastline crossed their bottom-line	N/A			devastated crossed bottom-line	judgment judgment	negative negative

of "stumbling" into and being "mortified" by the scene of pollution in a village, as emphasized by the high-probability modal adjunct "absolutely"; the negative appreciation embedded in the description of "heaps of garbage . . . amassed on water"; and negative social and moral judgment on the scale of pollution ("devastating") and crossing personal "bottom-line."

All instantiations of interpersonal meaning in this part are complemented by the speaker's paralanguage. Screenshots of the speaker's paralanguage at selected clauses (clauses 42 and 49) are provided (Figures 8.7–8.10) and described.

Clause 42: for example, on a surfing trip to Bali, Andrew Cooper and Alex Schulze were absolutely mortified seeing the amount of trash

Description: The speaker frowned, shook his head, and looked downward (see Figure 8.7). His lips were pressed firmly together, with corners down, indicating his frustration (see Figure 8.8).

210 *Ouyang Qianhua (Tasha) and Fu Ai (Ivy)*

Figure 8.7 Paralanguage at clause 42–1   *Figure 8.8* Paralanguage at clause 42–2

Figure 8.9 Paralanguage at clause 49–1   *Figure 8.10* Paralanguage at clause 49–2

Clause 49: for Andrew and Alex, the sight of this devastated coastline crossed their bottom-line

Description: The speaker's lips were pressed firmly together, with corners down (see Figure 8.9). He first reached out his hand with palm down, then pointed his finger down, showing his frustration (see Figure 8.10).

As is shown above, the speaker's negative facial expressions such as frowning, pressing lips firmly together and gestures such as shaking head and pointing fingers down are consistent with his verbal language of "being mortified," "devastated," and "crossed their bottom-line."

Clause-level assessment of chosen interpreters' output was again conducted. Table 8.9 presents their recapping of the interpersonal meaning resource chain. HFS recapped the young man's feeling of being "mortified," described the scene of pollution as "overwhelming" and the scale of pollution "hardly acceptable."

Effects of non-verbal paralanguage 211

Table 8.9 Interpreters' recapping of appraisal resources in part 1 of case 2

Clause	Type of attitude	ST resources	Resource recapped by HFS	Resource recapped by MFS	Resource recapped by LFS
42 + 45 + 46	negative affect	absolutely, mortified, stumble, struggle	吓到了 (mortified)	none	none
46+47	negative appreciation	heaps of garbage, amassed on water	水里…垃圾太多了 (in water … garbage overwhelming)	none	none
49	negative judgment	devastated, crossed bottom-line	难以接受 (hardly acceptable)	none	愤怒 (angry)

This substantiates our discourse-level assessment that "negative attitude embedded in the story of part one was generally recapped" by HFS. LFS, on the other hand, only recapped the social/moral judgment of the scale of pollution to the feeling of the two young men, saying that they were "very angry."

MFS lost the whole chain of interpersonal meaning resources and his performance deserves more discussion here. One may argue that the loss of interpersonal meaning in MFS's output can be a result of the substantial deviations in terms of the ideational meaning. Yet this research holds the view of SFL (see section 2.1) that interpersonal and ideational meaning should be analyzed separately as they fulfill different functions. For instance, if we keep the ideational meaning of the MFS's output unchanged, interpersonal resources can still be mobilized to make whatever world experience being represented as "unpleasant." Mobilization of the interpersonal resources can be triggered by verbal or paralanguage alike. And if this would be the case, MFS's output would deviate from the ST only in the ideational, but not the interpersonal strand.

Throughout part 1 of Case 2, HFS looked at the speaker for 13 times, MFS looked at the speaker 4 times, and LFS did not look at the speaker at all. In addition, throughout Case 2, the numbers of short gaze are 30, 8, and 0 for HFS, MFS, and LFS, respectively. If we put together the gaze data in Case 1, the numbers of short gaze for HFS, MFS, and LFS are 50, 21, and 0, respectively.

Analysis so far indicates that a general positive correlation does exist between the capturing of paralanguage and the recapping of interpersonal meaning in the two cases. In these two cases, HFS recapped 82% of interpersonal meaning instantiations when he looked at the speaker and multimodal complementarity was achieved, followed by MFS 33% and LFS 0%.

To sum up, from the rough counting in Case 1 and 2, and also from the general statistical results presented in the quantitative analysis subsection, it seems that HFS – the one who looked at the speaker rather frequently – did recap interpersonal meaning more completely and accurately. But our data, as examined within the analytical framework and theoretical perspective proposed by this research, cannot explain why MFS did not outperform LFS in general and in these two particular cases.

5 Discussion

This chapter aims at exploring the relation between the capturing of non-verbal paralanguage and the quality of meaning transfer in consecutive interpreting. An innovative aspect of this research is that it broadens the scope for multimodal research in interpreting by zooming into an under-researched area of consecutive interpreting. Under this specific context, three research questions are proposed, and the analyses in section 4 are attempts to find answers to them. Quantitative analysis shows that 66 of the 80 (83%) clauses carrying interpersonal meaning are complemented by the speaker's interpersonal paralanguage. Moreover, the complementarity of meaning is also reflected by the individual performance of student interpreters. For example, when looking at the speaker at these clauses, HFS recapped 66% of the interpersonal instantiations, whereas in places where no complementarity was observed, he only recapped 16% instantiations – a considerable difference of 50%. This shows that non-verbal para-linguistic resources largely accentuate meaning in the speaker's verbal speech.

The quantitative analysis also illustrates a varied performance of the interpreters from different frequency groups (Table 8.3). Throughout the speech, HFS recapped 58% interpersonal meaning instantiations, 18% and 16% more than MFS and LFS, respectively. When there was multimodal complementarity, the gap between HFS and MFS was widened to 30%. On top of that, the qualitative analysis of Case 1 and Case 2 further compares the accuracy of the interpersonal meaning transfer of the three interpreters. HFS, still the one reported most short gaze, a total of 50 in the two cases during the chosen segments, recapped the interpersonal meaning resources more fully at both the semantic and clause level. A particular observation worth mentioning is that HFS apparently outperformed MFS and LFS in transferring interpersonal meaning carried by semantic resources of appraisal. However, no major difference was noticed between the three interpreters in rendering meaning carried by lexico-grammatical interpersonal resources such as speech function, modal verbs, and modal adjuncts. This may be due to the fact that lexico-grammatical interpersonal resources are more free-standing, whereas the semantic meaning of appraisal words is intertwined with the ideational meaning. A possible assumption is that interpreters can process and capture the interpersonal meaning of the appraisal words better when they manage to receive the interpersonal indications of the paralanguage that goes along with these words. This assumption can be further explored in future research. In addition, Case 2 indicates that loss of interpersonal meaning in interpreters' output could be a result of substantial deviations in the ideational meaning. Although this research holds the view of SFL that interpersonal and ideational meaning should be analyzed separately as they fulfill different functions, more research should be devoted to making the point valid. To recap, we can generally conclude that the interpreter who looked at the speaker most frequently recapped the highest percentage of the interpersonal meaning realizations (Table 8.3) and best captured the more implicit interpersonal resources of appraisal.

However, neither the quantitative nor the qualitative analysis was able to explain how exactly the capturing of non-verbal para-linguistic elements is related to the recapping of meaning in the interpreters' output. For instance, though MFS only recapped 30% of total interpersonal meaning instantiations, 56% were recovered when she did not look at the speaker. Moreover, LFS was still able to recap 32% of interpersonal meaning instantiations without even looking at the interpreter at all. In addition, both analyses illustrate that LFS somehow outperformed MFS, though only by a small vantage, which the analytical framework and theoretical perspective proposed by this research are not able to explain.

To some extent, that proves our analyses are not exempt from limitations: the message rendered in the target language is only the observable result. To study the impact of para-linguistic resources on meaning transfer, a holistic approach should be adopted to take into account the complexity of the whole interpreting process, as interpreting is a cognitively demanding activity where a lot is going on in the interpreter's mind. It is quite impossible to fully understand the interpreter's inner perceptions by focusing exclusively on what is displayed. On the part of interpreters, varied competence in memory, note-taking, and multitasking could affect their output. On top of that, interpreters' output may also be constrained by sound, pace, and prosodic factors such as intonation, rhythm, and tone of the speaker. To consolidate our preliminary finding and explain what's not completely solved in the present research, the aforementioned variables should be included in future research. On the other hand, results in this research are derived from only one mock conference with one speaker and nine interpreters involved. Therefore, the results might not have universal reliability as the data used is limited. Consequently, future research should include a larger corpus, involving more interpreters and multiple experiments.

Albeit the limitations, this research does indicate quite a close relationship between interpreters' capturing of paralanguage and interpersonal meaning transfer in their output. The more frequent an interpreter's short gaze is, the more likely he/she is to produce consistent and complete interpersonal meaning in his/her output. In this respect, the present research can shed light on the teaching of interpreting, and we will bring the discussion on teaching in the context of China where the data of the research is collected. For instance, student interpreters in China are trained to leverage para-linguistic resources to express meaning in the reproduction stage so as to better interact with the listeners. This is due to the fact that public speaking is one of the core training modules of conference interpreting (Zhong 2001). However, emphasis has rarely been put on whether student interpreters should look at the speakers and capture their para-linguistic resources in the input stage to interpret meaning carried by other modes of expression. Several factors may have contributed to this problem. For instance, interpreter training in China emphasizes authenticity in course materials (Zhong 2007). Spontaneous speeches recorded from real-life conferences are thus encouraged in classroom activities (Wang 2015). However, the trainers, who work as on-site interpreters, are only able to audio-record the meetings, whereas para-linguistic resources deployed by different speakers are lost. On top of that, mainstream interpreting textbooks only provide audio recordings as supporting materials. These, coupled with limited infrastructure in the interpreting lab, more or less result in a neglect of para-linguistic resources in teaching. The lack of guidance on the capturing of multimodal meaning resources can be a major drawback in interpreting training. Trainers cannot assume that students have the innate ability to process information from different channels. The evanescent nature of interpreting requires interpreters to multitask and split their attention wisely in a matter of seconds. There is often an extra effort needed to receive visual input from the event. With years of experience, most professional interpreters have developed an empirical or intuitive sense of what impact speakers' paralanguage is having on their output, therefore attend to those resources quite naturally while listening. Yet student interpreters with meager experience are either busy taking notes or not aware of the need to capture speakers' paralanguage, so they need to be trained systematically in this regard. This research, by comparing the performances of student interpreters, further proves that it is necessary to look at the speaker at the listening stage, and hence, encourages trainers to develop pedagogical practices that can contribute to increasing awareness of para-linguistic resources. Suggested practices include (1) encouraging students to split their attention from taking notes to attending to the speakers while listening; (2) showing students videos of interpreting events and analyzing different choices made by professional interpreters and the results; and (3) organizing specific classroom activities such as mock conference to make the training more in line with real-life scenarios, thus augmenting the effect.

Apart from having the potential to improve China's interpreter training, this research is also relevant in informing the interpreting industry of the process norms of this profession, thus helping to create a favorable working environment for practicing interpreters. From the authors' experience of working as conference interpreters, an often-encountered misconception from the clients is that as long as interpreters can hear the speakers, they can communicate the speakers' intended message accurately, faithfully, and completely. Due to this misconception, interpreters sometimes work as an invisible conduit, being placed in a corner of the venue or even outside the venue where visual access to the speakers is barely guaranteed. However, our research suggests that limited visual access to the speakers may result in an inadequate transfer of meaning. Therefore, the industry stakeholders should be advised to provide interpreters with a proper working environment where they can not only hear the speakers' message clearly but also see a close-up of the speakers so as to observe all the non-verbal signs that are part of the message.

6 Conclusion

Based on the SFL inspired social semiotic framework and lexico-grammatical analysis, this empirical research has explored how interpreters' choices of looking or not looking at the speaker have affected the interpersonal meaning transfer quality in their output. A mock conference involving one speaker and nine qualified student interpreters was organized, followed by a careful analysis of the speaker's verbal speech, paralanguage, and the interpreters' short gaze and output. Findings suggest that non-verbal para-linguistic elements could facilitate interpreters' rendition of the speaker's input. Interpreters having more frequent eye contact with the speaker during the input process presented meaning more accurately and more completely in their output than those who did not. However, within the analytical framework and theoretical perspective proposed by this research, the exact relationship between capturing of non-verbal para-linguistic elements and interpersonal meaning transfer in interpreters' output remained to be further explored. Thereby, future research is suggested to extend the research to larger-scale data, involve more interpreters and multiple experiments, and to take into account more variables of the interpreting process and prosodic features of the speech. That said, the research does have strong implications on both interpreting pedagogy in China and the norms of the profession.

References

Baker, M. 2006. "Contextualization in Translator- and Interpreter-mediated Events." *Journal of Pragmatics* 38: 321–337.
Bateman, J. 2008. *Multimodality and Genre: A Foundation for the Systematic Analysis of Multimodal Documents*. New York: Palgrave MacMillan.
Bateman, J. and K-H. Schmidt. 2012. *Multimodal Film Analysis: How Films Mean*. London & New York: Routledge.
Bednarek, M. and H. Caple. 2012. *News Discourse*. London & New York: Continuum.
Bot, H. 2005. *Dialogue Interpreting in Mental Health*. Amsterdam: Rodopi.
Cokely, D. 1992. *Interpretation: A Sociolinguistic Model*. Burtonsville, MD: Linstok Press.
Crystal, D. 2001. *Language and the Internet*. Cambridge: Cambridge University Press.
Davitti, E. 2012. *Dialogue Interpreting as Intercultural Mediation: Integrating Talk and Gaze in the Analysis of Mediated Parent-Teacher Meetings*. PhD Thesis, School of Arts, Languages & Cultures, University of Manchester, UK.
Davitti, E. 2013. "Dialogue Interpreting as Intercultural Mediation: Interpreter's Use of Upgrading Moves in Parent-teacher Meetings." *Interpreting* 15(2): 168–199.
Davitti, E. 2015. "Interpreter-mediated Parent-teacher Talk." In *Linking Discourse Studies to Professional Practice*, edited by Alatriste Lubie, 176–200. Clevedon: Multilingual Matters.
Eraslan, S. 2008. "Cultural Mediator or Scrupulous Translator? Revisiting Role, Context and Culture in Consecutive Conference Interpreting." In *Translation and Its Others: Selected Papers of the CETRA Research Seminar in Translation Studies 2007*, edited by Pieter Boulogne. Available from www.kuleuven.be/cetra/papers/papers.html
Gile, D. 2004. "Conference and Simultaneous Interpreting." In *Routledge Encyclopedia of Translation Studies*, edited by Mona Baker, 40–45. London & New York: Routledge.
Goodwin, C. 1981. *Conversational Organization: Interaction between Speakers and Hearers*. New York: Academic Press.
Goodwin, C. 2001. "Practices of Seeing Visual Analysis: An Ethnomethodological Approach." In *The Routledge Handbook of Visual Analysis*, edited by Theo van Leeuwen and Carey Jewitt, 157–182. London & New York: Routledge.

Halliday, M.A.K. 1978. *Language as Social Semiotic: The Social Interpretation of Language and Meaning*. London: Arnold.
Halliday, M.A.K. 1994. *An Introduction to Functional Grammar*. London: Arnold.
Halliday, M.A.K., and Ruqaiya Hasan. 1989. *Language, Context, and Text: Aspects of Language in a Social-Semiotic Perspective*. Oxford: Oxford University Press.
Halliday, M.A.K., and Christian Matthiessen. 2004. *An Introduction to Functional Grammar*, 3rd ed. London: Arnold.
Hatim, B. and I. Mason. 1990. *Discourse and the Translator*. London: Longman.
Hatim, B. and I. Mason. 2002. "Interpreting: A Text Linguistic Approach." In *The Interpreting Studies Reader*, edited by Franz Pöchhacker and Miriam Shlesinger, 254–265. London & New York: Routledge.
Hood, S. 2011. "Body Language in Face-to-face Teaching." In *Semiotic Margins: Meaning in Multimodalities*, edited by Shoshana Dreyfus, Susan Hood, and Maree Stenglin, 31–52. London: Continuum.
Jewitt, C. 2006. *Technology, Literacy and Learning: A Multimodal Approach*. London & New York: Routledge.
Jewitt, C. 2008. "Multimodal Discourses Across the Curriculum." In *Encyclopedia of Language and Education*, edited by Nancy H Hornberger and de Mejía, 357–367. New York: Springer US.
Jewitt, C, ed. 2009. *The Routledge Handbook of Multimodal Analysis*. London & New York: Routledge.
Kade, O. 1968. *Zufall und Gesetzmäßigkeit in der Übersetzung: Beiheft zur Zeitschrift Fremd- sprachen I*. Leipzig: Verlag Enzyklopädie.
Kendon, A. 1990. *Conducting Interaction. Patterns of Behaviour in Focused Encounters*. Cambridge: CUP.
Kirchhoff, H. 2002. "Simultaneous Interpreting: Interdependence of Variables in the Interpreting Process, Interpreting Models and Interpreting Strategies." In *The Interpreting Studies Reader*, edited by Franz Pöchhacker and Miriam Shlesinger, 111–119. London & New York: Routledge.
Knox, J. 2007. "Visual–Verbal Communication on Newspaper Home Pages." *Visual Communication* 6(1): 19–55.
Kress, G. 2003. *Literacy in the New Media Age*. London & New York: Routledge.
Kress, G. and T. van Leeuwen. 2006. *Reading Images: The Grammar of Visual Design*, 2nd ed. London & New York: Routledge.
Lang, R. 1978. "Behavioural Aspects of Liaison Interpreters in Papua New Guinea: Some Preliminary Observations." In *Language Interpretation and Communication*, edited by D. Gerver and H. Sinaiko, 231–244. New York: Plenum Press.
Liu, Y. and K. L. O'Halloran. 2009. "Intersemiotic Texture: Analyzing Cohesive Devices between Language and Images." *Social Semiotics* 19(4): 367–387.
Martin, J. R. 1992. *English Text: System and Structure*. Amsterdam: John Benjamins.
Martin, J. R., and P.R.R. White. 2005. *The Language of Evaluation: Appraisal in English*. London: Palgrave Macmillan.
Martin, J. R., and M. Zappavigna. 2019. "Embodied Meaning: A Systemic Functional Perspective on Paralanguage." *Functional Linguistics* 6(1): 1–33.
Martinec, R. 2000. "Types of Processes in Action." *Semiotica* 130(3–4): 243–268.
Martinec, R. 2001. "Interpersonal Resources in Action." *Semiotica* 135(1–4): 117–145.
Martinec, R. 2005. "Topics in Multimodality." In *Continuing Discourse on Language*, edited by Ruqaiya Hasan, Christian Matthiessen, and Jonathan Webster, 157–181. London: Equinox.

Mason, I. 2012. "Gaze, Positioning and Identity in Interpreter-mediated Dialogues." In *Coordinating Participation in Dialogue Interpreting*, edited by Claudio Baraldi and Laura Gavioli, 177–199. Amsterdam: John Benjamins.

McKee, R. and J. Davis, eds. 2010. *Interpreting in Multilingual, Multicultural Contexts*. Washington, DC: Gallaudet University Press.

Ngo, T. 2018. "Gesture as Transduction of Characterisation in Children's Literature Animation Adaptation." *Australian Journal of Language and Literacy* 41(1): 30–43.

Ouyang, Q. 2018. "Assessing Meaning-dimension Quality in Consecutive Interpreting Training." *Perspectives* 26(2): 196–213.

O'Toole, M. 1994. *The Language of Displayed Art*. London: Leicester University Press.

Pasquandrea, S. 2011. "Managing Multiple Actions Through Multimodality: Doctors' Involvement in Interpreter-mediated Interaction." *Language in Society* 40: 455–481.

Pérez-González, L. 2014. "Multimodality in Translation and Interpreting Studies." In *A Companion to Translation Studies*, edited by Sandra Bermann and Catherine Porter, 119–131. Chichester: Wiley-Blackwell.

Pöchhacker, F. 2016. *Introducing Interpreting Studies*, 2nd ed. London & New York: Routledge.

Pym, A. 2008. "On Omission in Simultaneous Interpreting: Risk Analysis of a Hidden Effort." In *Efforts and Models in Interpreting and Translation Research*, edited by Gyde Hansen, Andrew Chesterman, and Heidrun Gerzymisch-Arbogast, 83–105. Amsterdam: John Benjamins.

Rossano, F. 2013. "Gaze in Conversation." In *The Handbook of Conversation Analysis*, edited by Jack Sidnell and Tanya Stivers, 308–329. Malden, MA: Wiley-Blackwell.

Royce, T. 1998. "Intersemiosis on the Page: A Metafunctional Interpretation of Composition in the Economist Magazine." In *Language and Beyond*, edited by Paul Joret and Aline Remael, 157–176. Amsterdam: Rodopi.

Royce, T. 1999. "Visual-verbal Intersemiotic Complementarity in The Economist Magazine." Available from www.isfla.org/Systemics/Print/Theses/RoyceThesis/ (Accessed April 24, 2014).

Royce, T. 2002. "Multimodality in the TESOL Classroom: Exploring Visual-Verbal Synergy." *TESOL Quarterly* 36: 191–205.

Setton, R. 1999. *Simultaneous Interpretation: A Cognitive-Pragmatic Analysis*. Amsterdam: John Benjamins.

Setton, R. and A. Dawrant. 2016. *Conference Interpreting: A Complete Course*. Amsterdam & Philadelphia: John Benjamins.

Stenzl, C. 1983. *Simultaneous Interpretation: Groundwork Towards a Comprehensive Model*. MA-thesis, University of London.

Unsworth, L. and C. Cléirigh. 2009. "Multimodality and Reading: The Construction of Meaning through Image-text Interaction." In *Handbook of Multimodal Analysis*, edited by Carey Jewitt, 151–164. London & New York: Routledge.

van Leeuwen, T. 1999. *Speech, Music and Sound*. London: Macmillan.

van Leeuwen, T. 2005. *Introducing Social Semiotics*. Abingdon, Oxon: Routlegde.

Wadensjö, C. 2001. "Interpreting in Crisis: The Interpreter's Position in Therapeutic Encounters." In *Triadic Exchanges. Studies in Dialogue Interpreting*, edited by Ian Mason, 71–85. Manchester: St. Jerome.

Wang, B. 2015. "Bridging the Gap Between Interpreting Classrooms and Real-World Interpreting." *International Journal of Interpreter Education* 7(1): 65–73.

Zappavigna, M., C. Cléirigh, P. Dwyer, and J. R. Martin. 2010. "The Coupling of Gesture and Phonology." In *New Discourse on Language: Functional Perspectives on*

Multimodality, Identity and Affiliation, edited by Monika Bednarek and J. R. Martin, 219–236. London: Continuum.

Zhong, W. 仲伟合 2007. 专业口译教学的原则与方法. (Principles and Methodology for Interpreting Training), 广东外语外贸大学学报 (*Journal of Guangdong University of Foreign Studies*) 3(3): 5–7.

Zhong, W. 仲伟合. 2001. 口译训练：模式、内容、方法. (Interpreter Training: Models and Methodology), 中国翻译 (*Chinese Translation Journal*) 2: 30–33.

Index

Note: Page numbers in *italic* indicate a figure and page numbers in **bold** indicate a table on the corresponding page.

actors 180–182, *181*; voice actors 121
addition 23–26, 83–85; of antithesis *83*; of metonymy and parallelism *84*; of punctuation marks 30–32; *see also* omission + addition
addressing terms: addition of 25–26; omission of 28
analytical frameworks 18–22, 196–198
analytical method and procedure 75
analytical process 5, 127, 171, 182, *182*
anaphora 72, 76, 85–87, *86–87*
angle 95–96, 130–131, 137, 184, *184*
antithesis 69–70, 75–77, 83–86, *83*, *85*
applications: intersemiotic shifts 36–38
appraisal resources 202, 206, **203**, **206**, **208–209**, **211**
architecture 134, 136, 184, *184*
Art of War, The 88; intersemiotic translation of RFs in 75–87; and its multimodal translation 73–75
audiovisual text (AVT) 16–17, 93, 172; addition 24; analytical framework 20–21, **20**; functions and applications 38; multimodality 18; omission 26; omission + addition 29–31; reasons and effects 39–40; roles of non-verbal modes 38; typographic transformation 34
audiovisual translation 2–3, 7–10; meaning codes in **93**

Belt and Road Initiatives (BRI) 10–11, 148, 165–166; data and methodologies 152–155; decision-making of political metaphor translation 163–165; description 155–156; metaphors in political communication 149; metaphors in translation studies 150–151; recontextualization of metaphors 156–163; three-dimensional framework of CDA 151–152
bilingual picturebooks 43–44; methodology 46–48; non-verbal paratexts 51–60; paratexts in picturebook translation 44–45; paratexts in the translation of picturebooks on Mulan 48–60; verbal paratexts 48–51; visual grammar 45–46
blurbs 140–141, *141*
book covers **133**, 140–141, *141*; of Cao Weifeng's translation *129*; *China's Bravest Girl* 52; compositional meanings 132, 139–143; data analysis of 134–143; establishing relations between participants 51–55; information value on *140*; interactive meanings on 130–131, 137–139; representational meanings 127–130, 134–137; of translated texts 125–126; type of elements on *139*; of Zhug Shenghao's translation *128*

carrier 171–172, 179, *179*, 182, 187
Chen Xi (Janet) xi, 11
Cheng'yu 158–159, **159**
China's Bravest Girl: The Legend of Hua Mu Lan 47, 52–61, *52*, *59*
circumstances 45–46, 172, 185–186, **186**
clause level 175–180, **203**, 207–208, **208**
coding framework: of compositional meanings 132, **132**; of interactive meanings 130–131, **131**; for multimodal analysis 126–132; of representational meanings 127–130, **131**

compensation 32–33
compositional meanings 5, 11; of book covers 139–143; coding framework 132, **132**
conceptual mapping 150, 154, 157, 159, 162, *162*
conceptual metaphor theory (CMT) 6, 149, 156
conceptual processes 5, 134–136, 143, 171–172, 182
conceptual representation 127, 134–135, *135*, 182–183
consecutive interpreting 192–193, 212–215; method 196–199; qualitative analysis (Case 1) 201–206; qualitative analysis (Case 2) 206–212; quantitative analysis 199–200; theoretical background 194–196
context 6; and Belt and Road Initiatives 165–166; contextualization 20–22, **22**, 46, 206–207; contextual metaphor 6; cultural 10, 44, 61–62, 91, 153; and the heroic image of Monkey King 92–93; multimodal 39, 67–73, 150; and non-verbal paralanguage 192–194, 196, 199, 212–213; political 149, 151; social 91, 144, 170; socio-historical 11; and tourism promotional materials of Macao 171–172, 184–185; *see also* recontextualization
corpus 22, 75, 133, 213; *see also* corpus analysis
corpus analysis 168–169, 187–189, 213; at clause level 177–180; data 173–174; ideational structure of video 180–183; interaction structure of video 183–185; methodology 175; relevant theoretical concepts 169–173; summary of findings 185–187; at word level 176–177
costume drama 17; *see also Zhenhuan Zhuan*
Cotai Strip 182, *182*
covers *see* book covers
critical discourse analysis (CDA) 18, 148, 151–152, 166
cultural connotations *see* expressions with cultural connotations

"Da Dao Zhi Xing" (DDZX) 148, 152–154, **153**, 161, **161**, 164
data 152–155, 173–174; *The Art of War* and its multimodal translation 73–75; *see also* data analysis; data collection

data analysis 94, 134–143, 17
data collection 95–96, 133–134, 198–199
decision-making 163–165
description 155–156
deviation operation 71–72, 75, 88
diachronic studies 124, 126, 144–145, 149
discourse analysis 189, 195; systemic functional approach to 170; *see also* multimodal discourse analysis
discourse assessment **202**, **208**

effects: intersemiotic shifts 38–40
emotions: and punctuation marks 23–25
endnotes 48–50
endpapers 55–56
equivalence 79–83; of parallelism *80–81*; of simile *82*
expressions with cultural connotations 20, **20**, 26–27, 32, 38–39

Fairclough, N. 148, 151–152, *152*; *see also* three-dimensional framework
Feng Dezheng (William) xi, 10
footnotes 48–50
foregrounding 156–159
forewords 50–51
frequency **159**, 161–162, 175, 197–202, **200**, 212
Fu Ai (Ivy) xi, 12
functions: intersemiotic shifts 36–38

Galaxy Macau on the Cotai Strip 182, *182*
gaze 130–131, 137–138, 183, 199–200, 211–213

Halliday, M.A.K. 9, 45, 126, 163; and the heroic image of Monkey King 93–94; and tourism promotional materials of Macao 170–172, 175, 177, 187; *see also* systemic functional grammar
Hamlet 10–11, 124, 143–145; book covers 127–132, *128–129*, 134–143, **138**, *142*; data collection 133–134
heroic image 59, 62, 91–93, 96, 120–123
high modality 184–185, *185*
HUMAN/FAMILY metaphors 155–156, **160–161**, 163–164; recontextualization of 159–161
hyperbole 70–71, 75–76, 85–86, *85*

ideational structure 180–183
IMAGE mode 18, **20**, 21–23, 26–27, 37–40

images 1–7, 9–12; and book covers of the Chinese *Hamlet* 125–127, 129–132, 134–137, *135*, 139–145, *141*; and the multimodal translation of *The Art of War* 70–73; and page layout 56–60; and paratexts in bilingual picturebooks on Mulan 45–46, 51–54, 60–62; and tourism promotional materials of Macao 169–170, 181–185, 187–189; *see also* heroic image; IMAGE mode; text-to-image translation practice
information value 5, 46, 132, 140, *140*, 143
interaction 180–185, 187
interactive meanings: of book covers 137–139; coding framework 130–131, **131**; of Hamlet and other human participants **138**
interlingual translation 1–2, 75, 173
interpersonal meaning 20, **201**, 212–214; clause-level realizations of **203**, **208**; method 196–199; qualitative analysis (Case 1) 201–206; qualitative analysis (Case 2) 206–212; quantitative analysis 199–200; theoretical background 194–196
interpreters **200**, **202**, **206**, **211**
intersemiotic analysis 4, 6
intersemiotic relations 126
intersemiotic shifts 1, 7, 10–11, 16–17, **20**, 40–41; addition 23–26; analysis 22–35; analytical framework 18–22; compensation 32–34; discussion of 36–40; functions and applications 36–38; and multimodality 17–18, **22**; omission 26–28; omission + addition 29–32; reasons and effects 38–40; roles of non-verbal modes 38; typographic transformation 34–35
intersemiotic translation 1–3, 7–12, 22, 67–74, 82–84, 88; addition 83–85; and Belt and Road Initiatives 148, 150–152, 154, 156–163, 165; equivalence 79–83; omission 77–79; replacement 85–87; of RFs in *The Art of War* 75–87; ST of 176–180; and tourism promotional materials of Macao 169, 173–174, 188; TT of 180–185

journey metaphors 155–159, 163–165

kinesics actions 95, **173**, 183, 187
Kress, Gunther 2–5, 9, 11, 66; and Belt and Road Initiatives 154; and book covers of the Chinese *Hamlet* 126–127, 130–132, 143; and the heroic image of Monkey King 93–95, 102; and paratexts in bilingual picturebooks on Mulan 45–46, 51, 54; and tourism promotional materials of Macao 169, 171–172, 175, 180, 184, 187; *see also* visual grammar

Lakoff, G. 149; *see also* conceptual metaphor theory
Lam Sut I (Michelle) xi, 12
Lei Sao San (Susann) xi, 12
lexical words 176, **176**
Li Xiaowei xi, 11
literal translation 154, 156–159
logic-semantic relation 7, 70–72, 75–77, 80–83, 86, 88
low angles 54, 96, 99, 105, 108, 137; vertical perspective 184, *184*
low modality *185*
Luo Tian (Kevin) xi, 11

Macao 168–179, 187–189; data 173–174; methodology 175; official news releases 174; online promotional videos 174, 180–185; summary of findings 185–187; tourism image 169–170; verbal resources in news releases 176–180
Martin, J.R. 194–197; *see also* social semiotic analysis
Martinec, Radan 7, 11, 126–127, 145; *see also* logic-semantic relation
material processes 99, 114, 120, 171, 177–178, *178*
meaning: meaning codes **93**; and punctuation marks 23–25; SFL perspective on 194; *see also* meaning transfer
meaning transfer 192–193, 212–215; analytical framework 196–198; data collection 198–199; interpersonal meaning 195–196; qualitative analysis (Case 1) 201–206; qualitative analysis (Case 2) 206–212; quantitative analysis 199–200; SFL inspired multimodal research 195; SFL perspective on meaning 194
metaphor **159**; analysis of **157**; conceptual mapping of *162*; contextual 6; omission of *78*; in political communication 149; recontextualization in the intersemiotic translation of BRI discourse 156–163; in source and target texts 155–156; translation analysis *152*; in translation

studies 150–151; *see also* HUMAN/ FAMILY metaphor; JOURNEY metaphor; metaphor analysis; metaphorical expressions; metaphor type; PLANT metaphor
metaphor analysis 6, 148, 151, *152*, **157**, 163
metaphorical expressions 149–151, 153–156, **155**, 158–160, 162, 164–165
metaphor type 155–156, **156**
methodologies 46–48, 75, 152–155, 175, 196–199
metonymy 66, 72, 75–76, 84–85, *84*
military 52–54, 56–59, 73–74, 85
modality 45–46, 131–132, **173**, 183–185, *185*, 196–197, 202–209
modal particles 20–21, 23, **20**, 29–30, 36–37, 40
Monkey King, image of 91–92
Monkey King: Hero Is Back 91–92, 120–123; analysis of scene 1 96–99; analysis of scene 2 99–102; analysis of scene 3 102–105; analysis of scene 4 105–108; analysis of scene 5 108–111; analysis of scene 6 111–114; analysis of 7 114–117; analysis of scene 8 117–120; data collection 95–96
Mulan 44, 46–48, 60–62; non-verbal paratexts 51–60; paratexts in the translation of picturebooks on 48–60; verbal paratexts 48–51
multimodal analysis 9–10, 92–95, *94*, 168–169; coding framework for 126–132; *Monkey King* **97**, **100**, **103**, **106**, **109**, **112**, **115**, **118**
multimodal complementarity 199–201, **200–201**, 205, 211–212
multimodal context 67–73, 150
multimodal discourse analysis (MDA) 12, 17, 171–173; overview of 3–7
multimodality 1–4, 6–10, 17–18, 148; and book covers of the Chinese *Hamlet* 125, 143; and non-verbal paralanguage capturing 192–193, 196; and tourism promotional materials of Macao 168–169, 172, 189
multimodal research 3, 193, 195, 212
multimodal texts 5–6, 43, 66–67, 75, 195; rhetorical figures in 70–71
multimodal translation 7–10, 73–75

narrative processes 5, 134–136, 143, 171, 180, 183
narrative representation 134–135, *135*, 180–182

news release *177–179*; verbal resources in 176–180
non-verbal modes 17–21, 36–38, 188, 197
non-verbal paralanguage 192–193, *204–205*, *210*, 212–215; method 196–199; qualitative analysis (Case 1) 201–206; qualitative analysis (Case 1) 206–212; quantitative analysis 199–200; theoretical background 194–196
non-verbal paratexts 47–48, 51–60; interplay between verbal paratexts and 60–61
non-verbal text 175–176

objects and their relations 45, 55–56
official news releases 174
off-screen 180–181, *181*
omission 23, 26–28, 77–79; of metaphor 78; of paradox and parallelism *79*; of repetition 30–32; *see also* omission + addition
omission + addition 29–32
online promotional videos 174
Ouyang Qianhua (Tasha) xi, 12

page layout 56–60
paradox 73, 76, 78–79, *79*
paralanguage *see* non-verbal paralanguage
parallelism 76–85, *79–81*, *84*
paratexts: classification of *47*; in picturebook translation 44–45; and publishing agencies' choices 61–62; in the translation of picturebooks on Mulan 48–60; *see also* non-verbal paratexts; verbal paratexts
para-verbal means 25–26
participants 4–5, 45–46, 94–95, 130–131, 134–139, 170–172, 179–187
phenomenon **171–172**, 181
picturebooks: on Mulan 48–60; non-verbal paratexts 51–60; verbal paratexts 48–51; *see also* bilingual picturebooks
pictures 55–56
PLANT metaphors 161–163
political communication 148–151
political discourse 148–149, 151, 158, 163–166
political metaphor translation 163–165
political persuasion 11, 149, 165
political translation 148–151, 165–166
prefaces 44–45, 50–51
processes, types of 5, 169, 171–172, **171**, 180; *see also* conceptual processes; narrative processes

promotional videos *see* online promotional videos
publishing agencies 61–62
punctuation marks 19–23; addition of 23–26, 29–32

Qian Hong (Sunny) xii, 10
qualitative analysis: Case 1 201–206; Case 2 206–212
quality assessment 197
quantitative analysis 199–201

rearrangement 161–163, **162**
recontextualization 124, 151, 153–155; by literal translation and foregrounding 156–169; by rearrangement 161–163; reasons for decision-making about 163–165; by selection 159–161
relations *see* objects and their relations; relations between participants
relations between participants 51–55
repetition 29–32
replacement 85–87, *85–87*
representational meanings *135*; of book covers 134–137; coding framework 127–130, **131**
representation: in news releases 176–180; objects and their relations 55–56; in videos 180–185; in visual grammar **172**; visual realizations of **186**
reshaption 70, 76, 86–87, *86–87*
rhetorical figures (RFs) 87–88; in *The Art of War* 75–77; in multimodal context 67–73; in multimodal texts 70–71; in the ST and TT *76*; translation strategies *77*; *see also* addition; equivalence; omission; replacement; verbal rhetorical figures; visual rhetorical figures

semiotic shifts 19, **19**, 40
Senado Square 182, *182*
sensor 179, *179*, 184–185
sensory coding orientation 184–185, *185*
simile 6, 76, 82–83, *82*, 88
social affinity 137, 183–184, *184*, 187–188
social distance 5, 46, 53–54, 137, 183–184
social semiotic analysis 6, 194–196, 214
socio-political reasons 164–165
Song of Mulan 47–48, 50, 56–58, *57*
systemic functional approach to discourse analysis 169–170
systemic functional grammar (SFG) 45, 94, 169–170, 187

systemic functional linguistics (SFL) 5, 7, 43, 126, 170, 193–197, 211–212

tagging 169, 199
taxonomy 67–71
text-to-image relation 148, 152–153, 156–159, 161–166
theoretical background 92–93, 194–196
three-dimensional framework 148, 151–152, *152*, 155
title pages 45, 47, 51, 55–56
titles 130, 133–134, 136–137, 140–141, *141*
token 99, 179, *179*
tourism 168–170, 173, 177, 181–183, 185, 187–189
transcriptions **24**, **26–29**, **31–35**, 172, 175, 199
transcripts 168, 201–202, **202**, 207
translatability 77, 80, 88, 150
translation *see* interlingual translation; intersemiotic translation; multimodal translation
translation method 34, 49, 153, 155–156, **156**
translation strategies 75–77, *77*, 79, 88
translation studies 1–3, 7–11, 16–19, 125–126, 153–155, 168–169; metaphors in 150–151
typographic transformation 34–35

van Leeuwen, Theo 4–5, 9, 11; and book covers of the Chinese *Hamlet* 126–127, 130–132, 143, 145; and the heroic image of Monkey King 93–95, 99, 102, 108, 114–117, 120; and paratexts in bilingual picturebooks on Mulan 45–46, 51, 54; and tourism promotional materials of Macao 169, 171–172, 175, 187; *see also* visual grammar
vectors 180–181, *181*, 183, 187, 194
verbal modes 19, 29, 38–40, 91, 165, 169, 192; and addition 20–23, 30
verbal paratexts 11, 47–51, 55–56, 58, 60–62
verbal resources 80, 168–169, 174, 182–183, 185, 187–188, 193; in news releases 176–180, *177–179*
verbal rhetorical figures (RFs) 67–70, 72, 74–79, 88
verbal texts 56–59, 126, 155, 159, 175–176, 194, 196
videos 174–175, 180–188
visual grammar 1, 5, 10; and book covers of the Chinese *Hamlet* 127, 131; and the

heroic image of Monkey King 93–94; and paratexts in bilingual picturebooks on Mulan 45–46, 48, 51–52; and tourism promotional materials of Macao 169–172, **172**, 175, 180–184, 187
visualized goal 180–181, *181*
visual metaphor 1, 6, 75, 78; and Belt and Road Initiatives 149, 153, 158, 163–164
visual realizations 185–187, **186**
visual rhetorical figures 66, 69–70, 72, 74–76, 85
voice actors 121

Wang Hui (Wanda) xii, 11
word level 170, 175–177
word lists 175–176, **176**

Xie Rosie Guixia xii, 11

Zappavigna, Michele 194–197; *see also* social semiotic framework
Zhang Meifang xii
Zhang Xiaoyu (Heather) xii, 11
Zhenhuan Zhuan (*Empresses in the Palace*) 10, 17, 22, 36–37, 40
Zhu Shenghao *128*, 133, 144